RULES *for* REAL ESTATE SUCCESS

Real Estate Sales and Marketing Guide

C. PEREZ

iUniverse, Inc.
Bloomington

Rules for Real Estate Success
Real Estate Sales and Marketing Guide

iUniverse books may be ordered through booksellers or by contacting:

iUniverse
1663 Liberty Drive
Bloomington, IN 47403
www.iuniverse.com
1-800-Authors (1-800-288-4677)

Because of the dynamic nature of the Internet, any Web addresses or links contained in this book may have changed since publication and may no longer be valid. The views expressed in this work are solely those of the author and do not necessarily reflect the views of the publisher, and the publisher hereby disclaims any responsibility for them.

Any people depicted in stock imagery provided by Thinkstock are models, and such images are being used for illustrative purposes only.

Certain stock imagery © Thinkstock.

ISBN: 978-1-4620-3801-5 (sc)
ISBN: 978-1-4620-3800-8 (hc)
ISBN: 978-1-4620-3799-5 (e)

Library of Congress Control Number: 2011914372

Printed in the United States of America

iUniverse rev. date: 9/7/2011

Contents

Preface

I entered the real estate business in 1978. The solid training I received from some of the top professionals in this business afforded me the opportunity to retire at an early age. This solid training built the foundation for my success. Years later, wanting to give back, to help others also find success, I decided to re-enter the real estate market, but as a college instructor/professor and trainer for national firms. After teaching my first college course, *"Real Estate Marketing,"* I soon realized that there is a lack of quality information on how to be successful in real estate sales and marketing. There are volumes of textbooks that have good information, but none are a "one source," well-organized, up-to-date, easy-to-follow, step-by-step textbook that students can read to obtain the information they need to build a successful career. Real estate is demanding enough without students and agents having to read hundreds of articles, books, and attending countless training sessions. There has to be a better source! This is the reason that I have written this textbook: to use my years of success and training to give students a unique insight of theory and real life practical skills in this profession with the information and options they will need to make better choices, in an easy-to-read, step-by-step guide for career success. This textbook will offer hundreds of ways to find business and how to drive it to you, which is the concept of marketing and selling. I believe that all agents have: the right to learn and know the information that will make them successful, the choice to select their career path, and the enjoyment of a successful career.

Introduction to Rules for Real Estate Success

"More than a Textbook…it's an essential Sales and Marketing Guide"

Why Real Estate: Each year, thousands of students will choose real estate as their profession. There are many reasons that you may have been drawn to this exciting, rewarding, yet demanding profession, some of which are the following: the opportunity to meet fascinating people and the freedom for independent employment. Perhaps you are more philanthropic in your efforts and feel compelled to contribute to society in some way, or you may see this profession as a way to help others fulfill their dreams. Or, is it for the enormous sums of money it promises? Yes, I know for a fact that real estate offers incredible wealth; however, before you decide to invest your time and money entering this career, you should know the truth; the income you can make and realistically, what is required to achieve that level.

Starting a Successful Career: Your enthusiasm and eagerness are strong now. However, statistics show that losing your motivation within the first two years of starting your real estate career is easy to do. Why is a real estate agent exuberant in the beginning, but later on, discovers enthusiasm often begins to wane? What is the problem? More importantly, what can you do to prevent becoming another sad statistic in realty? Is there a proven set of rules, when applied correctly, that will yield a successful real estate career? Is there a common thread with successful agents from whom you can learn and pattern? The answer is a resounding *yes*! A successful career in realty is 90% of building the right process, which is a consistent set of rules that top producers understand and apply. This book includes many examples and practice exercises that you will find useful in starting your career.

Achieving Success: This textbook is designed to help ALL agents, whether part-time or top producers, attain success in reaching their goals. In just twelve easy-to-follow chapters, you will learn hundreds of ways to find business and equally important, hundreds of ways to drive it to you. Consider this textbook an essential reference book for your entire career. It will give you the absolute best information and options so that you can make decisions that will lead "YOU" to success.

Being Prepared: Imagine having a crystal ball at your disposal that will allow you to accurately anticipate what your prospects are going to say to you the day before you meet them! Wouldn't this be an enormous advantage in preparing your best response? Wouldn't this type of advantage give you the confidence to go beyond what you normally would have in pursuing the sale? This book gives you that crystal ball. It is a fact in real estate that you will be asked the same questions time and time again, but in a thousand different ways. Regardless of the form taken, the answers are the same. A simple truth to remember: "Real estate success is really simple. You need to remember the 30 best answers for the most common questions you will be asked." This textbook gives the common scripts for nearly every question you will ever encounter so that you can confidently address them.

Theory vs. Practice: Bookstore shelves are filled with Real Estate Theory books. What makes this textbook unique is that it will give you proven "best practices" that will bring you success, especially in:

- Converting "For Sale by Owners": to "Sellers"
- Converting "Open House prospects" to "Buyers"
- Using the right words for expired listings
- Knowing the right reasons for staging
- Finding Success working with Sellers and Buyers
- How to introduce yourself to win clients

- Succeeding at door-to-door sales
- Knowing how to present the best offer, YOUR offer.
- Making cold-calls that work
- Addressing common house features
- Turning callers into prospects and prospects in clients

Decision Making: You have the right to know what is involved in building a successful real estate career. In this business, you will have to make several difficult decisions. For example, you will need to decide: if you want to be a full time or part-time agent and what Brokerage Company will fit your needs. Will you generalize or specialize? Will you be a Buyers or Sellers Agent or both, and why? In what areas of real estate are you willing to invest? This textbook gives the information you will need so you can confidently make the right decisions.

This textbook will also guide you to:

Chapter 1

This chapter helps you make a better career choice by giving you employment insight with the information and options that you need to know. This chapter also addresses:

- Selecting the brokerage firm that is right for you
- Preparing yourself before licensure – the 30 day waiting period for your license
- Preparing after you receive your license, developing a 30 day action plan

Chapter 2 Ethics and Consumer Protection Laws

This chapter helps you understand the various federal and state acts that are vital in real estate sales and marketing, and the vital role ethics will play in your career.

Chapter 3 Developing Goals, Business Planning, and Time Management

This chapter is designed to help you search your goal and the level of income you want by:

- Designing an effective business plan
- Developing reachable goals
- Organizing task and outlining your career path
- Having the time to promote your business

Chapter 4 Technology for Real Estate Agents

Use technology to build your successful career by:

- Using social media to build a streamline of prospects
- Using technology to effectively mass market to thousands
- Using software to stay in contact with hundreds of prospects and clients

Chapter 5 Professionalism and Salesmanship

This chapter helps you to:

- Build your professional image
- Learn to work like and known as a superstar
- Always have the right answer for nearly every question you will ever encounter

Chapter 6 Real Estate Marketing

Find and turn prospects and investors into clients by:

- Selecting the best marketing tools that is right for you
- Developing a marketing strategy that works
- Selecting and developing the right marketing ideas
- Budgeting for your marketing strategies
- Building confidence in meeting new people
- Knowing how to categorize your prospects to sell for the greatest dollar
- Designing effective business cards, letters, and marketing material

Chapter 7 Prospecting for Sellers, Part I

Build a pipeline of sellers by:

- Knowing how to find and turn prospects into clients
- Being effective in working with sellers
- Being effective in door-to-door sales
- Knowing how to capitalize on your listings

Chapter 8 Prospecting for Sellers, Part II

Build a referral system by knowing how to:

- Find and turn For Sale by Owners into clients
- Build rapport and win over sellers
- Overcome sellers' objections
- Service your listings

Chapter 9 Property Staging

Know how and why to do the following:

- Stage correctly for sellers and buyers
- Give your listings the competitive edge to encourage better offers
- Help buyers emotionally connect to the property
- Enable sellers to emotionally disconnect from the property
- Encourage both parties to buy and sell, making negotiations much easier
- Make it easier for sellers to move and pack
- Give the impression of a well-maintained property that indicates few if any repairs
- Make it easier to clean, maintain, and show because of less clutter and greater space
- Overcome views on outdated property
- Give the property the appearance of a larger, more comfortable home
- Shorten the time the property will be on the market

Chapter 10 Prospecting for Buyers

Know the most effective ways to find and work with buyers by:

- Being effective in establishing rapport with Buyers
- Categorizing buyers/prospecting
- Preparing and qualifying your buyers to increase your closing percent
- Previewing and selecting the right housing for your prospects
- Overcoming buyer's objections
- Building a buyer's referral system

Chapter 11 Financing Real Estate

Close more transactions in a shorter amount of time by:

- Understanding real estate finance
- Knowing the details for a quick closing and funding
- Knowing when you have qualified buyers
- Knowing how to improve credit scores

Chapter 12 Closing and Post Services

Understanding post-closing services; you will be able to work in the following areas:

- Forbearance agreements
- Loan Modification/Repayment Plans
- Broker price opinions (BPO)
- Short sales
- Banks in real estate owned (REOs) properties

Acknowledgement: Several people were helpful in putting this book together. I would like to thank Professor Dorothy Lewis, for her great wisdom and advice, my many students for their encouragement, Houston Community College Professors Jeannine Horn, Etta Smith, and Emily Marchand for their editorial services, and special thanks to my wife and children for their endless patience and for understanding why I was compelled to write this book.

CHAPTER 1
Real Estate Success

Objectives:

Understand the following:

- What will be required to achieve the level of success you want
- The decisions you will make for a successful real estate career
- What to expect as a real estate agent
- How to prepare for a the real estate career
- How to overcome common pitfalls in real estate

Can you be Successful in Real Estate Sales?

Real estate is not for everyone, but if real estate is for you, there is a systematic process that can lead you to success. However, before you decide to invest in this career, you have the right to know what is required to achieve the level of success you want, and what is the realistic income you can make. To help you with making a real estate career choice, this chapter will introduce four crucial areas that you will face.

Four Crucial Areas (D.E.P.P.) You Will Face as a Real Estate Agent

1. Decisions,
2. Expectations,
3. Being Prepared, and
4. Pitfalls you will encounter.

Decision Making

In this business, you will have to make several difficult decisions. For example, you will need to decide if you want to be a full time or part-time agent, the type of training you will obtain, and the type of Brokerage Company in which you will be comfortable. Will you generalize or specialize? Will you work with buyers or sellers, or both? Will you obtain a mortgage license? What type of marketing will you use, and in what areas of real estate are you willing to invest in? The most important decision you will make is whether you can make a commitment to yourself. Once you have decided, you can start implementing your plans and goals. Later, you can always adjust your goals, but for now, you need some direction. Schedule a meeting with your broker, manager, or a career coach. Below is an introduction to serious decisions you will have to consider which are covered in greater detail in Chapters 7-10.

- Marketing approach
- Full-time vs. part-time self-employment
- Job vs. career choice
- Generalization or specialization agency
- Single vs. multiple license
- Buyer vs. seller agency or both
- Virtual vs. physical marketing
- Salary vs. commission income
- Small vs. national franchise brokerage
- Type of commission agreement
- An action plan

Deciding on Your Marketing Approach

The following chapters hold many suggestions about how to find business and how to drive it to you. This is the concept of marketing and sales. Tom Hopkins says, *"Selling is a two part component: one is to find people to sell, and two is to sell to people you find."* While the following chapters offer hundreds of ideas, you cannot use them all. Instead, try to find a few marketing ideas that works best for you. Try to develop a working model. You can adjust the model later to suit your own needs and style. Your selection should be based on a good return on your money, whether you enjoy it, and how comfortable you are using it. The more comfortable you are using a marketing idea, the more likely you will devote enough time to it for success. We are all different and prefer one marketing or sales technique over another. Whatever you decide, make sure you give it enough time to work and enjoy what you have selected. Good ideas may take several months and an investment of money, but nearly all proven ideas will work, provided a sufficient amount of time and money is invested. A mistake many new agents make is trying new marketing ideas without giving the previous ideas enough time to work.

Deciding Whether to Work Full-Time or Part-Time

You will have to decide if you are going to be a full-time or part-time real estate agent. To help you decide, answer the following questions: "If I were selling my home, the biggest investment of my life, which agent would I use?" Who would most likely be there when you needed them? Who would most likely be committed to his/her work and be able to service your property 100% of the time? You would want the best, someone who would give you 100% of his/her effort, and has made a commitment to his/her career rather than treating the work as just a job.

It is understood you are entering this business to increase your earnings. However, success in real estate is rare for the part-time agent. This is not to say it cannot happen, but it takes a remarkable person with time management and an understanding of the information presented in this text. For this reason, most brokers are reluctant to hire part-timers unless they are either paying a monthly desk fee or have plans to become full-time. Not everyone is able to start working as a full-time agent, if this is your case; the material in this book is designed to help you quickly reach your goal so you too can enjoy a successful and rewarding career.

Decide to Generalize or Specialize

Another decision you need to make is whether you will be a generalist or a specialist. You will most likely have to generalize during the early part of your career; nearly all agents do. At some point, you will need to decide whether you want to continue being a generalist (i.e., a "jack of all trades" selling real estate, insurance, mortgages, and property relocation, or helping both buyers, and sellers) or if you want to become a specialist, the expert in a certain market. An agent who is a specialist may work with only buyers or only sellers, within certain income brackets, or in a particular location. Most top producers are specialists. For instance, top athletes who specialize in one position generally get paid more because they are considered the best in their field of work.

If you decide to specialize in working with only sellers, focus your attention on taking care of your sellers. If you are a buyer's agent, focus your attention on how to best serve your buyers. Focusing on anything else is a distraction. Another reason top producers specialize is due to the amount of work, time, and money it takes to be an expert in a particular area. How to become a specialist is discussed in later chapters. After all, the top 10 percent of successful agents are specialists, while the bottom 90 percent are generalists. The common belief is that agents should do it all, be a one-stop shop. On the surface, this seems like a good way to make extra income; however, this is not true. Imagine you are having a medical procedure. Do you want a general practitioner or a specialist? If you are having a complex procedure, you probably want a specialist, and are even willing to pay extra. Since housing is the biggest investment for most buyers, they will also want a specialist, the expert, especially for the same price.

One-Stop Center Decision

Many real estate offices provide several options for buyers and sellers. A one-stop real estate office or a real estate broker may offer residential real estate, commercial real estate, leasing, mortgage lending, insurance, investments, and title work services. Attorneys, surveyors, appraisers, interior designers, engineers, investors, hard money lenders, and real estate schools may be housed in the same office. This concept was developed to make home purchasing easier, less expensive, and more attractive to consumers. Real estate buyers and sellers shop or go to one office instead of going to different people and locations. The real estate broker could offer discount fees, since he/she would receive fees from two or more sources. Since the broker can control more resources, it is easier to legally resolve any problems and be able to close on time. If the broker acts as the real estate agent and loan officer, many transactions can be saved because he or she has both licenses. Many agencies consider this practice unethical; however, there are federal and state forms for this type of arrangement. Sometimes this helps push a sale through when the closing would not have funded with only one license.

Rules for Real Estate Success

Before deciding on working with buyers or working with sellers, decide which group will prove more profitable. Which group costs more and takes more time to work with, buyers or sellers? Usually, the answer is buyers. Searching for buyers is an expensive exercise, which can be frustrating. Many agents start working with both to get a better understanding of the selling cycle. Later, they will decide if they prefer to concentrate on one group over the other. As you will discover, many agents simply enjoy working with buyers. If you would rather work with buyers instead of sellers, that's understandable, but be aware of the cost and frustrations associated with working with buyers. Chapter 10, *Prospecting for Buyers*, provides several tips to help reduce the cost and frustrations of working with buyers.

For every house sold, there is an equal number of buyers and sellers (or the 50/50 rule). Today, over 73% of buyers search the Internet for their housing needs before searching for an agent. This is an important statistic which you will need for planning your marketing approach. Planning your marketing is discussed in Chapter 6. Buyers will usually call the agent who holds the housing inventory, thus leading to a possible increase in the agent's income. Chapter 7 discusses how to increase the number of buyers who call on your listings. The more inventory you hold, the greater the percentage of calls you will receive. More signs mean greater exposure. The bottom line is agents who focus on sellers have over 80% more business than agents who work with buyers. Skillful agents who understand agency rules will sell at least 50% of their listings if they adopt the marketing and sales strategies mentioned in the chapters with statistical sources to follow.

Virtual vs. Physical Marketing Decisions

You will have to decide whether to use old methods of marketing or try new technology. Before computer technology, agents prospected by farming/harvesting, cold calling, door-to-door sales, and using regular mail. This has changed. The future of real estate marketing is clearly the Internet by using social networking, software, cloud computing, and online services. While the Internet may have virtually endless boundaries, let us look at previous marketing techniques. Farming, cold calling, and door-to-door sales may be old-fashioned, but they still work, therefore, many agents are comfortable prospecting this way. Old-fashioned prospecting is discussed in Chapter 7, *Prospecting for* Sellers, to help you understand how each marketing method works. Having many options and using them all is almost impossible. Considering time and your monetary resources, are you comfortable using old reliable methods, or are you willing to understand and invest in the future of technology? Try to find new ways of using technology with old fashion prospecting.

Deciding on Commission or Salary Decision

You will need to make the decision to work for commission only income or salary income. Deciding how you would like to be paid for your services is a serious decision to make. Most brokerage companies are commissioned only. If you do not sell, you are not going to get paid. Coming into the office and working from 8:00 a.m. to 8:00 p.m., seven days a week will not earn you a paycheck. You must close a deal. A transaction may take several months to close, or worse, it may take several months to put a seller and buyer together, and then take several more months to close the deal.

Nearly every broker has his/her own commission structure, which can range from 100% of the commission to being paid 50% of the commission. You must decide what is best for you. A 100% commission broker may have a pricey monthly desk fee and/or not offer the tools you need, while a 50/50 commission plan may not have such a fee and it provides substantial training. The 50/50 commission broker is paid for availability to you. Keeping half of a commission is a significant incentive for the broker to want to help you and train you to become a better salesperson. Be aware that some 100% or even 50% commission brokers may have little incentive or are unable to help you become a super star. As you prepare to obtain your real estate license, you may want to visit several brokerage offices for information on training, support, fees, and commission structures. Study the different commission structures to find out what works best for you. If you choose a broker with a nice commission structure, but it ends up not working out for you because of the many additional fees, or they do not have the training to take you to a higher level, you can always transfer to another broker.

Deciding on an Action Plan

Are you in the habit of making excuses, such as why you did not finish your assignments? Was it due to a lack of time, or were you watching your favorite television show? If sales are slow, it may be due to the economy or it could also be your mindset. If you think sales are slow because of the economy, you are just blaming the economy. Instead of blaming the economy for slow sales, make the decision to readjust your plans; look into additional marketing techniques or mail-outs. Try something different. such as: door-to-door sales, start a farming plan, open houses, or turn your attention to short sales and investment properties. If you need more leads, start a listing campaign. Hundreds of ways are available to promote your real estate services. We all have comfort zones (the least amount of stress for the greatest reward), but continued drops in sales is an opportune time to rethink goals and plans. As you leave your comfort zone, do not be afraid to make mistakes. Business mistakes become learning opportunities.

What to Expect from a Real Estate Career

What to Expect

While thousands of individuals choose real estate as their new career, the public frequently hears about the lucrative investments and the money some agents make. The public is unaware, however, the degree of effort those agents made in order to obtain their income. Therefore, before starting your career success, giving some employment insight into this business to you is only fair. Let us examine what you should expect from this business.

Expect to Be a One-Man Show

Being self-employed in real estate is much the same as being the CEO of a company except you will be doing it alone, without the help of specialists. Keep in mind that corporations hire accounting specialists to do the paperwork, financial managers to prepare budgets and taxation, upper managers to design plans, CEOs to establish goals and make decisions, lawyers to make legal decisions, marketing departments to create ideas to attract customers, salespeople to sell the products, and human resources to keep everyone happy. As a real estate agent, you are essentially a CEO without any of these people to support you, unless you are willing to pay for their services. No one is going to set goals or develop a well-executed business plan for you. No one is going to tell you how you are going to sell houses. Being a self-employed agent means you are an army of one – you must be all of these specialists yourself. In preparing for this type of career, you must be willing to treat your new career as a real business.

You will need to learn (or at least be aware of) taxes, budgeting, accounting, legal issues, marketing, sales, as well as setting goals, and devolving a business plan. More specifically, you must transform yourself, which will require you to do things you have never done before. You will have to learn new things and learn how to do them differently. Think about your new real estate career this way, *"You cannot succeed in business unless you understand business."* Secondly, *"The greater you understand business, the greater the opportunity for business success."* Community colleges are an excellent resource for business courses. Invest in your career; do not just take the minimum number of courses to obtain a license, but sign up for business courses that will advance your career. The advantage is that you have the opportunity to earn more income than any other type of employment. What other types of work makes it possible for an average person to earn millions?

Being self-employed as a real estate agent essentially means *"No Work, No Money."* Business is not going to come to you. The fish is not going to deliberately jump into your boat. You are not going to sit in an office while customers line up waiting to see you. Most likely, it will be you looking for business, not business looking for you.

Being an employee usually means getting a regular paycheck regardless of how you perform. Self-employment means getting paid on the amount of business you are able to produce. For those agents who understand marketing and sales, the amount of potential earnings are unlimited. An optimistic person views this as an advantage for limitless opportunity. Why be limited to a regular paycheck? Why not get paid on performance? A real estate career gives you the opportunity to be self-employed with an infinite amount of income versus remaining an employee and bringing home the same paycheck week after week.

Expect to be Accessible

Success in real estate requires your availability to work with your applicant's timetable. Unlike most 9-5 jobs where you are off on weekends, you must be prepared to work longer hours. This includes weekends and peak summer months. For example, during the summer while children are out of school, real estate and mortgage lending experience a high volume of activity. Over 80% of sales occur then. The busiest time for real estate agents is weekends and evenings, when most people are off from work. Your work hours will be the opposite of school or the traditional 9-5 business person's because your availably should be that of your clients. For more information, refer to Chapter 5, *"Real Estate Professionalism."*

Expect a Demanding Career

This business is also becoming exceedingly demanding. Today's sophisticated real estate consumers have more information available and more options from which to select. There are over 130 websites promoting properties and For Sale by Owners. Nearly every real estate person has a website designed to capture prospects. Technology is helping agents find more clients and with greater marketing material. The savvy agent will find ways to use new technology mixed with old prospective methods. In the past, there were only a few types of lenders. Today, there are various mortgage lenders: prime, sub-prime, FHA, VA, banks, wholesale, retail, and hard-money investors, all armed with the latest tools such as the Internet, mortgage software, credit software, and AU Systems, not to mention the thousands of new real estate professionals entering this business every year. All of this technology, with more and greater options, is making the real estate business increasingly more demanding for some agents, while providing countless opportunities for others. Chapter 4 will address technology for real estate agents.

Expect Highs and Lows in Real Estate

You will experience highs and lows in monetary and emotions in this business. The financial rewards can be gratifying; nevertheless, the workload can be overwhelming and disappointing. As a new agent, your income will be seasonal. Since most sales occur during and around the summer months, most of your income as a new agent will occur during these months. Sales are usually sluggish during the winter months; therefore, if you do not plan ahead financially and save money, your winter may be long and lean. Once you establish yourself, sales and income will become more evenly spread throughout the year.

Moreover, your emotions can take you on a rollercoaster ride. Your experiences may vary from seeing faces of a young family moving into their first home to seeing a family's dream shattered by an uncontrollable event.

Expect to be Ready, Willing, and Able

Not all students/agents are suited for a career in real estate. Having unsullied business skills, strong work ethic, and confidence is still not enough. You must enjoy working with people. After all, real estate is the business of servicing people. You will attain success if you are willing to work long hours while you enjoy helping your clients or customers achieve his/her dreams. *"To be successful you must be ready, willing, and able to do what other agents won't do."* In real estate you will often hear the statement, "in order to make a sale you must have a willing, ready, and able buyer or seller." The truth is, it is "YOU" who must be *"ready, willing, and able."* This text presents the knowledge you need to prepare yourself, but it is up to you to have the confidence and put in the effort if you want success. Agents will not do what is required because of several reasons; the biggest reason is fear. Most agents, over 90%, will not knock on a stranger's door or start a conversation with a stranger to ask for their business. Mail-outs, phone calls, and emails all work to some degree, but agents who are ready, willing, and able to meet face-to-face and are comfortable with engaging prospects will likely take the business. Upon entering this business, you will notice how agents justify their reason by saying, *"I don't have enough time,"* when really, it is the fear of rejection and/or the lack of willingness to put-forth the effort.

Review the statistics on mail-outs, meeting prospects and overcoming the fear of prospecting in Chapter 7 and 8. The smartest agent, the most honest, or the hardest working agent will lose the opportunity to the agent who happens to be in the right place at the right time. In fact, it is up to you to be *"ready, willing, and able to be there"* at the right time. You must be comfortable being in front of prospects. Har.com indicates the person who first meets the sellers has a 58% chance of winning the listing, followed by 27%, and 11% while the fourth agent has less than a 7% chance of winning the listing.

Rules for Real Estate Success

Being Prepared

In preparing for a new career there are several things you should be aware of, which are:

- The importance of practicing and role playing scripts
- Willing to Make a Commitment
- Developing Confidence
- Quality Training
- Preparing for Licensure

Practicing and Role Playing Scripts

One of the best ways to build your real estate career is to always be ready by studying and role playing scripts. Agents tend to ignore this type of training. Top agents do not role play because they like it; they practice role playing because it is what professionals do. Do top athletes practice? Can you read a book on how to swim without practicing? Would you let a doctor perform a complicated operation from simply reading a text or let him/her wing it on you? Of course not, how silly is this? A statement by Peter Abrahams is applicable here, *"To get where you want to go, you cannot only do what you like."* Chapters 5, 7, and 8 will discuss "opportunity" moments and knowing how to respond with the very best answers. Knowing how to respond takes much practice, but the information is here to start you in the right direction. Teachers employ several mnemonic strategies for young students to help them to remember and understand, Here is a common rule teachers use, *"Tell me and I'll forget, show me and I'll remember, but involve me and I'll understand."*

Developing Confidence by Being Prepared to Answer Common Questions

If you had a crystal ball and you knew what your prospects were going to say the day before you met them, wouldn't this be an enormous advantage? Knowing this would give you time to prepare for your best response. It is a fact that in your career you will be asked the same questions or hear the same answers over and over again, but in a thousand different ways. Nevertheless, the answer is the same. A simple truth is as follows; *"Real estate success is really simple, you need only to remember the 30 best answers for the most common questions you will be asked."* Now that you are waiting for your license, this is an opportune time to address them. There are common scripts for the following that will address nearly every question you will ever encounter. Chapters 5-10 will cover the most commonly asked questions/answers and how to address them with the best possible scripts. However, if success is your goal, you should have at least two scripts ready for each of the following 15 areas starting your career:

1. For Sale by Owners	9. Closing the sale
2. Open houses	10. Working with buyers
3. How to present an offer	11. Introducing yourself
4. Working expired listings	12. Follow-up on leads
5. Door-to-door sales	13. Marketing rental houses
6. Making phone calls (cold calls)	14. Absentee property owners
7. Converting callers into prospects	15. Floor duty
8. Asking for referrals	

To jump-start your career, you should try using scripts to farm for expired listings and For Sale by Owners. Scripts are an excellent tool for new agents since most top producers will be preoccupied with working their referral system. In real estate, when we get these common types of questions/answers, we call them "opportunity moments." In your career you will be asked the following questions, but how much more successful will you be if you have the very best reply for the following questions? Knowing the best scripts removes barriers for opportunity.

- *Hello, how are you?*
- *What do you do?*
- *How is real estate?*
- *No, I do not need your help!*
- *What commission do you charge?*
- *We have a friend in the business.*
- *We'll call you back.*
- *We'll try to sell it ourselves.*
- *Why should we use you?*
- *We have an agent.*
- *We are just looking.*
- *What do you want?*
- *No, thank you!*
- *Are you MAD?*

When the right moment presents itself, if 90% of what you say, how you say it, and when you say it will determine your success, don't you want to be ready? My definition of LUCK is *"Being prepared when opportunity presents itself."* For example, look at sports, such as baseball or football. Those amazing plays you so enjoy do not just happen. Great athletes will practice and practice, preparing for the right moment to put their talent and skills into action. In your case, you can be prepared by always knowing the very best words and adjusting each script to match your personality and constantly practice role playing, waiting or looking for your opportune moment. Now, you understand why top producers look forward for people saying "No" to them? They're waiting with the perfect reply. Remember, your words should have a natural flow. Nearly every profession believes in "theory and practice," so why should real estate be any different. In fact, real estate is the only working field where a majority of agents think they have the right to call themselves professionals without practicing.

Ready to Make Small Talk

There is opportunity everywhere we go. Coffee shops, theaters, grocery stores, and sport events are filled with people who are starving for conversation. Chapter 5 will introduce how to make small talk.

Preparing Scripts for Common Home Features

Knowing how to address common housing features is also important. All houses will have different grades of granite countertops, wood flooring, carpet, gas or electric appliances, air conditioning, and roofs. To the buyers, what are the benefits and cost factor of each? Which of the following examples gives the greatest benefit?

An inexperienced agent may say the following:

"The property has beautiful granite countertops." or *"Nice wood floors!"*

You have the opportunity to sound professional with confidence by saying the following:

"This property has beautiful granite countertops. Granite is a siliceous type of stone. It is very durable, making it hard to scratch, and difficult to wear. You can even use it as a cutting board. Each natural granite stone is unique, one of a kind in the world. It is sanitary, easy to clean, and does not harbor bacteria. Natural stone goes with almost any type of décor. Replacing natural stone is also very affordable."

"Nice wood floors. There are basically three types of wood floors: solid, engineered, and acrylic impregnated. Now, can you feel the warmness? Have you notice as we walk on it, it is not noisy like tile? Hardwood flooring is very

durable, easy to maintain, ecologically sound, and healthier than carpet. It may be refinished many times to last decades. The Environmental Protection Agency has said today's indoor air quality is one of our leading health threats. Wood flooring is a necessity because not only is it durable, but also because it sets the stage for a warm and healthy family environment."

While waiting for your license, research common interior and exterior features, and practice your scripts and responses until you are comfortable. Each house you will show or list has common features, and you will want to take advantage of the opportunity. Think about developing your own scripts for ongoing dialogues. Chapter 5 addresses building dialogues. Sellers are delighted when you know enough about the intricacies of their home that you can attract more sophisticated buyers. If you were going to sell your home would you want the agent who can talk about his/herself or the agent who knows the intricacies of your home? Chapters 5-10 offer several scripts for each category.

Gaining confidence takes practicing and role playing the different common situations, contracts and other forms required for your business. Have your broker review your work, contracts, and presentations. For ideas on which forms to practice, pursue some of your broker's closed files. Examine the HUD-1 and other documents you will present to future clients.

Willing to Make a Commitment

Be willing to commit your time and efforts to building your successful business. Over 1,700,000 real estate agents work in the U.S. and Canada and 500,000 new agents sign-on each year. Unfortunately, over 80 percent of them will not achieve success and less than 20 percent will make the majority of the money. A major reason for the disparity is the lack of commitment and the will to succeed.

Now, before you go any further, you need to follow-up with a decision to take the next critical step - a commitment to take your career path seriously. Unless you take this step seriously, no amount of training, coaching, wishing, advertising, or skill-building will help you reach the end result, success. Oliver Wendell Holmes (1809-1894) says *"He has half the deed done who has made a beginning."*

Building Confidence with a Commitment

Ed Dorris from Universal Sales Systems (an excellent training source) states that health has a strong relationship to success. He further remarks, "Take a hard look at yourself, get naked, and stand in front of a full mirror, and then ask yourself, "How physically appealing am

I to my spouse or loved one?" This last comment is a bit harsh, but you are beginning a new career, and change for success is never easy. To be honest, do not stand in front of your mirror unless you are willing to make a change and a commitment to yourself.

Change is hard, sometimes more difficult than we expect. Take a physical look at yourself and decide what changes you *must* make. Do you need to lose ten pounds, tone-up, or just change your hairstyle? Make one of your goals to lose ten pounds in six weeks. Now, plan how you are going to do this. How are you going to step outside of your comfort zone? One small way is to make a list of your unhealthy eating habits, and then write on colorful paper how to correct them. Post the list where you can see it every morning. This list may include no candy or sweets, no eating after 8:00 p.m., or no snacks between meals. Getting in shape goes a long way in building self-confidence. How are you going to start physical self-confidence? There are thousands of textbooks to read about this subject and hundreds of places to go for help. As for making a list of your eating habits, treat it as a contract, a commitment to yourself, a contract you cannot break! Then, after meeting this goal, you are ready for a larger goal, maybe this time to lose 12 pounds. Meeting goals, even small ones, will boost your confidence level.

The theory is, if you feel good about yourself both mentally and physically, you will build confidence about yourself, about your abilities, and about your working environment, which means more success - likewise, more money. The more successful your working environment becomes, the more confidence you will have. It is a self-perpetuating cycle. Clients will also notice your positive outlook. In other words, you will exude self-confidence. You couldn't hide it if you wanted to.

Being Able by Developing Confidence

Buyers and sellers want someone who demonstrates mental confidence, someone who is assertive, but not overly aggressive. You must believe you are providing something of value or something only you can best provide. You must be totally prepared to have the very best answers (scripts) for any questions your clients may have and you must practice, practice, and practice to build confidence. Knowing how to answer your prospects' concerns will significantly increase your level of confidence. You must have a clear understanding of what your duties are and what your clients must do. If it is selling their house, how exactly will you do this? Is there a clear comprehensive action plan, and are those steps in writing? What clients do not want is an agent who appears as if he/she has no idea what to do but 'will figure the steps out eventually.' If you work with buyers, develop a clear plan on how you will help them find their home. If you are working with sellers, know every step in winning the listing, marketing, and selling the listing. The following chapters include many step-by-step examples. Your goal should be to rewrite your own script versions and adjust your action plans as your career moves forward. If your action plan is in writing, show yourself all the steps you will take and exactly what your customers and clients should expect from you. As you write and perfect the steps for the many situations, your confidence will start to develop. For now, keep it simple (KISS-Keep It Simple Stupid) and then later, you can add more steps for the different situations you will encounter. Your clients will feel comfortable because you know exactly what to do to meet their needs. More importantly, you will start building self-confidence.

Being Prepared with Quality Training

Students leave school with basic knowledge and high hopes of being the next Donald Trump, but then fail. This is mostly because they fail to take the necessary courses for learning successful sales skills and marketing techniques, the interwoven building blocks to success. Students enter the real estate business to make money, which requires creating sales opportunities, closing transactions, and getting referrals for more business. However, many students are taking only the required courses for a license to sell real estate and are failing to take additional courses on *"How to Sell."* Also, students often complain about having to take courses on ethics, not understanding why it is so important. From a legal standpoint, there are many reasons to be an ethical business person. From a sales person's viewpoint, trust is the main component for building a successful business relationship. Be sure to make a long-term investment in your career by taking the courses that will help you prosper. Building ethical business practices is discussed in further detail in Chapter 2.

50/50 Training Rule

Some brokers' training programs may include the 50/50 rule. Namely, new agents spend 50% of their energy in marketing and the remaining 50% in sales. Marketing and sales are not the same. You must do both. Your marketing strategies should be attracting consumers, balanced with your sales approach, which includes innovative ideas on how to sell the product. Do not make the common mistake many new agents make of spending thousands of dollars in a marketing campaign without knowing how to make the sale. Sales approach will be covered in Chapter 5 and marketing strategies in Chapter 6.

Beware of Seminar Craze

As you enter this business, you will start receiving all kinds of "dog &

pony" marketing invitations from independent training speakers. All of these so-called "*free*" power-building seminars have good information, but do not fool yourself; they do not have the magic formula for a real estate career. There is no formula to make you rich in 21 days if you purchase their $800 DVD or pay $2,000 for a one-year coaching membership. These motivational speakers do not have anything new. Most of the motivational or marketing material is a rehash from older material. This does not mean you should not attend these seminars. You can always improve or refresh yourself once you get past the fluff and puff. To start your training, if your brokerage does not have the quality training you require, I recommend the national, state, and local associations which are particularly selective about the type of training and speakers who offer valuable information to its members. While this text will prove extremely helpful, I also recommend investing in audio programs for motivation and personal training. Zig Ziglar, the foremost American sales trainer, coined the term "*Automobile University*" to describe audio program training because you can listen to it and learn while you are traveling. Colleges and private schools offer a wealth of courses as well.

The OPECC Training Rule

For new agents, the best way to start a career selling real estate is by following the OPECC rule, which is as follows:

- **O**bserve
- **P**ractice/role play, see Being Prepared by Practicing and Role Playing Scripts
- **E**valuate, see Chapter 3, Developing Goals, Plans, and Time Management
- **C**ommitment, see Willing to Make a Commitment
- **C**onfidence, see Developing Confidence

Observing Top Producers

As a new agent, it is necessary for you to start observing top-producing agents. Seasoned agents who are already battle-scarred from spending years in a demanding career usually make accomplished advisors. As you talk with top producers, you will find they all have something in common: commitment to be the best, enjoyment of their work, and focus on their goals.

A top producer's advice is priceless. He/she is one of a few people able to find ways to overcome the tension of change in this profession. Can you make a change or leave your comfort zone without some degree of stress? Not everyone is willing or able to make changes to achieve a higher level of professionalism. Getting to the top takes a considerable amount of discipline. It is this desire to compete that makes top-producing agents excel. Like anyone who is confident, he/she wants to share knowledge. These top producers are successful because they have developed the strong interpersonal sale skills that customers like. When an office manager or top producer extends his/her help, take full advantage of this invaluable opportunity. However, not all top-producers are willing to share their secrets. In this case, ask a top producer if you can be his or her apprentice for a month or longer in exchange for their trade secrets. You may have to pay part of your commissions for the training and the knowledge you gain, but in the long run, it will be worth it.

Preparing for Licensure

Upon entering this business there are many activities that you can start with. You will need to be aware of the following:

1. How to select the right brokerage firm.
2. How to prepare before licensure – the 30 day waiting period for your license.
3. How to prepare after you receive your license - developing a 30 day action plan to get you started.

Selecting a Brokerage Firm

Students and new agents often ask about what criteria they should consider when selecting a brokerage firm. The main factors you should consider are: ethical values, name recognition, training opportunities, and the tools necessary for your success, followed by office location and commission. Yes, as a new agent, commission should be your last concern; however, it will probably be your first as a seasoned agent. Below is a list of what to look for in selecting a brokerage firm:

1. Look for a firm where agents tend to work together. The more united the firm is, the more profitable you will be.
2. After selecting a broker, try to meet each of the agents. Seasoned agents have a wealth of knowledge and can be a good mentoring source. Check to see if there are top producers who would appreciate a good assistant, or consider having a partner with whom you can work as a team. Partnerships are helpful if you decide to specialize.
3. Ask your broker about office and individual specializations. Ask if the office has a mentoring system. Also ask about training and education, commissions, and office policy.
4. Ask about office dues, such as desk fees, or the unknown hidden fees you will find after receiving your first check and how the brokerage firm is using technology.

5. Drive around the office and check the signage. If the office has a good reputation, it should have most of its listings near its location. Check the parking lot. Is there plenty of parking?
6. Find out what services the firm offers to new agents. Find the type of office support who will answer phone calls and how calls are directed.
7. Find out how the office staff greets other agents' customers and answers phone calls.
8. Find out how much the firm spends in monthly advertising for the office and agents?
9. Find out how the management structure works; every broker has different levels of management control. While one broker may have strict control, another may allow you plenty of freedom.
10. The following table should prove helpful in selecting a brokerage firm:

How to Select Brokerage Firm	How Brokers Select Agents
1. What are the ethical values of the office and the broker?	1. What are your views and ethical values?
2. What is the broker's office image?	2. Are you neat, and do you present a professional image?
3. What is the broker's knowledge and experience?	3. Are you trustworthy?
4. How long has the broker been in business?	4. Do you have good character?
5. What are your office costs?	5. Are you disciplined?
6. What are the company's goals and mission statement?	6. Will you produce?
7. What type of brokerage firm is it (single or multi-agency)?	7. Are you a full-time or a part-time worker?
8. What is the broker's character?	8. What are your views on long-term employment?
9. Does the office have a strong federal and state compliance system?	9. Are you and your family flexible with your work hours?
10. What types of in-office training programs are available?	10. Are you a team or an individual player?
11. What tools do they offer?	11. Are you committed and serious about working?
12. What are the office staff, equipment, support, supplies and desk space?	12. Are you willing to educate yourself with their training programs? Are you a good reader and writer?
13. What type of technology is available (websites, software, and hardware)?	13. What is your means of transportation?
14. What is the management-to-agent ratio?	14. How far is the brokerage firm from your home?
15. How many listings and agents are there?	15. In term of personality, will you take control or are you passive?
16. What is the present agent-to-listing ratio?	16. Do you have enough money saved for one to three months?
17. What advertising fees are covered by the broker?	17. Do you have other sources of income?
18. How far is the brokerage firm from your home?	18. Do you have computer and software skills?
19. Is the office clean and organized?	19. What types of automobile insurance do you have?
20. How is the office environment and setting?	20. What types of licenses do you have?
21. Is the office staff courteous when answering telephone calls and greeting customers?	21. What is your employment history?
22. What are the office policies and procedures?	22. What is your level of education?
23. What is the dress code?	23. What are your goals?

How to Select Brokerage Firm	How Brokers Select Agents
24. How much floor time do you get, and how many leads are offered to agents? 25. How many sales meetings are there? 26. What sales material is provided? 27. What is the advertising budget? 28. What is the office turnover rate (retention factor)? 29. What will be your cost of E and O Insurance? 30. What type of customer and employee parking is available? 31. What are the desk space arrangements and fees? 32. Do you get office keys? 33. What hours can you use the office? 34. Can you work as either a full-time or a part-time agent? 35. What type of commission structure is available (100%, tier, or flat)?	

Pre-License Exercises - The Waiting Period

Once you have finished your courses and passed the state exam, there is a 30-45 day waiting period before you are officially licensed. Until then, you are not allowed to practice; however, you can use this time to start preparing to enter the real estate industry. The following is a list you can use to start preparing before obtaining your license. Information on how to do the following is in the coming chapters.

1. Start a savings plan. You will need around $800-$1,200 for memberships. Do you plan to use the real estate association services or not? If your broker is a member, then you must also become a member. Consider paying the following membership fees and legal dues:

    - State Real Estate Commission
    - National Association of Realtors ®
    - State Association of Realtors ®
    - Local Association of Realtors ®
    - *MLS* ® & Supra Keys System

2. Design a preliminary marketing plan, including your photographs, business cards and introduction letters. See Chapter 6.
3. Meet with brokers, marketing companies, and software vendors regarding which types of software to purchase.
4. Begin a database of people you know. Your yearly goal should be to double your list.
5. Ask your broker or manager if they have any scripts that you can use to start studying.
6. Obtain prices on iPad/laptops/desktop computers, digital cameras, printers, jump drivers, portable hard drives, file cabinets, shredders, and wireless Internet services. Most agents use a wireless laptop computer but are switching to iPads/smart phones with cloud computing.
7. Ask about Internet security. Smart phones/iPads have access to many of the wireless/cloud applications that are useful.
8. Search for a web designer/web master for developing a website. Most of the larger companies have pre-designed websites and tools already prepared. Investigate weblogs, cost of hosting, and training classes so you can do your own updates. Check your local association to find out if it offers free web space. Also, search for classes on web designing and their cost. You have about 30-45 days to learn basic web design.
9. Purchase some type of mapping system, such as a key Map book, a GPS for your car, or a smart phone application.
10. Make sure you have the necessary auto requirements and insurance. Speak to your insurance agent about liability insurance. It is wise to invest in a four-door car if you do not already have one. Become familiar with rules for transporting clients in your vehicle when showing them properties.
11. Research cell phones and wireless network providers for rates and services.
12. Meet with a tax adviser to discuss which items are deductible and to ensure that you pay your share of taxes and take all your deductions.
13. Search for open houses and go to as many as possible. Understand for what is involved. How do other agents stage properties? What kind of fliers are they designing? Are they using flags, banners, or balloons? How many signs should you use? What time of day should you post your signs? How can you improve what other agents are doing?
14. Take a look at what other agents are doing, compliment the agents on a job well done, ask for their advice, and take notes. The more you write, the more they talk. Do not forget real estate is a small world, and you'll be seeing these agents again; asking their advice is complimenting them. If you want the very best information, won't you go to the best source?
15. Start thinking about how you are going to be unique and what services you will offer. This will separate you from the rest of your competition.
16. Make a list of what you have to offer your clients and/or customers, such as education, credentials, specific skills, time, and financing.
17. Research pricing on business cards and memorandum pads as well as other forms of advertising.
18. Start a scrapbook and gather information from other agents' mail-outs and various types of letters. Ask your friends for help in collecting advertisings.

19. Ask your broker which software he/she has. You will need the following types of software, which many brokers already have:

    • Efax/Fax broadcasting and Email distribution,
    • Printing mailing labels and designing marketing material
    • Setting up databases and spreadsheets
    • Management/scheduling, accounting, and taxation
    • PDF converting documents
    • Digital photo editing and movie making
    • Goal setting and planning
    • Web design

20. Consider developing your personal website, or investigate how much it will cost to have one designed professionally. Most of the larger firms and *MLS* have free websites for their agents. Compare yourself to your competition, look at other real estate agents' websites and think about how you can build a better mouse trap.

21. Expand your business by networking and joining trade associations.

22. Attend community activities and be an active member. Remember to keep your career a priority and do not get caught up in too many social activities.

23. Start thinking about which areas to farm, ask your broker for his or her opinion on the best areas in which to farm, and conduct some research to determine if there is another agent farming the areas you want. Consider how you plan to farm, and what your broker thinks would work best. Research what farming tools top producers are using.

24. Get a physical examination and ask your doctor about a health plan before you start your career move. Starting a new career is new and exciting, but it is also stressful. You need to be in your best health. Not only will you feel better about yourself and have more confidence and energy, but you will improve your personal image as well. Consumers enjoy working with energetic agents who have a positive attitude about their work and themselves.

25. Let people know you are getting your real estate license. (Do not forget you are not certified to sell yet!) You have 30-45 days of planning to remind everyone you know that you are going to have your real estate license soon and will be ready to work for them.

26. Collect business cards from other agents. This will be helpful when you are thinking about taking photographs and the design of your business cards, letterheads, and other forms of advertising. Do you want photos that have a relaxed or business finish? What colors and types of clothing will you wear when posing for the photographs?

Post License Exercises - 30 Day Action Plan for Licensed Agents

Once you are licensed, you should implement a 30-day action plan. Think about it this way: success is habit-forming, but so is failure. What you do in the first 30 days will affect your new career move. Start your new career in the right direction. If you wish to attain success in this business, plan your first 30 days carefully, and give it much consideration. You will have only one chance at this.

1. Have your marketing material ready: business cards, introduction letters, press releases, and action plan.
2. Volunteer for floor time. Start your Google.com/local and Amazon account. See Chapter 4.
3. Work with your office mentor program and assist in open houses, search for expired listings, or answer phone calls during floor time.,
4. Sales is about meeting and interacting with people and for this you will need to have your power scripts ready. Again, you must know how to approach your prospects, and always know what you will say. Start practicing/role-playing the scripts that you will use. Chapters 5-10 have the scripts to get you started. It is up to you to adjust your scripts to match your personality.
5. You should have already stated your goals and designed plans to achieve your goal. Modify your goals when/if necessary. Talk with family, seasoned agents, office managers, or your broker about adjusting your goals. At the end of each day, work on your action plan for the next day.
6. Start contacting individuals on your list by phone, letter, email, or in person.
7. Keep letting your friends know you are in the real estate business.
8. Start "*farming.*" Do a mail-out in your neighborhood or a door–to-door campaign in your market area. List how many houses you will visit each week in your action plan. Know your neighbors by name. Develop a system on how you will personally reach every person in your "*farm*" area at least four times a year. Be aware of news you can share with homeowners in your "*farm*" area.
9. Find and study your competition.
10. You will need to pick an area to farm, so before you leave the office every day, pull MLS prices from different neighborhoods. Take a different route to your work, home, or when you go shopping. Become familiar with pricing in different areas. Once you have covered all the areas you are concerned with, start all over again. You should make this a habit. Why? To keep an eye open for "*For Sale by Owner*" properties. Price and product checking is common in this business. Grocery stores do this all of the time.- it is about competition. Storekeepers are always searching for the competitive edge by knowing their competitors' prices and products. Keep an organized binder of all of your work. This will enable you to give buyers and sellers a better idea of home sales and pricing history later.
11. Develop a system for checking expired listings in your farm and nearby areas. Each morning for the next 30 days, call on expired listings. Start in your "*farm*" area or where you live or work first and then work outward. How far outward you plan to search for expired listings will depend on you

and your broker. Set your location guidelines and start those searches. You should already have your marketing material ready.

12. Begin your action plan by contacting FSBO prospects and looking through old office files. You can also print an expired list every morning, and call people listed as "For Sale by Owner" from websites or in the newspaper. Have your friends look for FSBOs as well. As for old company files, get permission from your broker first. You do not want to start calling and mailing material to someone else's clients.

13. Be sure you have the names, phone numbers, and email addresses of all the agents in the office, and be sure the other agents in the office know you. You can get to know the other agents in the office by presenting them with a letter of introduction and posting your information on the office communication system.

14. Set a scheduling plan for floor time with the broker to determine the hours you will be in the office.

15. Do role playing such as: answering phone calls, meeting customers, meeting For Sale by Owners, and handling objections.

16. Plan your own open houses. How many open houses will you have per month? These open houses do not have to be your own listings. They can be company listings. Talk to listing agents to set-up the rules and start scheduling the hours and dates. Make your fliers early and begin planning for your open houses as early as possible.

17. Start collecting staging material. Buy items for future open houses when you find good deals and when you can afford to do so. Staging is discussed in more detail in Chapter 8, *Property Staging.*

18. By this time, you should have determined what type of technology you will use. Now is a good time to develop a long-term budget plan.

19. Urge your company to place an announcement in a local newspaper. Use your article as a part of your presentation package.

20. Make it a rule that when you are working, work 100%, but when you take time off, make it 100% personal. Eat good meals, take regular walks, and do something just for yourself! When you get home, schedule enough time for family matters. The next one will be difficult but try to keep work and family time separate so you can enjoy both.

21. Be punctual. If the staff work day starts at 8:00 a.m., then reset your reporting time to 7:00 a.m. The point is to develop good habits. You have many things to do in the next 30-45 days, so you need every minute to achieve all of them.

22. Always keep your vehicle clean, organized, filled with gas, well maintained, and ready for showings. Did you know over 80% of people will judge you by what you wear, drive, and how clean your car is?

23. Look at your office. How clean is it? Is your desk clean and well organized? Buy an organizer and filing system to keep your files safe and out of the way.

24. Read and understand office policy. Create form letters, postcards, or shop for real estate books and software that have the pre-designed items you need.

Reasons for Failure

There are several reasons that new real estate agents fail. Below is a list of the most common reasons:

- Failure to get information on how to be successful in their career
- Failure to receive sufficient basic sales and marketing knowledge
- Failure to learn how to balance a successful real estate career with their personal lives
- Failure to understand the importance of goal setting, planning, and time management
- Failure to understand how a real estate business should be a long-term career, not a temporary job
- Failure to understand the importance of having good values and/or ethics

Failure to get Quality Information on How to be Successful

A career in real estate holds a high failure rate, perhaps as much as 80%. In my opinion, this failure rate starts in the real estate schools. Most real estate schools teach information about how to acquire a license and how to pass the state exam, but inadequately teach their students information about how to become successful as real estate agents and/or brokers. However, students who read this textbook will find that the valuable information in the twelve chapters can change their careers.

Failure to Balance Work and Life

Having a successful home life is a critical component in building a successful real estate career. Due to the nature of the real estate business, your home life and your career as a real estate agent present a symbiotic relationship. Success in both of these areas of your life is largely dependent on your ability to manage your time. How to accomplish this balance is discussed in more detail in Chapter 3, *Time Management*.

Failure to Set Business and Personal Goals

Even the most erudite agents will fail as a result of their inability to establish plans and goals. Many agents fail to understand that real estate is a true business where goals, plans, and research are a fundamental part of success. You must focus on how to implement plans to achieve these goals. Students will often ask, *"Why do we have to read about goals and plans?"* The answer is this: having goals and plans are the road map to your success, which will be discussed in more detail in Chapter 3. Successful business people make plans. But, rest assured that their decisions are not based on what they like or what they want to do, but what is required. For example, as an employee, would you say, "No, I will not do what is required." to your boss? Probably not. Therefore, being self-employed, why would you not do an activity, when you know that activity is required to succeed? Every day, real estate affords agents the freedom of many activities. However, you must also do what is required first, this is why setting your business plan and establishing personal goals is very important.

Mapping Your Career (Short vs. Long-Term Career)

Another reason that new agents have short careers is the approach they take to sales. Agents will enter the real estate market expecting quick results, but after a few unprofitable months and an empty bank account, they will try another occupation. They have not learned enough to possess the adequate tools to compete in this business. As you go through this book, you will learn valuable information that you can use in your career. All reputable salespeople understand that sales should be considered a career, not simply a job. How you decide to sell real estate will depend on your job vs. career views. The main difference between a job and a career is the way we view jobs: a short-term way of income versus a long-term investment, even a lifetime commitment. You must understand that for most of us, there is no magic formula. Before you can expect any kind of reward, you will, you must, experience several months of training and practice As a real estate agent, you must be committed to a long-term career investment and have vision about your new career. Vision is the ability to see where you want to be in six months, one year, or five years and knowing how to get there. Planning is essential to assuring your ability to reach your destination. Refer to Chapter 3, *How to Map your Career*.

Importance of Having Good Values

As you start your new career, selectivity of the people you work with is important. Ed Dorris states, "In every office there are two types of co-workers: Cheerleaders and Ankle Grabbers." Cheerleaders are co-workers who will support you, but Ankle Grabbers are those agents who become jealous and do or say things to hinder you from a successful career. Mark Twain (November 30, 1835–April 21, 1910), the great American humorist, says, *"If you pick up a starving dog and make him prosperous, he will not bite you. This is the principal difference between a dog and a man."* So, keep away from people who try to belittle your ambitions.

Every office has its share of agents who harbor negative views on real estate or sit around complaining about the market, clients, and other agents. We call them Negative Ned and Negative Nettie. Perhaps a closing didn't go well for them or some other deal fell through, causing their negative viewpoint. To them, it is much easier to do nothing than to "*do what other agents won't do.*" Stay away from such cancerous people and remain positive in your career. However, chances are that they simply are too lazy to do what is required to enjoy success. Steer away from this cancerous negativity and remain positive on your goals.

Ed Dorris also says, "Whenever someone makes a negative comment, before you react, ask yourself. "Is it out of malice or ignorance?" It is usually out of ignorance, but what is more important is whose ignorance is it, yours or theirs? The only way you will know if it is due to ignorance or malice is to listen or ask for more information. If it is due to malice, what caused a person to believe such a thing? If it is from ignorance, can you help that person? The point is this: if you listen and process what the person is saying, you will not be the ignorant one.

Who's the Monkey?

If you are in an office where you have to work with such agents, think of the monkey principle. If you were at a zoo and a monkey made an obscene gesture, would you be offended or would you find it funny? Of-course, it would be funny, because the monkey doesn't know what it is doing; it is simply reacting to its audience. Think of these negative agents as such-most of the time, they are unaware of their actions. More importantly, make certain that you don't react negatively and, likewise, become the 'monkey.'

CHAPTER 2
Ethics and Consumer Protection Laws

"It's not hard to make a decision when you know what your values are." – Roy Disney

Objectives:

Understand:

- The six values which determine ethics
- Advertising laws under the Truth in Lending Act
- The purpose of the Real Estate Settlement Procedures Act (RESPA)
- Section 8 of RESPA
- Fair Housing Act

Be aware of

- Laws to protect your clients
- The National Do Not Call rules
- State laws regarding advertising by real estate agents

Terms:

- Advertisement
- Agency
- Annual Percentage Rate
- Antitrust Laws, Price Fixing
- Deceptive Trade Practice Act
- Competency
- Ethics
- Fair Housing Act, FHA
- Fee packing

- Fidelity
- Integrity
- Kickbacks
- Morals
- National Do Not Call Registry
- Real Estate Settlement Procedures Act
- Section 8 of RESPA
- Truth-in-Lending Act, TILA, Reg. Z
- Values

Ethics/Consumer Protection Laws

Rules for Real Estate Success

Today, there are several federal and state laws designed to protect consumers' rights throughout the real estate transaction. Ideally, most people grow up understanding values, morals, and ethics; however, our lawmakers have proposed the minimum legal concept of morals and ethics. These are called Federal and State Regulatory Acts. While the words *morals*, *values*, and *ethics* are considered synonymous, each word has its own specific definition.

- **Morals** are the feelings of what is right and wrong as a community or group.
- **Values** are the beliefs of an individual or culture, but they are not always the same as ethics. For example, the desire to be wealthy or to be honest is a value. Choosing to be an ethical person is more of a choice than a value. Having high ethical standards, however, is a value.
- **Ethics** are what we perceive is right or fair, and how our ethical belief influences our decisions and behavior in society. Your own ethical standards are generally higher than those standards established by our laws or legal concept of what is wrong or unfair. As a real estate agent, you must identify and follow the conditions outlined in Regulatory Acts and understand when and how to apply these regulations. It is especially important for you to understand what is right and fair for your customer during the transaction and to act on this knowledge by making a conscientious decision.

Ethics and Legal Requirements

As we discuss various federal and state acts, you will begin to understand the importance of ethics and the Regulatory Acts, as well as the vital role they will play in your real estate business.

Before entering the real estate industry, be sure you understand ethics and legal requirements. If you understand these laws, you are less likely to make mistakes that may cause you to lose your license. This chapter includes six of the most important consumer protection acts for real estate marketing and sales.

Federal, State Laws and Guidelines Concerned with Marketing and Sales

1. Ethics and Trust
2. Truth-in-Lending Act, TILA, Reg. Z
3. Real Estate Settlement Procedures Act, RESPA, (referrals vs. marketing)
4. Fair Housing Act (FHA)
5. Deceptive Trade Practice Act (DTPA)
6. National Do Not Call Registry

Ethics and Trust

Making ethical decisions can be difficult when they conflict with your objectives. Would you be comfortable if your mortgage lender accepted false information in order to provide your buyers a loan?

There are fundamentally six values that determine ethics. These are the cornerstones of real estate ethics today:

1. Honesty and fairness
2. Integrity
3. Loyalty
4. Responsibility
5. Caring
6. Disclosure

Building Trust/ Having Honesty

It is necessary to understand how trust plays a vital role in being successful. The number one rule in real estate sales is *"Consumers will use your services if they trust you are the right person for the job."* What consumers want is trust and honesty.

Sellers trust that you will get the job done, get the best price, and be completely loyal and honest to them. Buyers feel the same way. The buying of property may be their biggest investment, their home, a place where they will raise their kids. They want someone who will be loyal, competent, honest, and most importantly, trustworthy. If they believe you lack these basic values, chances are you will not be successful. The road to success begins with commitment followed by trust. Clients will not refer you to their friends, family, or anyone else if the feeling of trust is not present when conducting business with you. Luck will not be enough to obtain and keep clients coming back, but trust and honesty will.

As with any kind of sales, *"You must first sell yourself before you can sell your product."* Selling yourself begins with trust, which is one of the values of ethics. The importance of having strong ethical values cannot be stressed enough. Ethics originated from the pillars of honesty, fairness, and responsibility. If you develop strong values, you will make sound ethical decisions. Ethics should be woven into the fabric of your professional career. Many factors contribute to having either a short or long-term career, but one of the most common factors is personal values. People must trust you are the best person for the job. As Mark Twain (1835-1910) so eloquently states, *"Always do right. This will gratify some people and astonish the rest."*

Trust is the First Step to a Successful Career

Real estate brokers and managers prefer agents who have strong business ethics and who view their real estate careers as a long-term endeavor. Brokers are usually busy; therefore, they try to separate productive agents from "wanna-be" professionals or "one-time wonders" when they sponsor an agent. Time is valuable to brokers, so they surely do not want to waste any of it. Training is also expensive; therefore, most brokers have some type of sponsoring guidelines. It is necessary to note that not everyone has the motivation or attitude to succeed in this business. As real estate brokers select agents, they try to opt for the career-minded ones rather than someone who is just looking for a job. If you view real estate as a career rather than a job, you are more likely to endure the highs and lows, making better ethical decisions the entire time. A career-minded employee is someone who makes decisions based on long-term rewards rather than short-term income. If you are career-minded, your reputation is what will build your referral base, which is your greatest asset. Brokers know the value of a good reputation. If their own office is going to survive, it has to be built on the reputation of its agents.

You should also be concerned with the office environment. Can the broker you chose provide the tools needed for your success? Can the office guide you to success? Does the office have the training, support staff, equipment, and technology you need to advance your career? Most importantly, how does your selected office ensure that office personnel are treated ethically and fairly?

You can find a brokerage firm with all of the latest tools, the best training, the nicest office, and the most advanced technology, but all of these criteria will not help if you do not have the determination to succeed and lack trustworthiness in this demanding career. It is a career where making ethical decisions will determine your future. How agents interact with the public and one another are also determined by office management and/or brokers. This is noteworthy because building an ethical reputation is difficult if the office itself does not have clear, ethical guidelines. Some offices have reputations for agents taking other agents' customers. If the office in which you are working is comprised of agents who partake in "backstabbing" and other unethical practices, it may be a good idea to transfer to another office where the agents use ethical practices and is demanded by the broker.

Ethical Decision: Honesty

A homeowner calls for a comparative market analysis or CMA. In order to get the listing, what would you do?

1. Research the price, add a ten percent increase, and let the homeowner believe you can get that particular price. After all, 90% of sellers want to believe their property is worth more and will accept the agent who brings the highest CMA.
2. Be honest, give the homeowner a realistic CMA, and hope your honesty will prevail. Let the homeowner know that you will only take listings that will sell, since the best chance of selling is at the beginning of the listing period, when the property is priced correctly.
3. Prepare an accurate CMA; give the homeowners the choice of listing at fair market price or marking up the price in hopes of getting a better offer. After all, most buyers will submit a discounted offer. This way they will get what they originally expected. If the property does not sell, they can always reduce the price. If they do this, however, they are taking the chance of overpricing the property during the beginning of the listing period, the time when sales are the strongest.

Why Should Buyers be Represented by a Real Estate Agent?

Buyers, like sellers, need a representative because there are many pitfalls and legal challenges in purchasing a house. You can help buyers gain knowledge about any property values, preparing contracts, property disclosures, federal requirements, the condition of the properties, and any necessary repairs. You can also protect them from being overcharged, known as fee-packing, by the lender.

As a real estate agent representing buyers, you have the fiduciary duty to protect your principal's best interest. As a real estate agent, you must abide by the Real Estate Canons of Professional Ethics and Conduct, which are comprised of three main characteristics:

- **Fidelity:** A real estate broker or salesperson while acting as an agent for another is a fiduciary. Special obligations are imposed when such fiduciary relationships are created.

a. As a real estate agent, your primary duty is to represent the interest of your client. Your position as your client's representative must always be clear to all parties involved. This does not mean you cannot or should not treat all other parties to the transaction fairly.
b. You must be faithful to your client, since the relationship is based on trust. You must also be both scrupulous and meticulous in doing your job.
c. You must not place your personal interests above that of your client's interest.

- **Integrity**: You have a special obligation to exercise integrity when discharging your responsibilities. You must be prudent and cautious in order to avoid misrepresenting anything, either by commission or omission.

- **Competency**: You are obligated to be knowledgeable. You should do the following:

a. Know market conditions and pledge to pursue continuing education on the intricacies involved in marketing real estate.
b. Be aware of national, state, and local real estate issues.
c. Know about new real estate developments.
d. Be judicious and skillful when doing your work.

As a real estate agent, you are a fiduciary with special obligations to your principal. In fact, you can lose your license and be liable for damages to your principal if you fail to show fidelity, integrity, and/or competency in relation to your principal.

Fiduciary Duties when Mixing Real Estate and Mortgage Lending

If you obtain both a real estate and a mortgage-lending license, you will be faced with several questions. Some of these questions include the following:

- What are my duties to my clients and customers?
- What are my duties to borrowers and lenders?

If the buyer is your client, then the same client services from real estate are extended into the lending field if you also want to be the loan officer. This relationship would be unusual because the borrower in mortgage lending is typically considered a customer to the lender, while a buyer in real estate can be either a customer or client. Therefore, if you act as both the loan officer and real estate agent for the buyer/borrower, while there are state/federal disclosures for this type of relationship, you will have blurred the relationship.

In real estate, the term **agency** refers to the relationship between two individuals, one having the legal power to act on behalf of the other while representing the individual's best interest.

- The person having power to act for another is the agent.
- The person being represented is the principal or client.
- The third party is the customer.

In real estate, either the client or customer can pay you. Your duty, however, remains the same: to know and protect your client and be honest with your customer. You have a fiduciary responsibility to the client. You do not have a fiduciary responsibility to the customer, but you should be fair and honest. You owe the following duties to your clients:

- Obedience – Faithfully perform your duties and follow your client's instructions, unless the request is either unreasonable or unlawful.
- Loyalty – Always act in the best interest of your client.
- Disclosure – Obtain relevant information and give information to your client.
- Confidentiality – Keep your client's information confidential. You cannot share any of your client's information without permission, even after the transaction ends.
- Accountability – Make sure to place all funds you receive from the client into a special non-interest bearing trust account that is separate from your personal or business account.
- Reasonable care and diligence – be careful of your responsibility to your client.

Formal Rules of Conduct

Your clients know you are a professional agent—for the most part; this is why they are using your services. However, they will appreciate some formal rules of conduct. Below are suggestions you may place on the back of your business card or in your buyer's presentation package.

The Seven Rules of Conduct I will abide by

Fidelity — I will always place your interests above my personal interests and the interests of all others.

Obedience — I will always be obedient to you within the law.

Loyalty — I will be completely loyal to you at all times.

Disclosure — I promise never to share any of your information unless I have your written permission.

Confidentiality — I promise to inform you of all important issues concerning your property, and I will protect all confidential information.

Accountability — I promise to earn your trust while handling your property valuables and caring for your home.

Reasonable Care and Diligence — I pledge to do my best to be informed of market conditions and to communicate all important issues to you as soon as possible.

Signature _____Date _____

Protecting your Buyers

If buyers are your clients, then is it your duty to protect your buyers? While mortgage lending is largely federally driven, real estate sales are more state-driven. In mortgage lending, it does not matter in which state the loan originated or what type of lender processes the loan; nearly all loans must meet the same federal requirements. Of course, there are a few exceptions, which may cause a mortgage loan not to fall under federal guidelines.

From a mortgage-lending standpoint, all loans must be processed the same way in every state and with every type of lender. Real estate sales are conducted differently from state to state; however, there are also many federal laws you must follow. Also, several federal laws were enacted to protect real estate consumers. In real estate, the most important federal laws for marketing and sales are the following:

Federal Acts	Purpose
Truth-in-Lending Act, TILA, (1968) Reg. Z	To promote the informed use of consumer credit by requiring disclosures about its terms and cost. The regulation also gives consumers the right to cancel certain credit transactions involving a lien on a consumer's principal dwelling.
Real Estate Settlement Procedures Act (RESPA) (1976), Reg. X	To effect certain changes in the settlement process for residential real estate will result in 1. More effective disclosure to homebuyers and sellers of settlement costs. The elimination of **kickbacks** or referral fees that tend to unnecessarily increase the costs of certain settlement services. 2. The reduction in the amount the homebuyer is required to place into escrow accounts established to ensure the payment of real estate taxes and insurance. 3. Significant reform and modernization of local record keeping of land title information.
Civil Rights Act (CRA), (1866)	For <u>all</u> citizens in the United States to have the same rights to inherit, purchase, lease, sell, hold, and convey real and personal property.
Fair Housing Act (FHA), (1968)	A law that makes it illegal to discriminate on the basis of race, color, religion, sex, national origin, physical handicap, or familial status in connection with the sale or rental of housing. These individual classes are known today as the "protected classes."
Antitrust Laws, Price Fixing	To prohibit monopolies and sustain competition in order to protect companies from one another and to protect consumers from unfair business practices.
Deceptive Trade Practice Act (DTPA)	To protect consumers from unfair and deceptive acts.

Truth-in-Lending Act

Rules for Real Estate Success

Under REG. Z, advertising, using any of the five-trigger terms below, requires the use of all five disclosures. *Advertisement* means a commercial message in any medium promoting, directly or indirectly, a credit transaction. Generally, advertising is when the consumer is left with the means to contact the promoters.

The five trigger terms are

1. The amount or percent of any down payment.
2. The amount of any payment.
3. The number of payments.
4. The repayment terms.
5. The amount of any finance charge.

All five of the following disclosures are required if any of the trigger terms are used:

1. The dollar amount of the loan
2. The down payment amount
3. The repayment schedule
4. The annual percentage rate
5. The total payment

The Truth-in-Lending Statement (TIL) is another disclosure form delivered within the third business day after completing a loan application. The TIL gives the consumer the **Annual Percentage Rate** (APR) within 1/8 of a percent. The original Truth-in-Lending Statement and the final TIL given at closing cannot be more than 1/8 difference. The APR is the interest and certain closing costs the buyers will pay at settlement. It is lawful for the lender to give a copy of any of the buyers' documents to you, the real estate agent. Asking buyers for their copies of documents, however, may prove helpful at closing.

Advertising is **a commercial message in any medium, promoting a credit transaction, directly or indirectly.**

Section 226.3 Exempt transactions This regulation does not apply to the following:

(a) *Business, commercial, agricultural, or organizational credit.*[4] {⁴ The provisions in § 226.12(a) and (b) governing the issuances of credit cards and the liability for their unauthorized use apply to all credit cards, even if the credit cards are issued for use in connection with extensions of credit that otherwise are exempt under this section.}

(1) An extension of credit primarily for a business, commercial, or agricultural purpose.

(2) An extension of credit to other than a natural person, including credit to government agencies, or instrumentalities.

(b) *Credit over $25,000 not secured by real property or a dwelling* An extension of credit not secured by real property, or by personal property used or expected to be used as the principal dwelling of the consumer, in which the amount financed exceeds $25,000 or in which there is an express written commitment to extend credit in excess of $25,000.

Section 226.16 Advertising

(a) *Actually available term.* If an advertisement for credit states specific credit terms, it shall state only those terms that actually are or will be arranged or offered by the creditor.

(b) *Advertisement of terms that require additional disclosures.* If any of the terms required to be disclosed under Section 226.6 is set forth in an advertisement, the advertisement shall also clearly and conspicuously set forth the following:[36d]

(1) Any minimum, fixed, transaction, activity or similar charge that could be imposed.

(2) Any periodic rate that may be applied expressed as an annual percentage rate as determined under Section 226.14(b). If the plan provides for a variable periodic rate, that fact shall be disclosed.

(3) Any membership or participation fee that could be imposed.

(c) *Catalogs or other multiple-page advertisements; electronic advertisements.*

(1) If a catalog or other multiple-page advertisement or an advertisement using electronic communication, gives information in a table or schedule in sufficient detail to permit determination of the disclosures required by paragraph (b) of this section, it shall be considered a single advertisement if:

(i) The table or schedule is clearly and conspicuously set forth; and

(ii) Any statement of terms set forth in Section 226.6 appearing anywhere else in the catalog or advertisement clearly refers to the page or location where the table or schedule begins.

(2) A catalog or other multiple-page advertisement or an advertisement using electronic communication complies with this paragraph if the table or schedule of terms includes all appropriate disclosures for a representative scale of amounts up to the level of the more commonly sold higher-priced property or services offered.

(d) *Additional requirements for home equity plans*

(1) Advertisement of terms that require additional disclosures. If any of the terms required to be disclosed under Section 226.6(a) or (b) or the payment terms of the plan are set forth, affirmatively or negatively, in an advertisement for a home equity plan subject to the requirements of Section 226.5b, the advertisement also shall clearly and conspicuously set forth the following:

(i) Any loan fee that is a percentage of the credit limit under the plan and an estimate of any other fees imposed for opening the plan, stated as a single dollar amount or a reasonable range.

(ii) Any periodic rate used to compute the finance charge, expressed as an annual percentage rate as determined under Section 226.14(b).

(iii) The maximum annual percentage rate that may be imposed in a variable-rate plan.

(2) *Discounted and premium rates.* If an advertisement states an initial annual percentage rate that is not based on the index and margin used to make later rate adjustments in a variable-rate plan, the advertisement also shall state the period of time such rate will be in effect, and, with equal prominence to the initial rate, a reasonably current annual percentage rate that would have been in effect using the index and margin.

(3) *Balloon payment.* If an advertisement contains a statement about any minimum periodic payment, the advertisement also shall state, if applicable, that a balloon payment may result.

(4) *Tax implications.* An advertisement that states that any interest expense incurred under the home equity plan is or may be tax deductible may not be misleading in this regard.

(5) *Misleading terms.* An advertisement may not refer to a home equity plan as "free money" or contain a similarly misleading term

Section 226.24 Advertising (a) *Actually available terms*
If an advertisement for credit states specific credit terms, it shall state only those terms that actually are or will be arranged or offered by the creditor.

(b) *Advertisement of rate of finance charge*
If an advertisement states a rate of finance charge, it shall state the rate as an "annual percentage rate," using that term. If the annual percentage rate may be increased after consummation, the advertisement shall state that fact. The advertisement shall not state any other rate, except that a simple annual rate or periodic rate that is applied to an unpaid balance may be stated in conjunction with, but not more conspicuously than, the annual percentage rate.

(c) *Advertisement of terms that require additional disclosures*

(1) If any of the following terms is set forth in an advertisement, the advertisement shall meet the requirements of paragraph (c) (2) of this section:

(i) The amount or percentage of any down payment.

(ii) The number of payments or period of repayment.

(iii) The amount of any payment.

(iv) The amount of any finance charge.

(2) An advertisement stating any of the terms in paragraph (c)(1) of this section shall state the following terms,[49] {49 An example of one or more typical extensions of credit with a statement of all the terms applicable to each may be used.} as applicable:

(i) The amount or percentage of the down payment.

(ii) The terms of repayment.

(iii) The "annual percentage rate," using that term, and, if the rate may be increased after consummation, that fact.

Real Estate Settlement Procedures Act (RESPA) (1976), Reg. X

Real Estate Settlement Procedures Act

Under RESPA, lenders are required to be more effective in providing advance disclosures of settlement costs to homebuyers and sellers. Under RESPA, lenders must give several disclosures in advance such as the following:

Section	Disclosures	Time of Delivery
Sec. 5	HUD's Special Information Booklet 1676-H	No later than three business days after the application was taken
Sec. 5c	Good Faith Estimate	Within three business days of the prepared application
Sec. 8	Affiliated Business Arrangement Disclosure	Required at the time of the referral; unless by phone, you will have three business days.
Sec. 4	HUD-1	One day prior to closing

Protecting Your Buyers

Under the Good Faith Estimate (GFE), the buyer is to receive the disclosure within the third business day after applying for a loan. The disclosure shows consumers how much they are expected to pay in closing costs. The lender's fee is a closing cost fee. So, if the lender's fees are much higher at closing or in the HUD-1 closing statement than on the GFE, the lender maybe engaging in what is known as **"fee packing."** The buyers will have original copies of the GFE so, if the lender does not have a good explanation for the different fees, you should have the lender explain the fees to your buyer.

Under the Gramm-Leach-Bliley Act, (1999), Privacy Act and Fair Credit Reporting Act, the lender cannot give information to you (the agent) because you are a third party. However, you may ask your buyer for copies of the GFE. The **HUD-1** which is the final settlement statement of charges must be made available one day before closing upon request to all parties to the transaction. You should request a copy of the HUD-1 from the settlement agent and compare it to the buyer's GFE. The GFE and the HUD-1 have the same cost items for the buyer. The difference between the GFE and the HUD-1 is the **GFE** is merely an estimate while the HUD-1 must be accurate and final. Your buyers are counting on you for this accuracy. Your buyer is a customer of the loan officer; thus, the loan officer holds no fiduciary responsibilities toward your client. The loan officer's fiduciary duties are to the lender. The loan officer, however, does hold a duty of honesty and fairness to your buyer. When there are fees, do not expect the loan officer to be loyal to your buyers. You are the one who must be loyal and responsible to your clients.

Real Estate Settlement Procedures Act (RESPA)

The Real Estate Settlement Procedures Act, commonly known as RESPA, has two primary objectives:

- To provide the consumer with timely disclosures as it relates to the cost and the servicing of loans
- To prohibit certain abusive practices, such as kickbacks, escrow amounts, loan servicing, or a sellers' requiring the buyer use a particular title company as a condition of the sale

Gifts to Promote Business or Kickbacks?

The act of gift-giving between real estate agents, title companies, insurance companies, and loan officers or affiliate members rarely helps promote business, and it could be viewed as an illegal referral fee, which is a violation under Section 8 of RESPA.

Giving away items as part of an advertising and marketing campaign is perfectly legal as long as the item(s) advertise and market the company name or logo and is open to all of its members. For example, a loan officer may legally give coffee mugs with a company logo on them to all real estate agents in the office as part of a marketing campaign. However, if the loan officer is selective, giving a free trip to a particular agent, this is considered a **kickback**. Giving a gift to a friend for referring his/her friends is also considered a kickback under RESPA. While some states have a safe limited amount to give, such as a fifty-dollar gift, RESPA has no dollar amount limit. In fact, RESPA specifies *"any fee"* or thing of value is a violation. Two of the most valuable gifts you can give someone are your services and your knowledge. If the agent or loan officer is not sure whether the referral fee is legal under the cost of marketing or an illegal kickback, do not give or receive it.

Where RESPA becomes a kickback issue under section 8 of RESPA is with marketing. Loan officers or real estate agents are not allowed to give or receive any type of kickbacks. Many agents ask what kickbacks are. A **kickback** is the act of giving or receiving an unearned gift. See Section 8 below for the definition of an unearned gift. What are the exceptions to RESPA? What are the violations for giving or receiving illegal gifts? Can advertising be considered a kickback? These are good questions that deserve to be addressed.

Ethical Decision, Kickbacks

If a real estate broker paid $500 for advertising on one page of a magazine, can he/she charge the loan officer $500 for 20% of the same space if the real estate broker agrees to give the loan officer an applicant yielding $5,000 in return?

Situation 1 Situation 2 Situation 3

Would this be good business if the loan officer paid an excessive advertising fee, and he earned $5000 on the loan?

What amount should the loan officer have paid for 20% of the advertising space?

What is wrong with this situation if the consumer paid regular price, but both the real estate broker and loan officer earned a profit?

Exceptions to RESPA

RESPA applies to all 1-4 family federally related mortgage loans except the following:

- Construction loans, unless the 1-4 family residential loan is used as, or may be converted to, a permanent loan by the same lender
- Loans on property of 25 acres or more

- Loans for business purposes, such as commercial or agricultural real estate
- Temporary loans converted to a permanent loan by the same lender
- A bridge or swing 1-4 family loan which is not covered by RESPA
- Vacant land, unless a structure or manufactured home will be constructed or placed on the real property within two years from the settlement of the loan
- Assumption without lender approval is when the lender does not have the right to expressly approve a subsequent person as the borrower on an existing federally related mortgage loan
- Loan conversions that are any conversion of a federally related mortgage loan to different terms that are consistent with provisions of the original mortgage instrument, as long as a new note is not required
- Secondary market transactions

Certainly, all gifts must be earned—an unearned gift or anything of value or consideration can be illegal in the housing industry. See RESPA's Section 8 rules on kickbacks below:

Real Estate Settlement Procedures Act

SECTION 8. PROHIBITION AGAINST KICKBACKS AND UNEARNED FEES

No person shall give and no person shall accept any fee, kickback, or thing of value pursuant to any agreement or understanding, oral or otherwise, that business incident to or a part of a real estate settlement service involving a federally related mortgage loan shall be referred to any person.

No person shall give and no person shall accept any portion, split, or percentage of any charge made or received for the rendering of a real estate settlement service in connection with a transaction involving a federally related mortgage loan other than for services actually performed.

Nothing in this section shall be construed as prohibiting the payment of a fee:
- To attorneys at law for services actually rendered or by a title company to its duly appointed agent for services actually performed in the issuance of a policy of title insurance or by a lender to its duly appointed agent for services actually performed in the making of a loan
- The payment to any person of a bona fide salary or compensation or other payment for goods or facilities actually furnished or for services actually performed

- Payments pursuant to cooperative brokerage and referral arrangements or agreements between real estate agents and brokers
- Affiliated business arrangements so long as

(A) A disclosure is made of the existence of such an arrangement to the person being referred and, in connection with such referral, such person is provided a written estimate of the charge or range of charges generally made by the provider.

(B) Such person is not required to use any particular provider of settlement services, and

(C) The only thing of value that is received from the arrangement, other than the payments permitted under this subsection, is a return on the ownership interest or franchise relationship.

Any person or persons who violate the provisions of this section shall be fined not more than $10,000 and/or imprisonment for not more than one year. The second time it is a $50,000 fine.

Any person or persons who violate the prohibitions or limitations of this section shall be jointly and severally liable to the person or persons charged for the settlement service involved in the violation in an amount equal to three times the amount of any charge paid for such settlement service.

No person or persons shall be liable for a violation of the provisions of section 8 if such person or persons proves by a preponderance of the evidence that such violation was not intentional and resulted from a bona fide error notwithstanding maintenance of procedures that are reasonably adapted to avoid such error. The Secretary, the Attorney General of any State, or the insurance commissioner of any State may bring an action to enjoin violations of this section. In any private action brought, the court may award to the prevailing party the court cost of the action plus reasonable attorney's fees.

Section 3500.5 Coverage of RESPA

(a) *Applicability*

RESPA and this part apply to all federally related mortgage loans, except for the exemptions provided in paragraph (b) of this section.

(b) *Exemptions*

(1) A loan on property of 25 acres or more.

(2) *Business purpose loans.* An extension of credit primarily for a business, commercial, or agricultural purpose, as defined by Regulation Z, (a) (1). Persons may rely on Regulation Z in determining whether the exemption applies.

(3) *Temporary financing.* Temporary financing, such as a construction loan. The exemption for temporary financing does not apply to a loan made to finance construction of 1- to 4-family residential property if the loan is used as, or may be converted to, permanent financing by the same lender or is used to finance transfer of title to the first user. If a lender issues a commitment for permanent financing, with or without conditions, the loan is covered by this part. Any construction loan for new or rehabilitated 1- to 4-family residential property, other than a loan to a *bona fide* builder (a person who regularly constructs 1- to 4-family residential structures for sale or lease), is subject to this part if its term is for two years or more. A "bridge loan" or "swing loan" in which a lender takes a security interest in otherwise covered 1- to 4-family residential property is not covered by RESPA and this part.

(4) *Vacant land.* Any loan secured by vacant or unimproved property, unless within two years from the date of the settlement of the loan, a structure or a manufactured home will be constructed or placed on the real property using the loan proceeds. If a loan for a structure or manufactured home to be placed on vacant or unimproved property will be secured by a lien on that property, the transaction is covered by this part.

(5) *Assumption without lender approval.* Any assumption in which the lender does not have the right expressly to approve a subsequent person as the borrower on an existing federally related mortgage loan. Any assumption in which the lender's permission is both required and obtained is covered by RESPA and this part, whether or not the lender charges a fee for the assumption.

(6) *Loan conversions.* Any conversion of a federally related mortgage loan to different terms that are consistent with provisions of the original mortgage instrument, as long as a new note is not required, even if the lender charges an additional fee for the conversion.

(7) *Secondary market transactions.* A *bona fide* transfer of a loan obligation in the secondary market is not covered by RESPA. In determining what constitutes a *bona fide* transfer, HUD will consider the real source of funding and the real interest of the funding lender. Mortgage broker transactions that are table-funded are not secondary market transactions.

Section 3500.14 Prohibition against kickbacks and unearned fees.

(a) *Section 8 violation*

Any violation of this section is a violation of section 8 of RESPA and is subject to enforcement as such under Section 3500.19.

(b) *No referral fees*

No person shall give and no person shall accept any fee, kickback or other thing of value pursuant to any agreement or understanding, oral or otherwise, that business incident to or part of a settlement service involving a federally related mortgage loan shall be referred to any person. Any referral of a settlement service is not a compensable service, except as set forth in Section 3500.14(g) (1). A business entity (whether or not in an affiliate relationship) may not pay any other business entity or the employees of any other business entity for the referral of settlement service business.

(c) *No split of charges except for actual services performed*

No person shall give and no person shall accept any portion, split, or percentage of any charge made or received for the rendering of a settlement service in connection with a transaction involving a federally related mortgage loan other than for services actually performed. A charge by a person for which no or nominal services are performed or for which duplicate fees are charged is an unearned fee and violates this section. The source of the payment does not determine whether or not a service is compensable. Nor may the prohibitions of this part be avoided by creating an arrangement wherein the purchaser of services splits the fee.

(d) *Thing of value*

This term is broadly defined. It includes, without limitation, monies, things, discounts, salaries, commissions, fees, duplicate payments of a charge, stock, dividends, distributions of partnership profits, franchise royalties, credits representing monies that may be paid at a future date, the opportunity to participate in a money-making program, retained or increased earnings, increased equity in a parent or subsidiary entity, special bank deposits or accounts, special or unusual banking terms, services of all types at special or free rates, sales or rentals at special prices or rates, lease or rental payments based in whole or in part on the amount of business referred, trips and payment of another person's expenses, or reduction in credit against an existing obligation. The term "payment" is used throughout Sections 3500.14 and 3500.15 as synonymous with the giving or receiving any "thing of value" and does not require transfer of money.

(e) *Agreement or understanding*

An agreement or understanding for the referral of business incident to or part of a settlement service need not be written or verbalized but may be established by a practice, pattern or course of conduct. When a thing of value is received repeatedly and is connected in any way with the volume or value of the business referred, the receipt of the thing of value is evidence that it is made pursuant to an agreement or understanding for the referral of business.

(f) *Referral*

(1) A referral includes any oral or written action directed to a person which has the effect of affirmatively influencing the selection by any person of a provider of a settlement service or business incident to or part of a settlement service when such person will pay for such settlement service or business incident thereto or pay a charge attributable in whole or in part to such settlement service or business.

(2) A referral also occurs whenever a person paying for a settlement service or business incident thereto is required to use a particular provider of a settlement service or business incident thereto.

(g) Fees, salaries, compensation, or other payments

(1) Section 8 of RESPA permits the following:

(i) A payment to an attorney at law for services actually rendered;
(ii) A payment by a title company to its duly appointed agent for services actually performed in the issuance of a policy of title insurance;
(iii) A payment by a lender to its duly appointed agent or contractor for services actually performed
in the origination, processing, or funding of a loan;
(iv) A payment to any person of a *bona fide* salary or compensation or other payment for goods or facilities actually furnished or for services actually performed;
(v) **A payment pursuant to cooperative brokerage and referral arrangements or agreements between real estate agents and real estate brokers. (The statutory exemption restated in this paragraph refers only to fee divisions within real estate brokerage arrangements when all parties are acting in a real estate brokerage capacity and has no applicability to any fee arrangements between real estate brokers and mortgage brokers or between mortgage brokers.);**
(vi) Normal promotional and educational activities that are not conditioned on the referral of business and that do not involve

the defraying of expenses that otherwise would be incurred by persons in a position to refer settlement services or business incident thereto; or
(vii) An employer's payment to its own employees for any referral activities.

The Department may investigate high prices to see if they are the result of a referral fee or a split of a fee. If the payment of a thing of value bears no reasonable relationship to the market value of the goods or services provided, then the excess is not for services or goods actually performed or provided. These facts may be used as evidence of a violation of section 8 and may serve as a basis for a RESPA investigation. High prices standing alone are not proof of a RESPA violation. The value of a referral (i.e., the value of any additional business obtained thereby) is not to be taken into account in determining whether the payment exceeds the reasonable value of such goods, facilities or services. The fact that the transfer of the thing of value does not result in an increase in any charge made by the person giving the thing of value is irrelevant in determining whether the act is prohibited.

Multiple services. When a person in a position to refer settlement service business, such as an attorney, mortgage lender, real estate broker or agent, or developer or builder, receives a payment for providing additional settlement services as part of a real estate transaction, such payment must be for services that are actual, necessary and distinct from the primary services provided by such person. For example, for an attorney of the buyer or seller to receive compensation as a title agent, the attorney must perform core title agent services (for which liability arises) separate from attorney services, including the evaluation of the title search to determine the insurability of the title, the clearance of underwriting objections, the actual issuance of the policy or policies on behalf of the title insurance company, and, where customary, issuance of the title commitment, and the conducting of the title search and closing.

Prior to the referral, the person making a referral has provided to each person whose business is referred a written disclosure, in the format of the Affiliated Business Arrangement Disclosure Statement set forth. This disclosure shall specify the nature of the relationship (explaining the ownership and financial interest) between the person performing settlement services (or business incident thereto) and the person making the referral, and shall describe the estimated charge or range of charges (using the same terminology, as far as practical, as Section L of the HUD—1 or HUD—1A settlement statement) generally made by the provider of settlement services.

Civil Rights Act of 1968, Fair Housing Act (FHA)

The Civil Rights Act of 1968 makes it illegal to discriminate on the basis of race, color, religion, sex, national origin, physical handicap, or familial status in connection with the sale or rental of housing. These individual classes are today known as the "protected classes."

While age is not a part of FHA, it is part of the Equal Credit Opportunity Act (ECOA).

The Fair Housing Act is Title VIII part of the Civil Rights Act, and it is overseen and enforced by HUD, which prohibits discrimination in all aspects of residential real estate.

The first violation under FHA is a fine of not more than $50,000, with a fine of not more than $100,000
for subsequent violations, in addition to civil damages and attorney's fees. All lenders are required to display the Equal Housing Opportunity logo and poster in all offices as part of the Fair Housing Act. A HUD logo can be downloaded from www.hud.gov.

- Logos are to be used when advertising mortgage loan products.
- When using multi-media advertising, you must also use a nondiscriminatory statement, such as *"equal housing lender."*

Deceptive Trade Practices

False, misleading, or deceptive acts or practices in the conduct of any trade or commerce are hereby declared unlawful.

The term "false, misleading, or deceptive acts or practices" includes, but is not limited to, the following acts:

- Passing off goods or services as those of another
- Causing confusion or misunderstanding as to the source, sponsorship, approval, or certification of goods or services
- Causing confusion or misunderstanding as to affiliation, connection, or association with, or certification by another
- Using deceptive representations or designations of geographic origin in connection with goods or services
- Representing that goods or services have sponsorship, approval, characteristics, ingredients, uses, benefits, or quantities which they do not have or that a person has a sponsorship, approval, status, affiliation, or connection which he/she does not
- Representing that goods are original or new if they are deteriorated, reconditioned, reclaimed, used, or secondhand
- Representing that goods or services are of a particular standard, quality, or grade, or that goods are of a particular style or model, if they are of another
- Disparaging the goods, services, or business of another by false or misleading representation of facts
- Advertising goods or services with intent not to sell them as advertised
- Advertising goods or services with intent not to supply a reasonable expectable public demand, unless the advertisements disclosed a limitation of quantity
- Making false or misleading statements of fact concerning the reasons for, existence of, or amount of price reductions
- Representing that an agreement confers or involves rights, remedies, or obligations which it does not have or involve, or which are prohibited by law
- Knowingly making false or misleading statements of fact concerning the need for parts, replacement, or repair service
- Misrepresenting the authority of a salesperson, representative or agent to negotiate the final terms of a consumer transaction
- Advertising of any sale by fraudulently representing that a person is going out of business; advertising must not be false, misleading, or deceptive.

National Do-Not-Call

Federal Trade Commission on Telemarketing Sales Rules

Rules for Real Estate Success

Real estate agents trying to solicit telephone leads should understand the Federal Trade Commission rules on telemarketing. The **telemarketing sales rules** (TSR) apply to any plan, program, or campaign to sell goods or services through interstate phone systems. This includes telemarketers who solicit consumers, often on behalf of third party sellers. It also includes sellers who provide, offer to provide, or arrange to provide, goods or services to consumers in exchange for payment.

The TSR prohibits deceptive and abusive telemarketing practices and protects consumers from unwanted late-night telemarketing calls.

- Calling times are restricted to the hours between 8 a.m. and 9 p.m.
- Telemarketers must promptly provide the identity of the seller or charitable organization and indicate the call is a sales call or a charitable salutation before making their pitch.
- Telemarketers must disclose all material information about the goods or services they are offering and the terms of the sale. They are prohibited from lying about any terms of their offer.

Starting October 1, 2003, telemarketers must connect their call to a sales representative within two seconds of the consumer's greeting.

This will reduce the number of "dead air," or hang-up calls, you get from telemarketers. These calls result from the use of automatic dialing equipment that sometimes reaches more numbers than there are available sales representatives. In addition, when the telemarketer does not have a representative standing by, a recorded message must play to let you know who is calling as well as the number from which he/she is calling. The law prohibits a sales pitch. The telemarketer must also stay on the line until at least 15 seconds, or until four rings have passed, in order to give you time to answer the phone.

Beginning January 29, 2004, telemarketers must transmit their telephone number, and if possible, their name, to the caller ID service. This will protect homeowners' privacy, increase accountability on the telemarketer's part, and help with law enforcement efforts.

The Federal Trade Commission's (FTC) amended Telemarketing Sales Rule (TSR) puts consumers in charge of the number of telemarketing calls they get at home. The amended rule created the **National Do Not Call Registry**, which makes it easier and more efficient for consumers to stop getting telemarketing sales calls they do not want.

The FTC began enforcing the National Do Not Call Registry on October 1, 2003. Phone numbers stay in the registry for five years, until the number is disconnected, or until it is deleted from the registry.

The law requires telemarketers to search the registry every three months and to synchronize their call lists with the phone numbers listed on the registry.

If telemarketers fail to update their database and continue to make calls while disregarding the National Do Not Call Registry, they can be fined up to $11,000 for each call. For more information about the National Do Not Call Registry, visit www.donotcall.gov. *A good example whether or not the* Do Not Call Registry applies is when calling a For-Sale-By-Owner. If you call a For Sale by Owner (FSBO) to *solicit* a person's business, you need to clear his/her phone number with the National Do Not Call Registry. However, if you call the FSBO because you have buyers and want to preview their property, you do not need to clear the Do Not Call Registry. You are allowed to call a homeowner as long as you are not trying to solicit his/her listing/business.

Title Insurance Companies

In the past, the legality of title insurance companies providing free marketing assistance to real estate and mortgage companies was nebulous. However, the 2004 HUD Commissioner's ruling made it clear that title companies, like any other settlement service provider, may not furnish any free assistance to any mortgage or real estate individuals or companies, since this would be a kickback violation under RESPA Section 8. The cost of assisting real estate or mortgage individuals is considered an unearned fee and is subject to a $10,000 fine and/or one year in prison for either taking or receiving such unearned gifts. This federal law is enforceable, regardless of the state real estate commissions' view on the gifts.

Rules for Real Estate Success

1. Visit (www.hud.gov) for information on HUD's Special Information booklets. While this booklet is required by all lenders, it has important information for real estate agents. You should read and adopt this booklet as part of your buyer's presentation kits. While it is not a requirement, real estate agents can include a HUD Booklet for buyers. There are several sources to purchase booklets.

2. In order to protect your clients from predatory lending and kickback fees, you should fully understand the Good Faith Estimate (GFE). Visit a title company and ask for help in understanding closing procedures and reading GFEs and HUD-1.

3. Visit grocery stores or any location where they have real estate magazines. These magazines are filled with advertisements—most ads are correct, but a few have legal issues. Study the format agents use to start a scrapbook of good ads. Read the Truth-in-Lending Act on advertisement for this exercise.

4. Work on sellers' and buyers' closing net sheets. Title companies and broker managers are good sources for this exercise.

5. Read and fully understand the Real Estate Settlement Procedures Act Section 8.

1. Ethics is
   A. How we perceive what is right or fair from our own values and the decision we should take.
   B. The feeling of what is right and wrong as a community or group.
   C. State or federal laws that govern behavior.
   D. The rules to conduct meetings.

2. Kickback laws are found in the
   A. Truth-in-Lending Act.
   B. Equal Credit Opportunity Act.
   C. Civil Rights Act.
   D. Real Estate Settlement Procedures Act.

3. Gifts from lenders to real estate agents are in what law?
   A. Legal under Reg. C
   B. Legal under state real estate laws
   C. Illegal under Section 8 of RESPA
   D. Illegal under TILA Reg. Z

4. Telemarketers can call between what hours?
   A. 9 a.m.-5.p.m.
   B. 8 a.m.-9 p.m.
   C. 9 a.m.-9 p.m.
   D. 7 a.m.-10 p.m.

5. Affiliated Business Arrangement Disclosure falls under which act?
   A. Truth-in-Lending Act
   B. Equal Credit Opportunity Act
   C. Civil Rights Act/Fair Housing Act
   D. Real Estate Settlement Procedures Act

6. The delivery time for the Good Faith Estimate is
   A. 24 hours.
   B. 7 days.
   C. One day before closing.
   D. 3 days after loan application.

7. Advertising in any media falls under which law?
   A. Reg. Z
   B. Reg. C
   C. Reg. B
   D. Reg. X

8. Which is <u>not</u> one of the fundamental values?
    A. Honesty and fairness
    B. Integrity
    C. Loyalty
    D. Awareness

9. Morals is
    A. How we perceive what is right or fair from our own values and the decision we should take
    B. The feeling of what is right and wrong as a community or group.
    C. State or federal laws that govern behavior.
    D. The rules to conduct meetings.

10. An agent is
    A. The person having power to act for another
    B. The person being represented
    C. The third party
    D. All the above

11. Fidelity is
    A. A fiduciary relationship between a real estate agent and client
    B. A fiduciary relationship between a real estate agent and customer
    C. The relationship between a Broker to both client and customer
    D. A special obligation to exercise when discharging ones' responsibilities.

12. Which is not a trigger term?
    A. The amount or percent of any down payment
    B. The amount of any payment
    C. The number of payments
    D. The annual percentage rate

13. The delivery period for the HUD-1 is
    A. One day prior to closing
    B. Three days after loan application
    C. No later than Three days before closing
    D. On day of closing

14. Fee packing is
    A. Illegal fees from lender to real estate agent
    B. Unjustified fees by the lenders
    C. Unwarranted advertising fees
    D. The annual percentage rate

CHAPTER 3
Developing Goals, Plans, and Time Management

Objectives:

Be able to do the following:

- Formulate goals
- Develop a business plan
- Implement time management
- Establish a budget
- Prioritize assignments
- Implement a plan and take action
- Evaluate the results
- Know your audience

Terms:

- Company marketing
- Goal planning
- Goals
- Individual marketing
- Institutional marketing
- Marketing plans
- Sales skills
- Target audience
- Tasks
- Time management

Developing Goals, Business Plans, and Taking Action for Real Estate Agents

This chapter will focus on real estate agents developing their business plans, which consist of five important parts: goal setting, time management, marketing, taking action, and evaluating the results. Many sales agents haven't made the distinction between goals, time management, sales, and marketing, and how important they are. In a nutshell, the following terms have been defined:

- **Marketing** refers to how agents attract people to their business, such as putting an ad in the newspaper.
- **Sales skills** refers to the manner in which agents personally interact with consumers in order to sell a product.
- **Goals** state a specific achievement desired to be accomplished within a specific timeframe.
- **Plans** are the framework for achieving the desired results.
- **Time management** is designing the framework to achieve the most productive work possible in the same amount of time.

Why is planning and time management so important? Agents can spend thousands of dollars in marketing, but without successful planning, selling skills, or time management, the expected result will not be encouraging. Therefore, before spending your time and large sums in marketing, it is prudent to understand time management, build sales skills, and plan to achieve your desired goals. Another important reason why many agents fail is because they do not realize that real estate is a business with real goals, plans, time management, and organization to achieve those goals. Real estate agents should act like the CEO of their business, to lead their company in the right direction.

Five Parts to Developing a Real Estate Business Plan

1. Developing Goals
2. Time Management
3. Marketing Plans
4. Taking Action
5. Evaluating the Results

Goal Setting and Planning

How do you set goals and plans and then commit to achieve those goals? More specifically, you need to decide what you want and how you plan to achieve them. Setting your career goals is similar to deciding where you want to go for your summer vacation. Should you go to Europe, Canada, or stay in the U.S.? Will your decision be based on funds, time, or interest? Will your summer vacation be a once-in-a-lifetime trip or an annual event?

Goals or objectives are what one plans to do or intend to achieve. In real estate, it's your carefully planned final decisions, considering your personal limitations, and assessing your resources to decide if the goal is feasible for you.

You must decide what you want from your real estate business. Will your business goals be short-term (i.e., just another job to earn extra income), or will they encompass a lifetime career? Do you have the funds required to start your new career? How do you plan to get there? Committing to your goal of actually working as a professional in real estate is much the same as getting to your planned destination for your summer vacation. To get to your destination, you wouldn't just start driving and hope to end up in the right place. You would get a map. Think of your goal and plan as a 'trip' to success that you map-out and set a course. Once you decide what you want, specify your goal. Part two is the planning stage, which is determining how to get where you want to go in the quickest and safest way.

Effective Goals Must Include the Following:

- In writing
- Realistic
- Clear and specific
- Based on a time schedule
- Measurable
- Based on levels of achievement
- Flexible
- Based on a reward system
- Personal
- Fun, fun, and more fun!

Putting Your Goals in Writing

Goals should be clear and in writing. By writing down your goals, you are one step closer to making a formal commitment to yourself. These written goals should include short, medium, and long-term goals. Not only should you have a clear contract with yourself, but simple notes can also give you direction. Each night before you go to bed, try posting your goals on your mirror so that each morning, you'll start focusing on what is important. For example, you might write something like this: "This month, I will list 20 houses on the MLS and sell 10 houses." Now, think about how you will accomplish your goal of listing 20 houses. You may already have a detailed plan, but try to think of fresh new ideas each morning. You should be thinking about marketing your real estate goals morning through night. Don't just trust your memory. The human mind is capable of holding only five to seven pieces of information at once. Instead, have a notepad and pen ready for those brilliant ideas that come to you in the middle of the night or while you are daydreaming during the day.

Making Your Goals Realistic

As you write your goals, keep in mind that they should be reasonable. For instance, is it realistic and practical to set a goal to sell a million dollars worth of real estate in your first season? Although your goals are personal, don't be afraid to ask for help in achieving them. Ask seasoned agents or management for advice on setting realistic goals. If you do not set realistic and attainable goals, you will be frustrated in the real estate business. Be realistic; however, don't be afraid to set high standards.

Making Your Goals Specific

Your goals should be specific—that way you can clearly see what it is that you want to achieve and know when you have achieved them. Once you clearly understand what you want to achieve, you can set specific standards for that achievement.

Things to consider when making specific goals may be as follows:

- How much do I plan to earn monthly? How much do I plan to earn in the first, second, and the third years?
- How many houses will it take to earn those amounts, based on my commission level?
- How many listings will it take for me to sell ten houses per month? Will it take 20 listings at the right price (with good marketing) to sell ten houses per month?

You need to develop a marketing budget and consider the following, even if your goals are clearly specified:

- How much of your income (i.e.,10-20%) will be used for marketing during the first year, the second year, and so on?
- What research will you conduct if you plan to get the most marketing for your dollar?
- How much (i.e., 20%) should you, as a new agent, (as opposed to a seasoned agent) spend on marketing?

If you set a goal to list five houses per month, think about whether or not the goal is realistically feasible. Think about this: if you actually closed four transactions and lost three loans in one month, will you have achieved your goal, or will you have lost ground instead? In order to gain five new listings per month, how many contacts are you required to make? How many letters will you send, how many doors will you knock on, or how many phone calls will you make? Statistically, for each listing, you will mail out one hundred letters, make twelve to sixty phone calls and visit 23 homes. For more information on sales statistics, read Chapters 5 and 7.

Setting Specific Goals for a Successful Career

Setting specific goals is difficult for some people. To help you set specific goals, follow the steps below:

- Make a list of all your goals, placing them into one of four broad categories: business, spiritual, personal, or health.
- Divide each broad category into sub-categories: long-term (i.e., it will take over ten years to achieve), mid-term (i.e., it will take over one year to achieve), and short-term (i.e., it will take one year or less to achieve) goals.
- Prioritize every section and category by order of importance.

Time Management

Managing Your Time

Why are setting goals and planning so important? Learning to set goals and planning demonstrates effective time management and decision-making. The purpose of **time management** is to perform the greatest amount of work in the least amount of time. As you get busier, the need for time management will become more apparent to you. You must learn to work with more customers in the same amount of time. The purpose of time management is to help you learn to take control of your time and your life, as well as to give you the flexibility to manage the daily surprises that we all experience from time to time. Try to envision goals as a road map that will provide you with detailed directions to your destination. It always helps to know where you are and the progress you have made. It will also enable you to see other possible choices should you decide to take a different route. You will be better prepared to make good decisions if you always know where you stand.

Many agents speak of time management as if they can control or are able to manage time. We can't manage the flow of time, but what we can manage is what we do with the allocated time that we do have (self-management). We make choices every day, and we are able to manage those choices, whether big or small. The most difficult part of time management or self-management is self-discipline. Even if you develop the most beautiful chart or outline to help you manage your time more effectively, successfully achieving self-discipline is more difficult if there is not an element of fun or reward to help motivate you to achieve your goals. Therefore, as you're developing all of your goals (short, medium, and long-term), remember to make them realistic, fun-filled, exciting, and challenging.

Scheduling a Target Date to Meet Your Goals

Make sure you set a specific date in which you hope to meet each goal. For example, instead of thinking, "I'll research how much my Realtor® fees are sometime next week," set a specific date. Without a specific date, procrastinating is simply too easy and can rob you of achieving your goal. Get your calendar or planner and set a specific time and day for each of your goals. It is easy to say, "I'll do it tomorrow" when you don't have your schedule planned, but if you know you have to accomplish step one today so that you can accomplish step two tomorrow, it will be much harder to procrastinate. Breaking your goal down into smaller steps also helps assure you that you will eventually reach your goal.

Sometimes you have to say "No" to your friends and co-workers in order to give yourself time to meet your goals. For example, if your best friend wants you to help him or her with some weekend shopping, but it would interfere with your goal of having two open houses per month, you have to say "No" in order to meet your own goal. You may feel guilty saying no, but think about it this way: whose goals are you achieving by going shopping with your friend?

Making Your Goals Measurable

In order to succeed, your goals must be specific and measurable. You must not generalize your goals (i.e., "I want to make a lot of money.") An example of a specific and measurable goal is "I want to earn $54,000 per year." You may have a chart similar to the one below to help you determine if you are behind or if you are ahead of your schedule for meeting your goal.

Income Goals $1,000 per week, $4,000 per month, $54,000 per year				
Property Listed in June	Contract Pending	Sales Price	Commission	%
7606 Linden, Houston TX		327,000	$19,620	6%
611 Uvalde, Houston TX		139,000	$4,170	3%
236 Evergreen, Deer Park TX		250,000	$7,500	3%
724 Dale St. Clear Lake TX	08/17/12	600,00	$12,000	2%
236 Shore Acres, Porte TX		417,000	$00	
			$43,290	
Net commission for 6 months $43290 X 60% = $25,974				

Breaking your goals down into measurable parts (i.e., daily weekly, monthly, annual, five-year, and lifetime goals) is helpful.

Goals must also have measurable levels of achievement. For instance, as you improve your marketing and sales skills, you should increase your expected returns. If you are able to earn $54,000 the first year, consider what you could earn in successive years

You may want to increase your earnings goal by $10,000 per year, or 10% per year, in order to reach the next level of achievement. You must have a measurable goal for how much more money you plan to make. Think about the CEO of any company—before making any decision, he/she wants facts and measurable details. You are the CEO of your business because at the end of the year, you are responsible for the end result of your business. Therefore, as the new CEO, how will you make your decisions to move the company forward? As the CEO, your job is to make the company grow with greater profits.

Making Your Goals Flexible

All goals must be flexible. In the above example, the agent has fallen short of the $54,000 per year goal. Therefore, the agent has the flexibility of making one of two choices: either drop the yearly goal, or update the next six monthly goals.

You will always make mistakes as a real estate professional—correcting mistakes is a part of being successful. Success will not occur without mistakes because none of us are perfect. Not making mistakes simply means you haven't tried enough. No one likes to make mistakes, but you must be willing to make them in order to grow.

Dale Carnegie says, "*The successful man will profit from his mistakes and try again in a different way.*" James E. Burke states, "*We don't grow unless we take risks. Any successful company is riddled with failures.*" Understand that making mistakes is a part of growth. You should not be afraid to make your share of mistakes, as long as you learn from them. An anonymous author asserts, "*Growth is never a mistake, unless we try again the same way.*"

In order to keep your goals flexible, review your status at the end of each day and at the end of each month just in case you need to readjust your plans; if so, you can readjust them as soon as possible. The key factor is to stay focused and committed in order to achieve your goals.

Making Your Goals Personal

Achieving your goals brings a sense of gratification; however, the fun is in the journey itself. Keep your plans to achieve your goals fun and exciting. As you stay focused on achieving your goals, you will build self-esteem. High self-esteem leads to improved confidence, which, in turn, leads to increased sales. The goal is to build a positive selling cycle. With each sale, your confidence builds, and soon, the momentum is moving in the right direction.

Always remember to keep your goals personal. Instead of aiming to outperform your competition, you should aim to stay ahead of yourself. Consider several goals, such as education, savings, yearly income, and retirement. Only you know how much income will be required to meet your personal goals.

Establishing a Reward System to Achieve Your Goals

Goals must include a reward system. The commission that you earn is certainly a good reward, but you should also set up a system of personal rewards. For example, what do you enjoy the most? Is it a fishing trip? Buying a new dress? Spending a night in Las Vegas? The reward is exclusively for you—something that you will be looking forward to. Indulge yourself! If you meet your weekly goal, buy that new dress you've been eyeing. If you meet your yearly goal, take that trip to Vegas you've been wanting. Let your close friends and family know about your reward system—you can even include them.

Making Your Goals Fun

An effective goal should have an element of fun to it. If you enjoy what you are doing, chances are you will be successful in your career. If your goals are set too high or are no longer exciting, then you need to readjust those goals to bring in an element of excitement. Success in business and enjoyment should go hand-in-hand.

For goal setting to be successful, you must develop a balance between business, family, and personal time. You should allocate enough hours for your personal time, business time, and family time with some emphasis on family requirements. It is important to note that if things are not going well at home, trying to achieve your other goals will be very uncomfortable. If you decide to work 40-50 hours per week, then you must set your goals so that you will not waste any of your time. Writing down your goals may take 20 minutes per day, but think about how much time you will save by following your plans. Writing down your goals on a daily basis will save you an average of one hour for every five minutes. It's also vital to identify the quantity of time that you will spend on working the business to ensure that you maximize those hours.

Suggestions for Goal Setting

Before you start writing down your goals, think about the following:
- What are your strengths, and what are your weaknesses?
- What do you enjoy most about selling real estate?
- Would you rather work with buyers or sellers?
- Do you plan to generalize or specialize?
- What other licenses do you plan to acquire?
- Are you planning to be a full-time or part-time agent?
- How long do you plan to stay in real estate sales?
- Do you or your firm have a mission statement?
- How are you going to balance your workload with family?

Marketing Plans

Business Planning

Planning is the framework to achieve goals. With careful planning, you will often foresee a problem that you are likely to encounter. The purpose of planning is to avoid problems. Think back to our example of using a road map to get to our destination. If there is a pending road problem ahead, a good road map will provide you with several options. That is to say, it's easier to adjust your plan to avoid an unforeseeable crisis than to deal with it unexpectedly.

You should make your goals clear and put them in writing. Consider whether you would prefer to use a daily planner or one of the many software packages available for planning or both. You can carry a daily planner or print your daily and weekly plans. The eight basic rules to consider when developing and implementing a practical and effective real estate business plan are as follows:

1. Do your research.
2. Know the reasons for developing a plan.
3. Determine your objectives.
4. Establish a budget.
5. Prioritize your task.
6. Implement the plan and take action.
7. Evaluate the results.
8. Target your audience.

Purpose of Developing a Plan

The whole purpose of planning is not to waste time, but to help you remember what's important and to get you where you want to be in the shortest possible time. While you may take hours or even a few days to design a plan, you will save weeks, months, or even years in achieving your goals. How many times during the week have you forgotten to do something? Keeping a daily planner handy enables you to write what you feel is important or delete items. You will always know where you stand or what is left to achieve before the day or week is over. As you work or are driving during the day, you will constantly think of new ideas. Those ideas can last a moment and are then gone, or you can keep track of them by adding them to your daily planner. Each day, you will have a plan, but during the day, you can perfect your plans. Below are suggestions for developing a workable plan:

- Determine your objectives.
- Outline your objectives.
- List the details required to achieve these objectives and be specific.
- Establish a budget—only you know your monthly expenses.
- Develop tasks to achieve your objectives.

Determining Your Objectives

What is that you wish to achieve? Your objective can range from being a top producer to making $500,000 per year. The next step is to determine how to meet your objective (that is, to outline your objective).

Outline Your Objectives and Listing the Details Required to Achieve those Objectives

You must have detailed plans in order to facilitate the fulfillment of your goals. Consider the following:

- In real estate, do you plan to work with buyers, sellers, or both, and in what area do you plan to specialize?
- Do you plan to cold call? If so, how many hours per week?
- What days do you plan to search for expired MLS listings? How many expired listings do you plan to call on per week?
- How do you plan to contact FSBOs, and how will you develop a script?
- How do you plan to contact each person you know?
- What type of information will you send to your contacts and how often?
- What are your plans for people who do not answer your email or mail-outs?
- What are your plans for staying current in your marketing areas?
- What do you know about your neighborhood, community development, or school's ranking, etc?
- Are you aware of the Do-Not-Call Registry, Can-Spam, and Fax-Spam?
- How are you going to let the public know who you are?
- How will you advertise and market yourself?
- How will you know which is the most effective marketing plan for you?
- What type of niche marketing do you plan to develop?
- What are your target areas?
- How are you going to get the public to want to buy your product or service, rather than simply considering it?
- What services do you plan to offer that are different from the rest of the mortgage and real estate community?
- What are your plans for new listings?
- What type of listing campaign will you have? Will your listing campaign be 30 new listings, an inventory of 30 listings or to set aside 30 days to get X number of listings? For example, once a year, maybe in March, just before the selling season starts, will you set aside 30 days to build an inventory of homes or a pipeline of buyers/borrowers? In your 30-day campaign, will you work only with sellers and ignore buyers, or will you categorize your buyers and still work with those buyers who need immediate help?
- If you decide to work the 30-day campaign, will you train an assistant to help someone with his/her files?
- What are your plans for preparing open houses?
- What type of direct marketing strategies do you plan to use?
  a) Geographic area
  b) Type of housing
  c) Mixing real estate and mortgage lending

- Will you have press releases or newsletters?
- Which of the following do you prefer, and how do you plan to research and become an expert in these fields?

Developing Goals, Plans, and Time Management

a) Working with buyers
b) Working with sellers
c) Working with buyers or sellers
d) Working with government foreclosures, VA/HUD
e) Working with local bank foreclosures
f) Working with upscale properties
g) Working with first-time home owners
h) Working with commercial real estate

- How do you plan to stage properties?
  a) Staging Open Houses
  b) Staging builder's model homes
  c) Listing vacant properties

- Make a list of marketing tools you have used, and indicate the one you like best. Keep records on how much money was used for each type of marketing and which ones were successful.

For example: **June 2011 Marketing**					
Post cards	500 mail outs	Cost $650	3 replies	Cost per lead = $1.3	5 hours
Calendars	300 mail outs	Cost $750	4 replies	Cost per lead = $2.5	10 hours
Brochures	800 mail outs	Cost $550	2 replies	Cost per lead = $.68	8 hours
Newsletter	100 mail outs	Cost $650	7 replies	Cost per lead = $.65	16 hours
Internet	***************	Cost $150	10 replies	Cost per lead = $.0002	60 hours

- In the above example, Internet marketing will give the highest yield per dollar, while mailing calendars will have the lowest yield. However, if you prefer to mail out calendars because you feel it's more personal and you have the funds and time to wait for your return, then do so, as long as you understand the numbers or cost per lead. There is no one right way. Marketing has different results for most agents. The key is to have fun and understand the cost factors of what you're doing.
- What are your plans regarding the various levels of marketing, and how much time and money are you willing to spend? Before you decide to advertise remember this quote, "All the advertising dollars won't sell the property, but a good agent will always sell a well-priced house."

Establishing a Budget

The cost of selling real estate is high. There will be many expenses, some of which you will be required to pay out-of-pocket before you will be allowed to sell real estate. In your budget plan, you will need to include membership fees for the following items:

- Realtors ®
- MLS ®
- Local Association of Realtors ®
- State Association of Realtors ®
- National Association of Realtors ®
- State Mortgage Association
- State Real Estate Commission
- Other memberships

Below is a chart reflecting levels of marketing dollars.

An estimate of the levels of marketing dollars you are expected to pay

0% - 10%_____ Institutional Marketing ____$____

0% - 20%_____ Company Marketing ____$____

70% - 100%___ Individual Marketing ____$____

Institutional marketing is the marketing amount paid by the franchise (promoting the franchise).
Company marketing is the dollar amount paid by the brokerage (promoting the broker and office).
Individual marketing is the dollar amount paid by the agent (promoting the individual agent). As the example indicates, most of the marketing dollars come from the individual agent.

Developing Tasks

Tasks are building blocks, basically, the simple things you must do to attain a major goal. Break each goal into single activities, and be specific. Your steps/tasks should be something you can actually complete before going on to the next task.

If your goal is to make $54,000 in listings per year, what will the individual tasks be? How will you plan your individual steps? While the items below are planning, the task is completing the individual steps. Again, to be successful, break your task down into steps that are as specific as possible.

- How many listings will it take to make $54,000?
- How can I gain $54,000 worth of listings?
- What materials are required?

Developing Goals, Plans, and Time Management

Prioritizing Tasks

On your list of objectives to achieve, specify which ones are most important. Make a list of what you have to do and then prioritize them. You should have a daily, weekly, and yearly goal list. The prioritized list can be broken into "must do," "should do," and "could do" tasks or a number system. Just because you dislike cold calling or door-to-door sales doesn't mean you should categorize it as a "could do" item. Prioritizing means doing what is most important first, not just what you enjoy doing. See an example of a marketing action plan below:

Check daily for expired listings in St. Claire Community (600 homes) • *1st day, call each expired listing* • *2nd day, mail out to all expired listing* • *3rd day, personally visit each expired listing* • *7th Day, start revisiting all expires* • *On the 1st and 15th day, mail out to all expired listings* • *On the 1st and 15th day, mail out to all For-Sale-by-Owners*	*Must*
Make appointments to visit at least 10 past clients.	*Should*
Stage an open house on Saturday for 1313 Mockingbird Lane.	*Must*
Design open house mail outs to 200 homeowners nearest 1313 mockingbird Lane	*Must*
Check the National Do Not Call List for homes in St. Claire Community, and call as many as possible to inform about open house.	*Must*
Do Door-to-Door farming for 50 homes in St. Claire Community.	*Should*
Update my MCE education.	*Must*
Make sure property is ready for open house three days in advance.	*Should*
Make sure open house kit is ready.	*Should*
Meet at least 20 new contacts.	*Could*
Attend real estate meeting on Tuesday.	*Could*
Plan floor time on Monday from 9 a.m.-noon; review all ads and flyers.	*Must*
Order new business cards.	*Could*

Taking Action

Rules for Real Estate Success

Implementing the Plan

The biggest obstacle to completing your tasks is procrastination. People procrastinate because they think the task at hand is either overwhelming or unpleasant.

If your task is overwhelming, you haven't broken it down enough. Maybe your outline is too general, you need more information, or your plans are disorganized. As you research information, the task will tend to shrink. You should divide your objective into the simplest activities, and prioritize each activity to make it clear and easier to achieve.

Overcoming objections to completing seemingly unpleasant tasks is a little different. To quit delaying a task that you don't like, meet the task head on-immediately. If you don't take care of the task immediately, it will be harder to avoid procrastination; it can even become a habit. Think about the task; it has to be completed sooner or later, so why not get to it as soon as possible? Be sure to reward yourself for completing each difficult or unpleasant task.

Evaluating the Results

Make sure you keep records of your goals. After each day, review how much you accomplished, and evaluate your performance. Keep notes on how you can improve or perfect your daily tasks.

Targeting Your Audience

To **target your audience** means to zero-in to whom you plan to market. Are you going to market to sellers in a given area, or are you going to do mail-outs for buyers in certain zip codes? Do you know what buyers are interested in, such as grant money or schools? For marketing to be effective (the greatest return for your money), you must know your audience. Casting too wide of a net is not the answer—in fact, it's very expensive. Starting small and building slowly is a better strategy. As you learn about your target area, increase your range. For example, think about where you live. First try mailing out 50 post cards or letters. Wait for replies, and then in a few weeks, try another 50 homes. Each area will have different results, so cautiously test your material. If you didn't receive any calls, take a second look at your marketing material. Did you target your audience?

1. Write your personal goals and be specific.
    *   First month's goal
    *   Six-month goal
    *   One-year goal
    *   Ten-year goal
    *   Lifetime goal

2. Organize your goals into categories.

3. Set a personal reward for each goal.

4. Plan how you will reach each goal.

5. Research the cost per goal.

6. Research the cost for each of the following:
    *   Local Association of Realtors®
    *   MLS
    *   Supra / lockbox system
    *   State association
    *   National association
    *   Other real estate fees in your area

7. Research the various software packages for goal setting and planning.

8. Visit an office supply store for the following:
    *   Mileage log book
    *   Software for goal setting and planning
    *   Daily planner
    *   Wall or desk calendar

9. Use your planner to design a weekly plan and the tasks for each day. As you read and start working, you will have to adjust your plans, but for now, you need a starting point.

10. Find your company's mission statement, and write you own career mission statement.

1. Goals are described as
   A. How the agent attracts people to their business.
   B. Sales skills refer to the manner in which agents interact with consumers in order to sell a product.
   C. Stating what you want to achieve.
   D. The design or framework for achieving the desired results.

2. The purpose of time management is
   A. To perform the greatest amount of work in the least amount of time.
   B. To measure success.
   C. To develop tasks.
   D. To evaluate results.

3. Planning is
   A. How the agent attracts people to his/her business.
   B. The manner in which agents interact with consumers in order to sell a product.
   C. Stating what you want to achieve.
   D. Designing the framework for achieving the desired results.

4. Goal setting must have which of the items to be successful?
   A. Clear/Specific
   B. Written
   C. Flexible
   D. Realistic
   E. All of the above

5. The purpose of developing a plan is
   A. To get to the destination with the least number of distractions.
   B. To have a clear idea where we are going.
   C. To have options if we encounter a problem.
   D. To measure the amount of activity.
   E. All of the above.

6. Institutional marketing is marketing by
   A. Franchise.
   B. Company/firm.
   C. Individual agent.
   D. None of the above.

7. Individual marketing is usually paid by the
   A. Franchise.
   B. Company/firm.

C. Individual agent.

D. None of the above.

8. The biggest problem with performing one's task is procrastination. People procrastinate because the task at hand is

    A. Overwhelming.

    B. Unpleasant.

    C. Not clear.

    D. All of the above.

9. Tasks are

    A. Stating what you want to achieve.

    B. The manner in which you personally interact.

    C. The building blocks, usually the simple things you must do to attain a major goal.

    D. All of the above

10. Target your audience is to

    A. Keep records of your progress.

    B. Zero-in whom you plan to market.

    C. Stating what you want to achieve.

    D. Designing the framework for achieving the desired results.

11. Sales skills refers to

    A. The manner in which agent attracts people to their business.

    B. The manner in which agents interact with consumers in order to sell a product.

    C. Stating what you want to achieve.

    D. The design or framework for achieving the desired results.

CHAPTER 4
Technology for Real Estate Agents

Objectives:

Understand:

The importance of

- Using today's information technology
- Having a business website
- Social networking
- Using digital imaging
- Global Positioning Systems (GPSs)
- What software packages are available
- Types of hardware that are available
- Developing virtual tours

Terms:

- Affiliated marketing
- Digital camera
- Flip video
- Movie Marker
- QR codes
- Search engine optimization
- Supra keys system
- Webcasting

- Blogs
- Domain name
- Global Positioning System
- Portable data transfer device
- Really simple syndication
- Social networking
- Virtual tour
- Webinar

Technology

Technology is another important factor you should consider if you are going to thrive in this business. Perhaps the most significant part of technology is the information available on the Internet which has not only changed how the world does business, but also how real estate and mortgage lending do too. For example, with the power of the Internet, we can mass market to thousands with the use of social media. The future of communication technology is how we will be able to communicate over the Internet.

The Future of Technology for Real Estate Agents

Today's technology trend is to promote a self-service public and do away with the ordinary real estate agent. Buyers and sellers are wondering why they should even use a real estate agent with all of the technology available to them. This is the reason that you must stay ahead of your competition and ahead of the public. The same technology that is causing the disappearance of the ordinary agent is the very information that will separate you from the rest.

Usefulness of Technology

Before the popularity of the Internet, real estate agents used books to place their listings. Depending on the area, these books were available two times per week to monthly subscribers. Since then, they have been replaced with the agents' directly inputting their own listings into Multiple Listing Services (MLS) on their websites. Previously, agents had to drive to the listing agent's office, pick up a set of keys, and then drive back to turn them in, but now agents call into a centralized showing service, and the keys are located at the property within special lock boxes.

In the last twenty years, much progress in two areas of technology, software and hardware, has been made. Of course, hardware is driven by software, but our interest in this chapter is to examine how technology directly affects real estate and how to use technology in business, marketing, and sales.

Software Technology:

- Information on the Internet
- Software
- Personal and business websites
- Professional domain name
- Efax
- Email
- Online prospecting
- Search engine optimization
- Social networking
- Web seminars or webinars
- Webcasting
- Webloging (blogs)
- Affiliated marketing
- Photo Story software
- Movie Maker software
- Virtual tours
- Internet businesses/online
- services

Hardware Technology:

- Cell phones and iPhones
- Wireless notebook computers
- Wireless/mobile printers
- Portable data transfer devices
- Flip videos™
- Digital cameras
- Global positioning systems (GPSs)
- Business computer network
- Supra keys system with special lock boxes
- Talking House™

Software Technology

Information on the Internet

In mortgage lending, the Internet is making loan processing almost paperless. Lenders no longer receive stacks of paperwork. Paper is being replaced by digital files, email, PDF files, efax, and cloud computing. On the real estate side, buyers have the same information real estate agents have, with the exception of the Realtor® MLS version. With the Internet, there is a wealth of information available. Buyers, as well as your competition, are all researching this information in order to gain a competitive edge. Right now, your competition may be surfing the Internet for new marketing material, searching what to add to their website, what online services are available, what is new in signs, and for anything else to give them an edge in this competitive field. For example, do you know which websites to obtain the following information from or how to set- up a community blog?

Software for Real Estate Agents

Software packages are available for the list below:

- Efax
- Fax broadcasting
- Email distribution
- Contact software
- Printing mail labels
- Designing marketing material
- Setting up databases
- Spreadsheets
- Loan document preparation
- Management/scheduling
- Accounting and taxation
- Converting documents
- Digital photo editing
- Digital movie making
- Goal setting and planning
- PowerPoint presentations
- Web design

The above list is only a sample of the many types of software packages available. Software enables real estate agents to reach hundreds, or even thousands, of potential customers and clients, economically design effective marketing material, and manage their businesses. There are software companies such as Microsoft™ and Adobe™ that have utility software as part of their packages.

Building Personal, Business, and Social Websites

Developing and hosting personal and business websites are another way to increase sales. Websites are becoming as common as business cards; nearly all agents have one or several. Like virtual tours, websites can be created with software, online services, or companies. The overall design of your website will largely determine if it will drive business to you. Because a website that will give an Internet high ranking will need constant updating for Internet search engines, it is ideal to have it designed by a professional web designer or SEO consultant "search engine optimization" or "search engine optimizer," preferably an SEO who is familiar with the real estate business.

Your website format should be easy to navigate; your personal information should be as brief as possible, while all other business information should be organized using links. Buyers and sellers search the Internet for information to help their housing needs, not to read about you. Websites should be designed to give the information buyers and sellers want, not for you to directly sell yourself. Think of it this way: the site should not push the viewer to you, but draw the viewer to your services. Do not think if you give too much information, prospects will not need your services. They will usually find your website useful and call when they are ready. If your site does not have the information, other agents will have it available on theirs. For a better Internet ranking, your site should be easy to navigate, with helpful public information links. It should also be well structured, with easy-to-read fonts, have several videos and photos with tags, and have an easy-to-remember professional domain name. Finally, since search engines favor websites that have links to outside sources, be sure to include plenty of links to all properties, community sources, limited personal information, a simple background, and email accounts for viewers to contact you.

Web space is unlimited and inexpensive, so you should not be afraid to post plenty of property pictures, videos, blogs, and PowerPoint presentations. Make sure that all your pictures and video files have key words, tags. This will increase search engines with finding your site. There are sites that will host your videos and pictures so you simply can link up to those sites. If sellers still have the original floor plan, post it. Have an introductory video of yourself. When buyers and sellers are trying to select an agent, they will appreciate a video of an agent with a warm, friendly smile. As far as designing a website, property images are the most decisive factor for buyers when searching for a home. Images and videos are a way of showcasing properties, to get a better website ranking, and to market yourself.

Your website should consider how buyers search for housing. Buyers' most common searching steps are: community or areas first, sometimes schools (young couples), neighborhood, agent, and then the house itself. Buyers usually search for homes from the outside-in, which are as follows: area, neighborhood, exterior and, lastly, the interior of the home. Should you decide to farm a neighborhood/community, be an expert, and post your specific information. What information should you post? Put yourself in the buyers' shoes. What would you look for in an area? Keep notes of what buyers are looking for. Ask sellers why they purchased their property, or survey the neighborhood. Here are a few suggestions:

- Education: public, private schools and colleges
- Medical: local medical services to medical centers
- City and county services: fire, police, trash pickup, water, and tax office
- Neighborhood sales: number of houses, average price, range, and turnover ratio
- Transportation services: bus, public road improvements, and maps

- Recreation: parks, sports, pools, waterways, golf, and community centers
- Entertainment: theatres, zoos, museums, dining, and night clubs
- Retail shopping: grocery, general stores, and malls
- Crime statistics

Agent Video

You should have professionally designed videos of yourself, **agent video.** Your videos should be in two parts, an introductory video to introduce yourself and to welcome the public, and an exit video to give your thanks for visiting your site, and to give consumers the information on how to contact you. Your video profile should be very short, a quick introduction, 30-seconds in length. Once you have your videos, you can add your introductory, testimonials, and exit videos to all your property listing. It is the constant viewing of your agent video that the consumer will remember. They will view hundreds of properties, but remember only one, YOU, the Star! You can also develop an educational video of you for your clients. The presentation can be how to stage, the importance of staging, the pricing of their home, or safety issues. You can use software like Movie Maker, by Microsoft™ which is likely to already be installed in your computer, if you are using Windows. You can post the video on your website or have professional physical copies made for less than $2.00 using professional video production companies such as kunsaki.com. Kunaki.com will allow you use their software or you can create your own front and back cover to your video jacket. Total price for the professional jacket, DVD, your message, and wrap will range from $1.00 to $1.99 each. Have your testimonials on video. Give your prospects the information to confirm that "YOU" should be their agent. Ask other agents if they would be interested in a collaborative project? This would separate you from the rest.

Other videos you can incorporate into your website are:

- Client testimonials
- How to stage
- Community video
- How to have an Open House
- Safety
- HOA videos
- Tips for FSBO

Search Engine Optimization (SEO)

Search engine optimization is the process of improving the ranking of a website or a web page in search engines. Internet search engines will search information request in order of videos, pictures, and word groups. Depending on the actively on the each website, search engine will determine the order it will appear on a search. For example, if you type the words real estate and the name of your city, the ranking or order will appear differently each day. The higher the ranking, the more likely consumers are to visit that site. You can have your web page SEO designed for local or global searches (Global SEO). Most agents will design for local searches.

Professional Domain Name

A **professional domain** name is important; it shows how serious you are about your career. There are several free domain name sites available, such as Yahoo, AOL, Hotmail, MySpace, or even Realtors.com; however, these domains do not look professional to the public. Purchasing a domain name and hosting a website is only a few dollars per month. Search engines also give professional domain names a better ranking. Domain names are supposed to drive leads to your website. If a buyer is searching for houses in Austin, Texas and types in the words, "houses in Austin," "Austin homes," or "Austin real estate," would your website turn up in the search results? It would have, if your domain name had the words "Austin" or "real estate" in it. Finding a good domain name has become difficult. Keep looking for a domain name that will give you maximum exposure. In choosing a suitable name, be sure to keep it short, common, easy to spell, and try to use a standard extension such as dot.com. You can always link different domain names to your master domain.

Efax

Efax, or Internet faxing, is converting paper faxes to paperless e-mail. Efax has many advantages over conventional faxes. One is the cost. Old traditional faxes require a dedicated phone line, paper, toner, and the equipment. The cost of efaxing varies; depending on the service contract, it is usually anywhere from $10-$25 per month. Receiving efax is usually free, depending on the service contract. Efax can be viewed, saved, and edited in color from any computer that has the software at any location. New software (eFax Pro) is making efax interactive with sound and motion. Efax can also be time-set or sent from any location. You can also keep track of all fax activities through your account. Overall, efax is cost effective and offers more options than traditional faxing.

Email

Email provides a better means of communication; it's fast, and the recipient receives it in seconds. No postage, envelopes, or paperwork is needed. There is no limit to the number of recipients or limitations because of distance to the recipient. It enables you to better manage your time. The reader cannot see or read your body language, you can email photos, graphics, or other vivid details to express your ideas to provide greater detail without interruptions. In other words, you control the communications. You can easily communicate with thousands of clients at a time. You can time-set your email (e.g., you can write your emails at 2:00 a.m. and send them at 2:00 p.m.). Email can be sent from remote locations using new phone technology, which means you can be fishing or playing golf while your boss thinks you are hard at work. You can create a colorful presentation of all your listings and send an email to thousands of prospects and agents with digital software. The importance of effective communication with past and present clients, building databases, and time management is discussed in upcoming chapters.

Email Effectiveness

While email does have its advantages over regular mail, its effectiveness can be improved. Below are basic rules for e-mailing:

- Keep emails short, direct, and interesting.
- Fill out the subject line.
- Always have a headline.
- Have a signature, which includes your name, phone numbers, and address.
- Check your email for mistakes and clarity.
- Send emails early in the day before people go to lunch.
- Organize what you want to say and use graphics and pictures, if possible.
- Ask for a response.
- Give your recipient the opportunity to opt out of receiving email from you.

Online Prospecting

Buyers who shop for houses or loans on the Internet, like all other buyers, should be categorized (covered in Chapter 10). Buyers want more control, so they are usually reluctant to reveal personal information to real estate agents. This is probably the reason they are shopping on the Internet. They do not want to be bothered with questions by some aggressive Realtor®, or they may want more control of searching on their own. Online shoppers tend to be better informed; they usually start early in their research and are aware of property values and financing requirements. Nevertheless, they are still quality buyers and deserve the same respect as traditional buyers. Online shoppers are information-gathering people, so they tend to welcome any information via email or website. Do not give up on these prospects; they will call you when they are ready to obtain more information. Ask what information they want, and give them specifically what they ask for; other information such as your resume may discourage further contact. If you have other information, such as a newsletter that they may want, first ask for permission before emailing it to them. Check for spelling and grammatical mistakes, keep emails short, and be sure the recipients of your newsletter can unsubscribe.

Social Networking

All too often younger people are using social networks such as Facebook™, Twitter™, or My Space™ to communicate, but now businesses are adopting social networking as in Linkedin™. **Social networks** are online communities where information is shared instantly. These social networks are multiplying. These free websites are growing more and more, and now adults and businesses are joining these social networks as well. Some of these websites offer several tools, such as videos, blogs, and free email. While there are several social networks, try to be selective. YouTube™ is a leading website for hosting your videos, which can present any number of ideas, such as how to stage a home, qualify for a loan, or even a presentation on the community you are farming. Here are a few well-known social networks:

- YouTube™(www.youtube.com)
- Facebook ™(www.facebook.com)
- MySpace™ (www.myspace.com)
- Twitter™ (www.twitter.com)
- Activerain™ (www.activerain.com)
- Squidoo™ (www.squidoo.com)
- Hubpages™ (www.hubpages.com)
- Digg.com/news (www.digg.com/news)

Social Media Marketing (SMM)

Through social media marketing came from the catch phrase "social media." **Social media** is a term used to describe Internet sites that allow users to participate in sharing of content. Today, social networking sites have become a venue for people to share thoughts, ideas, information, and allow interactive dialogue among people who share similar interests. It allows you to keep in contact with your friends, friends' friends and beyond. Social media is about establishing connections with friends and family.

Computer-savvy people are now learning how social media sites can create a virtual web stretching further than your normal scope of contacts. Social media has allowed us to monitor and pass information faster and easier, and today there are thousands of real estate professionals on the major social media sites like LinkedIn™, Facebook™, and even Twitter™. Therefore, if you are not using them, you should be. Social media must be one of the tools you use in your marketing toolbox. No other place can allow one to put a human face on real estate, connecting and communicating with so many people in such a short time, all in the comfort of your own home or smart phone. Using social media will bring people to you instead of your trying to find people you knew 10, 20, or 30 years ago.

Facebook™

Facebook is by-far the most effective way to connect with lost friends, allowing people to share their lives with one another. Facebook has, by popularity, grown into an established resource for real estate promotion because it embraces the free flow of information and provides a kind of public forum where you can thoroughly publicize your interest. Social media forums all have beneficial aspects to allow you to connect and re-connect with friends, family, past clients and soon-to-be clients.

Blogs

The term "blog" is short for "web-logs" or "web-logging." **Blogs** are chronological journals over the Internet or online diaries with the latest entries on top by date. It serves as an online media, such as a discussion forum. Blogs can be personal or for business. The entries can be by one person or by all of its members. Blogs can be simple or very business-like, with graphics and paid advertisements. Blogs can be part of websites or stand alone. The best thing about building blogs is it is inexpensive to maintain and easy to create. Type in the word "blogs" into your web browser and you will get hundreds of websites that will host or build your blog. Most web designers can be helpful here.

Word Press and Blogger are examples of free public blog services that have pre-formatted pages, allowing users to publish written text with photos, making them perfect for home sellers to display information regarding their property as well as providing pertinent links to various related sites. While these tools are useful for finding out a little about a person and for providing contact information, other real estate professionals are setting themselves apart by creating Blogs and other web resources to provide industry information from which many will benefit. Jump into conversations, leave comments on blogs, share news items you find appealing to people in your social networks and for people with whom you are connected, and become an online source of information.

Rules for Real Estate Success

Importance of Community Blogging

The purpose of community blogging is to attract and develop regular community viewers. Blogging can help you keep information current, establish a relationship with visitors/members, develop a climate of trust, and set you apart as a community leader. It is also an easy and a cost-effective way to share relevant information. When viewers are able to read your comments on a particular subject, they will have a better understanding of your ethics and values.

Marketing Blogs

So, how can a weblog be helpful in your marketing and sales? It is a convenient way to communicate with a selected group of people. For example, you can post new listings in your farm area, enter pictures or websites, tell the neighborhood about upcoming news, and let other community members post their ideas or comments about whatever happened at the last town meeting. It is a good way for neighborhoods to communicate with one another. Specifically, you set the topic, and other members can easily voice their opinions. For example, you may post a topic about the safety of our kids walking to school. You can then post an entry and let others write in their comments. Before long, you have a long string of entries; you can then suggest having formal meetings. Any viewer can log in at any time and catch up with current news by going back to past entries. Blogs can be open to the general public or to a selected few members.

In a community discussion forum, it is essential to set the host as an expert, an authority in a certain subject. For example, in real estate, the topic could be *"How to have a Successful Open House"* or *"Property Staging."* The host would start by writing an article or entering a comment on the blog while other people in the same social network reply.

Commercializing Blogs

Blogs can be used for other real estate information, such as how to protest taxes, how to stage your home, or information about a new law. You can even have what is called affiliated advertisements to monetize your blog. This means you can make money by letting other people advertise on your website or blog. Again, there are several websites, which will match your blog to the paying customers. Type "blogging services" or "blog match" into your browser and you will see several sites that will match your blog to paying customers. Should you decide to commercialize your blog, pick affiliates who are consistent with your topics. For example, if you are working with buyers, affiliate with a good mortgage lender. If you decide to work with sellers, look for affiliates who will complement your content;

in this case, lenders, home repair centers, appraisers, and title companies or even insurance companies. Be careful about using too many affiliates. Using too many ads may make your blog look suspicious to viewers. The whole idea in the first place is to create trust with viewers.

Affiliated Marketing

Affiliated Marketing is when a company has agreed to pay the host a commission to help sell its product. Internet ad payments will depend on three basic payment systems. One is the pay per click, pay per lead, or pay per sale. If your visitor clicks the ad space or clicks and does a particular thing, a small amount of money will go to your account. The basic rule is the more active your blog becomes, the greater the chances are of visitors clicking on one of your affiliated ads. While Internet ads can boost your income, it will take time to establish profitable blogs.

Twitter™

Twitter™ is a micro-blogging utility site that can generate plenty of interest for your property. Use Twitter to post every time you update your property listing blog, which can automatically update your Facebook™ message board. Facebook™ pages that integrate personal interactions are usually likely to succeed because they offer people something they are actually interested in, and they are connected to other social media pages (i.e. Twitter™, Facebook™, LinkedIn™...) Twitter is advantageous if you plan to start up a conversation and are ready with quick responses. If you fire-off an impressive comment on Twitter, it will spark conversation, but if you are not there to respond/reply, the topic dies rapidly.

Add your Twitter accounts and the RSS address to your blog post. **Really Simple Syndication** (**RSS**) is a way to subscribe to websites and help save viewing time on the Web. Learn how to use Twitter, Facebook™, LinkedIn™ and Blogging to generate traffic for your lead generation system.

There has been much conversation about the use of Social Media in real estate. People fail at social media in real estate because they use social media for socializing, not doing business. As a Realtor®, you know the value of social media, but despite your best efforts, you may still be struggling. How can you change your social media luck?

Below are Five Ways Realtors can Find Success in Social Media:

1. Have a plan. While social media can be a powerful tool, you must come up with a strategy for success. Devote about an hour per day to social media, 30 minutes in the morning and 30 minutes in the evening. Without proper planning and implementation, it will take you much longer to get results.

2. Create useful and engaging content. In order to engage people through social media, it is important to provide them with content that informs, something they can use to help in their decision making that helps reiterate the things you may have already told them. Being a likable person does not necessarily mean people will care about what you have to say unless you can give them a reason to keep coming back. Below is a list of places you can find exceptional content.

Resources for Finding, Engaging, and Useful Content for the Real Estate Professional

Your website	
Company website	
Local MLS board	
Regional association	
Your local newspaper website	
Inman News	www.inman.com
Twitter	www.twitter.com/inmannews
Facebook	www.facebook.com./inmannews
Trulia	www.trulia.com
Zillow	www.zillow.com
House Logic	members.houselogic.com
Realtor.com	www.realtor.com
Altos Research	www.altosreserch.com
HGTV Frontdoor	www.frontdoor.com
Realty Trac	www.realtytrac.com
Street Advisor	www.streetadvisor.com
NabeWise	www.nabewise.com
Outside.in	http://outside.in
BizJournals	www.bizjournals.com
Flicker	www.flickr.com/explore
Reddit	www.reddit.com
StumbleUpon	www.stumbleupon.com

3. If you delegate, do so wisely. If you decide to delegate social media to someone else or a company, be sure to delegate carefully. It is permissible to have someone help you, but keep a close eye on what he or she is doing and be sure to continue to delegate only some, not all of the social media

work. Your own personal interaction should always be present. This is what makes social media work. If you are not a "people person," then you may find it necessary to hire an assistant or intern who is, but keep yourself involved at some level. Learn what works for you; the more you do it, the better you will become.

4. Listen in lieu of hard selling your listings. Remember, "People do not like to be sold to; they want to buy from." This fact holds true in social media. Develop relationships with your social media fans before advertising your listings. If you listen closely to your fans and followers, you will begin to know which ones may be interested in one of your listings. It is much easier to sell to someone who needs what you are selling. Try to integrate topics that maintain their interest. Selling is about fulfilling a need. Incorporate things they are actually interested in daily, such as community events, market statistics, and local school information, into your social marketing sites. The more you listen to them, the better you will become at fulfilling their needs. This is when social media becomes very powerful.

5. You must be consistent. As with most "advertising" the more you invest, the greater the return. Invest in your time, find useful resources, and keep up with the trends of this ever-changing venue. If you can afford it, you should consider paying for tools to help monitor your social media. It takes time and dedication to succeed in social media. There may not be immediate returns, but over time, and if you are consistent, you will eventually see a return on your investment.

Webinars/Webcasts

Webinars are web-based seminars in which the presentation is conducted over the web. The presentation is in real time and interactive. The viewers and presenters are able to interact with one another in real time. Webinars are becoming a popular form of training because of the low cost and ability to reach viewers at home or in their office. Webinars can be recorded and edited for future use. Once webinars are edited, they can be broadcasted as webcast files. **Webcasts** are prerecorded files, which lack the interactivity webinars have. To view a webinar or a webcast file, the viewer needs only three things: an Internet connection, a phone, and a computer or a smart phone. For the presentation, presenters can bring in other software tools, such as Word, PowerPoint, Excel, photos, and the Internet. While webinars are an excellent form of training, they do not present the opportunity for marketing; however, the prerecorded webcast version can be a great marketing tool. These files can be posted on websites giving agents the professional grade. Webcast files can literally have any type of information for consumers to view, such as how to stage a home, how to pack, how to improve credit scores, or how to have open houses. The list on what to post on web sites is limitless.

Photo Story Software

Photo Story software by Microsoft™ is digital storytelling using pictures, graphics, audio, and web publishing. Photo Story is an easy-to-use and inexpensive software package designed for the non-technology savvy person. Pictures or graphics are uploaded and then dropped into an orderly system with all kinds of special effects and audio. Later, these files are saved in different formats for presentations, shows, DVDs, or into a website. While Photo Story is very kid-friendly, real estate agents can use the same software to create listing presentations to be shown during open houses, to pick up FSBOs, to be included on websites, for social networks or to help buyers and sellers understand the real estate process. The stories are endless. All you need is a computer, digital camera, a story telling software package, and some imagination to be the next Steven Spielberg. While Photo Story is a Microsoft product, there are several software packages that will produce the same results, but they may cost a bit more.

Movie Maker Software

Movie Maker, a Microsoft™ video software package also designed for the non-technology savvy person and just as easy to use as Photo Story. It is an effective software package for making movies that can be applied to real estate. It is an inexpensive way of producing virtual tours that can easily be edited and uploaded to your website or listing site. Many software packages, like Movie Maker, are available to produce the movie making results you want. What is interesting is you may already have a version of it. Movie Maker is installed on most computers, which operates on Windows™.

Virtual Tours

While digital pictures allow prospects to view the property, **virtual tours** were designed to give prospects the sense of being at the location. Depending on your local Realtor Association, you are even able to add a quick commercial to the front and back of each video. The commercial can either feature you as "the star" or a professional actor who is introducing your services or listings. If you do the commercial yourself, each time prospects click on one of your listings they will see you again, over and over. They will remember your face, while they tend to forget names or listings.

Video tours are always helpful for pre-open house videos. Make short videos with just enough information to cause viewers to visit your open houses.

You can have videos of the neighborhood that you are farming. This would include schools, parks, new projects, people from the civic association, educators' welcome, shopping areas, and any items of interest.

Virtual tours range from picture slide shows like a PowerPoint presentation to highly interactive 3-D virtual tours. Creating virtual tours can come from do-it-yourself software or online services. There are free hosting websites like QIK.com or YouTube.com on which you can submit video presentations. QIK.com has a live two-second delay platform. QIK.com allows you to post live presentations from which your viewers can use mobile phones to access. Through the power of the Internet, prospects can view virtual tours anytime they wish and at its best stage. We will discuss how to stage a property in Chapter 8. Creating and posting on your website or copying virtual tours to DVD/CD format are a fairly inexpensive way of using today's technology. These virtual tours can be emailed to prospects, distributed during open houses, or used to impress potential sellers. The cost of virtual software and equipment can range from a few hundred dollars to several thousand. For a few hundred dollars, it is certainly a worthwhile venture. Before purchasing software, you may want to do some research since hundreds are available. Ask your local college computer department or computer store for suggestions, or even someone who is active with virtual tours in the office. There are also several online companies that will provide the software and can host the website for a fee.

Internet Schools and Training

Real estate and mortgage Internet schools (distant education) are becoming popular. Internet courses give students flexibility with their schedule; they no longer have to drive and actually be in class. What is new? Online schools now have the ability to use more technology, such as iPhones, webinars, webcasts, and Blackboard™. These extra perks give students the feel of the traditional in-class structure from any location with the use of a smart phone.

Hardware Technology

Smart Phones/iPads

Many smart phones and iPads are available, the two best smart phone standards by most real estate agents are BlackBerry™ and the iPhone by Apple™. Cell phones and iPhones with Internet connectivity enable real estate agents to reply to incoming messages instantly. iPhone by Apple™ is the new wonder in phone technology. With thousands of business applications available, there's an application for almost any business function. Whether you need to get organized, attend an online meeting, map out the best routes, or work on your files, iPhones have almost unlimited possibilities for business users. You can track leads or manage your pipeline. iPhones are useful for managing your sales prospects by keeping you up-to-date with critical information. You can work on your accounting, generate an invoice, or record tasks for a follow-up. The next technology wonder is the iPad, with information using cloud computing. Since large storage devices are no longer practical, cloud computing is storing your files or accessing your software from a remote system that can be hundreds of miles away. None of your files or software will be stored in your device; it would be an empty shell, the same as when you purchased it from a retailer. Your Internet remote can be miles away, not just a few feet. You obtain your information by using your access codes.

As long as the buyers/borrowers have Internet access, you can send pictures of houses with information while on the road or send and receive text messages with this technology. You can also take pictures using your high resolution cell phone/iPhone. Use the Internet to find whatever information you may need. Take pictures to be used for designing flyers, ads, or for multi-listing services.

QR Code

QR code is a matrix, or a two-dimensional bar code. QR codes can be used to read text, open a URL, or display pictures with the use of a digital camera phone. The QR codes are modules arranged in a certain square pattern. There are several sites that can create QR codes of your listings for free or for a small charge. A prospect can take a picture of the QR code and view your entire listing on his/her smart phone. The capacity of a standard QR code is 7,089 numeric characters, or 4,296 alphanumeric characters. While there are several types of data codes, Data Matrix and QR codes are the most common ones in the United States.

Wireless Notebook Computers

Just a few years ago, agents had to decide whether to invest their funds in buying a desktop computer or to go mobile. Since the price of computers has dropped, it is now affordable to have both. There is no question that computers are a requirement in this business. There are several software packages to load, perhaps thousands of pictures, plenty of marketing information, and hundreds of letters. Moreover, memory is inexpensive. It is advantageous to use notebook computers, iPads, and portable printers. You can access the Internet from any location, make corrections to documents on-site, or stop at the neighborhood Starbucks and do some work while enjoying your coffee. Do not go out and buy the largest laptop though. In fact, the smaller, the better, as long as you are comfortable reading the screen, using the keyboard, and have the speed, and memory you need. After carrying your computer bag for a few days, you'll realize why smaller and lighter is better.

Portable Data Transfer Devices

Portable storage devices have several names: jump drives, memory sticks, flash drives, thumb drives, pen drives, key drives, portable hard drives, and USB flash drives. A **portable storage device** (USB drive) functions as a data storage device that fits into your computer's USB port. This allows you to easily carry your files with you or transfer them from one computer to another. It serves as a backup in case your computer crashes. These devices come in all shapes and sizes and are small enough to carry in your pocket. In real estate or mortgages, this can be helpful in transferring information between computers, in open houses, between home and work, or the client's computer.

Flip Video™

Flip Video™ is a small hand-held video camera to take digital pictures or video. What makes the Flip Video™ different from other digital cameras is its simplicity in uploading files to social networks and in editing videos for websites. Flip Video™ makes it easy to develop property tours or digital pictures of properties. It is also small enough to carry in a shirt pocket, easy to start shooting, and easy to edit music or sound. The problem with using Flip Video™ is the MP4 format. Older video software programs are unable to recognize the MP4 format. In this case, you will have to convert the files to an older or different format. Another problem is the lens power. For those deep shots you will need a camera that can deliver better optical zoom.

Digital Cameras

Another pricey tool is the digital camera. **Digital cameras** have the capacity to take thousands of still photographs on a single memory device and often even have the capability of capturing video and audio. In digital cameras, you have the following four options:

- Ultra compact (point and shoot with limited features)
- Compact (point and shoot with extra features)
- SLR (single-lens reflex)
- Cell phone

The ultra-compact point and shoot cameras are small and designed for easy use. Compact cameras can fit in your shirt pocket and usually have a better optical zoom. For real estate, you will need the wider zoom

(24mm) for those MLS pictures and telephoto capability (135 mm) for those close-up shoots. The larger SLR cameras have interchangeable lens but can be expensive. There are many compact cameras under $200 that will work for most agents. A good start is one with 12 mega-pixel and 12X optical zoom.

Images are stored in TIFF, RAW, NEF, and JPEG (Joint Photo Experts Group) formats. JPEG is the most common format designed to work with continuous tone photographic images, which takes image data and compresses it; however' the more you compress, the more information you will lose. When shopping for a digital camera, consider pixel count, optical zoom ability, image stabilizer, and storage formats. Pixel count is the number of individual pixels it takes to make an image. Pixel count varies between 1 million (*1 Mega-pixel*) to around 15 million (*15 Mega-pixels*). Digital cameras use three color channels: red, green, and blue. A 1 million mega-pixel camera will produce one million tiny squares, or pixels, of each color. These colors added together will produce over 16 million possible combinations. A 3-megapixel, or 3-million pixel count camera is the minimum quality camera to purchase for real estate photographs. Storage formats come in several different forms, such as Compact Flash (CF), Micro drive, Sony Memory Stick, Secure Digital (SD), Multimedia, and camera interface technologies, such as USB 1.1 and USB 2.0. For storage capacity, a 4GB storage device is a good place to start. Another important feature is the optical capability, both in zoom and stabilizer. A zoom 1-X camera will produce a single 35 mm effect whereas a 3-X camera will produce 105 mm (3x35=105). The higher the number means a greater telephoto. The lower the number means wider optical lens. In real estate, you will need from 24-105 mm.

Digital Camera Usefulness

Digital cameras are useful for taking pictures of houses, kids, pets, group pictures, pictures of the closing or of the family moving into the house, creating a twelve month calendar, or even a photo book. What is interesting is that very few people actually take pictures of their home. Making yearly 12-month calendars for clients of their homes, with your company information included on it, is helpful for clients remembering your services. Multi-listing Services (MLS) requires several photos of each listing. While camera phones are replacing the traditional point and shot cameras, they do not have the lens power of traditional SLR cameras. Pictures are important, and with a good wide zoom lens, you will be able to showcase those beautiful features the property has. Good pictures will encourage interest in your listings. The advantage of using a digital camera is you can take hundreds of still pictures, select the best, and delete the rest. For marketing, pictures of clients and properties are useful for family calendars. You can always make several copies for your clients to mail to other family members. Ask your clients if they would like you to make copies. If they would, ask for a count and have them ready for mailing. Do not forget to include the most important part of the calendar; namely, your advertisement in each picture. Select the best twelve pictures, and enhance them for a twelve-month calendar.

Tips for using a digital camera are as follows:

- Use the camera's highest resolution.
- Consider the lighting; natural lighting is better than camera flash. When using your flash it is best when the subject is less than 8 feet away; otherwise, turn off the flash.
- Take as many pictures as possible, and have plenty of memory in order to do so.

After each set of pictures, delete the unwanted ones on-site — do not wait.

- Get as close to the subject as possible.
- Use a wide lens for wide shots.

Global Positioning System

The **Global Positioning System** (GPS) transmits precise microwave signals, enabling GPS receivers to determine their location by speed, direction, and time. GPS was developed by the Department of Defense. In 1983, President Ronald Reagan issued an order making GPS available to American civilians for free. Today, GPS has become widely used as a worldwide aid to navigation. GPS comes in several applications: in cell phones, handsets for walking or hiking, for boating, and even for the real estate agent's automobile. Armed with GPS receivers, users can accurately locate where they are and easily navigate where they want to go, whether walking, driving, flying, or boating. This navigation system will greatly help you avoid getting lost and easily navigate to your destination. When buyers are viewing several homes, it is difficult to always know the quickest routes, so they are depending on you to know the best ones. This will not only lessen frustration, but help with gas savings as well.

Supra Key System

The **Supra Keys System** consists of special computerized lock boxes used by real estate professionals across the United States. They are made to easily attach to any doorknob or railing. Each box has a storage compartment to hold keys. This allows you to go directly to the house for showings and records who has access to the property. To use a supra key system, you are required to purchase computerized entry keys, a service contract, and lock boxes for each house. You can purchase noncomputerized lock boxes as well. These combination lock boxes function the same way, but you will need a special combination code to access the keys inside the box.

Talking House (www.talkinghouse.com)

Talking House uses radio technology. With Talking House, you purchase radio transmitters to send short radio waves about the product you are selling. Talking House is useful for listings, open houses, and office messages. The procedure is simple. You can prerecord a message into the digital transmitter, the transmitter sends out radio signals, and prospects turn their radio to your station to hear the prerecorded audio.

1. Research how you will develop your website. Talk with a web designer about what information your website will offer. Ask about the design cost and monthly fees. Most Realtors® associations have free web space and templates for its members.

2. Search the Internet for a professional domain name.

3. Ask web designers about including blogs as part of your website.

4. Movie Maker and Photo Story programs are installed on most PC computers as a part of the Microsoft® package. The version will depend on the Microsoft® package. Create a few story lines using photographs and videos, add titles. Later, with the use of a digital camera, Flip Video™ camera, or Internet websites like qik.com you can create live tours for each property.

5. Start thinking about an induction video of yourself that you can add to all your listings, and check with your local *MLS*® to make sure you are able to insert a pre and post video into your listings.

6. Make sure you are able to use all the technology that is available in your office, such as scanners, copiers, lockboxes, GPS, that you know how to fax or email from your office.

7. Research if your office has QR coding.

8. Shop for the right type of digital camera that you will need; also, find out if classes are offered on using your camera.

9. Design a plan from which to research and purchase from the following items:

    *   Portable data transfer devices
    *   Cell phone/iPhones/iPad
    *   Global Positioning System
    *   Flip Video
    *   Photo-editing software
    *   Digital camera

10. Research how you can use the following social networks to market yourself:

    *   Facebook.com
    *   Myspace.com
    *   Twitter.com
    *   Squidoo.com
    *   Linkedin.com

1. A professional domain name
   A. Is recognizable by Internet search engines.
   B. Shows the seriousness of the agent.
   C. Is cost-effective.
   D. All of the above.

2. Webinars are
   A. A form of web-loggings.
   B. A web-based seminar where the presentation is conducted over the web. The presentation is in real time and interactive.
   C. A form of efaxing software.
   D. Using microwave signals that enables GPS receivers to determine their location by speed, direction, and time.

3. Social networking is/are
   A. A group of online communities discussing a common interest.
   B. A web-based seminar where a presentation is conducted over the web. The presentation is in real time and interactive.
   C. Chronological journals over the Internet or online diaries with the latest entries on top by dates.
   D. Digital storytelling software, using pictures, graphics, audio, and web publishing.

4. Blogs are
   A. Online communities that discuss a common interest.
   B. A web-based seminar; the presentation is conducted over the web. The presentation is in real time and interactive.
   C. Chronological journals over the Internet or online diaries with the latest entries on top by dates.
   D. Digital storytelling software using pictures, graphics, audio and web publishing.

5. QR codes are
   A. A matrix or a two-dimensional bar code. QR codes can be used to read text, open a URL, or display pictures with the use of a digital camera phone.
   B. The number of chronological journals over the Internet or online diaries with the latest entries on top by dates.
   C. A 1 million mega-pixel that will produce one million tiny squares of each color. These colors added together will produce over 16 million possible combinations.
   D. Using microwave signals, enabling GPS receivers to determine their location by speed, direction, and time.

Technology for Real Estate Agents

6. Global Positioning System is
    A. A web-based seminar; the presentation is conducted over the web.
    B. The number of chronological journals over the Internet or online diaries with the latest entries on top by dates.
    C. A 1 million mega-pixel that produces one million tiny squares of each color. These colors added together will produce over 16 million possible combinations.
    D. Using microwave signals, enabling receivers to determine their location by speed, direction, and time. This is used as a worldwide aid to navigation.

7. Virtual tours are useful for
    A. Using microwave signals to enable receivers to determine their location by speed, direction, and time. They are used as a worldwide aid to navigation.
    B. The number of chronological journals over the Internet or online diaries with the latest entries on top by dates.
    C. The agent who is physically touring the property with the buyers.
    D. A 3-D property tour to give prospects the sense of being at the location from a remote location.

8. Portable data transfer devices is/are
    A. Small devices that fits into a UBS port which functions as an external memory drive, useful for sharing data.
    B. A small camera which takes video and audio with the capacity to take thousands of still photographs.
    C. Digital software.
    D. A fax broadcasting system.

9. Useful for sending a large number of letters to clients is
    A. Efaxing
    B. Fax broadcasting
    C. E-mail distribution
    D. All of the above

10. Computerized lock boxes used by real estate agents is/are
    A. Talking houses.
    B. MLS systems.
    C. A Supra Key System.
    D. Combination lock boxes.

CHAPTER 5
Professionalism and Salesmanship

Objectives:

Understand the importance of

- Building a professional image
- Business etiquette
- Reading body language
- Having strong communication skills
- Being Prepared by knowing the best replies to objections

Know how to do the following:

- Use the Unique Selling Proposition.
- Use the Theory of Small Commitments.
- Apply the Rule of Benefit.
- Be empathic.

Know what the following are:

- The four main purposes of designing advertising material
- What prospects expect from their real estate agent

Terms:

- ABCs of real estate
- Business etiquette
- Direct approach
- Finding a winning way
- Kaizen
- Power scripts
- The rule of benefit

- Body language
- CSIR
- Ethics
- First awareness
- Personal assistants
- Professional image
- Unique Selling Proposition

Selecting a Real Estate Agent

Buyers and sellers do not wake up and suddenly decide to hire a real estate agent. They usually go through a selection process.

The selection process generally follows this pattern:

1. Buyers and sellers will first decide they either need to buy or sell real estate now or in the near future.
2. If an agent is not already chosen, buyer/sellers will look on the Internet, or ask family, or friends for recommendations. As stated before in Chapter 1, 47% of buyers and 58% of sellers will choose the first agent they meet, while 52% of sellers will consider the recommendations from friends and family.
3. At this time, one or two agents are interviewed, and a decision is made.
4. The actual buying or selling process begins.

Professional Image

The purpose of building a professional image is to be prepared and to be the first person prospects will think of when they are in the real estate selection stage.

Be Prepared-Knowledgeable by Developing the Following Ten Items

1. Company image
2. Personal image
3. Duties and responsibilities
4. Preparation
5. Professional services
6. Social skills and etiquette
7. Business etiquette
8. Character
9. Professional attire
10. Communication skills

Company Image

Choosing a brokerage firm is a serious decision for a prospect to make. Brokers understand the importance of company image. Most brokers have policies and guidelines for protecting their image. As a new agent, maintaining your company's image while building your personal image is particularly beneficial to you. Here are some suggestions on how to build a successful company image:

- In real estate, most brokers prefer to work with full-time agents, as opposed to part-timers. Part-time agents require more attention and create a greater liability for brokers. This is a potential problem for anyone leaving a steady job for a career in real estate. One option is to share the workload and commission with other agents. In doing so, however, it may lead to questions such as, how will the money and workload be divided? Who will keep the consumer in his/her database for further referrals? What are office policies? Will other agents have the time or interest that you and your buyers expect? How will this type of relationship build your image or the company's image? How to become a successful part-time agent will be discussed in this text and subsequent chapters.

- Implementation of expected policies and procedures concerning earned fees and a code of conduct for staff will help in building and maintaining the company image. Even if one or more agents provide excellent services, what the company does as a whole will determine the financial future for all of its agents.

- The success of a business depends on its members working as a group. When two or more persons work together to produce a result not obtainable independently, it is called **synergy**. When a company has synergy, not only will the company be more productive, it's agents will also reap the rewards.

- Most businesses have a central theme that consists of a color scheme, logo, and business statement, or motto. When designing marketing material, avoid changing the central theme of the company.

- Companies usually work hard to create an image based on several variables, including: ethics, product knowledge, fair pricing as well as effective and efficient service. It is sound practice to view and learn from commercials sponsored by the larger firms, such as Prudential, Century 21, Keller Williams, Re/Max, and Coldwell-Banker. Many of these advertisements have the tendency to project a specific image geared toward reaching the minds of American consumers and motivating them to become loyal to their brand.

Personal Image

First Impressions

Consider this real estate rule: *"Prospects will decide to hire you based on their first impressions of you, and their referrals will be based on their last impressions of you."* Since impressions are paramount, what image do you want your name to represent?

Building a Professional Image

Rules for Real Estate Success

Salesmanship begins with building a professional image. As you start any career, thinking about your personal and professional image is vital. **Professional image** is a projection of your personal characteristics, such as manners, qualities, and values. These characteristics encompass the image and reactions that first come to mind to anyone who knows you or hears your name. The goal is to build your professional image in such a way that when your prospects are in the selection stage, your image is already established ahead of the competition. For example, think of the best actress for a remake of *The Wizard of Oz*, or choose the best-known real estate agent from a well-known firm. Who first comes to mind? The person whose professional image stands out the most does. The point is, when the public thinks of a notable person or decides they need a real estate agent, your name should be first on a very short list or first in your clients' mind, creating **first awareness** so you are the first person they will first contact.

Building Your Image

- Be proactive. Do not wait for your broker to ask you in what areas you need help. Speak to well-trained agents and managers. Do your research and ask your broker questions. You may have to identify ways to increase your real estate knowledge.
- Be ethical in your practices. Make sure your prices are comparable. Be honest, and always provide exceptional service. Do not forget that in sales, you must first sell yourself before you can sell the product. The rule is *"Once you sell your ethics, then the product will sell itself."* In Chapter One, the Realtors® survey shows 43% of buyers and 29% of sellers pick the agent based on reputation, honesty, and trustworthiness.
- Always keep your word.
- When engaged in marketing, not only are you bringing in business for yourself, but more importantly, you are building your company and your professional image. As you prepare your marketing material, include material to build your public image as well. Always keep in mind how you want the public to view you. An example is an open house sign. Every time you meet someone and every open house sign you place is an opportunity to build your image. Advertising material should promote the following three elements:

1. Your company's professionalism
2. Your public image
3. The property

- Every house you list creates an opportunity for your image to build in your surrounding communities.
- Image building is an ongoing endeavor. It should be a permanent process of your real estate career.
- Display your degrees and certificates. Nearly all top-producing professionals have their professional accomplishments displayed for potential clients' viewing.
- Have your facts ready. For example, research your areas and find the percentage of houses listed compared to the sold prices. This way you can inform your prospects, *"In this area, my average of selling my listings are at 98% of listed price while my competition is selling for 79% of the listed price. As you can see, it is the great service that we provide that will get you the highest price."* These are public facts which will help your prospect make an astute decision.

Duties and Responsibilities

Unique Selling Proposition

You have the duty to give your clients what they expect from your services. In order to win your prospects, you must clearly convey the types of services you offer, which your competition does not. Set yourself apart from the rest. A good way to accomplish this is by using the Unique Selling Proposition. The **Unique Selling Proposition (USP)** is a marketing concept introduced by Rosser Reeves of Ted Bates and Company during the 1940s. USP is based on the idea you are advertising a product so unique, consumers will want to switch products. The idea is called a proposition tagline. An example of a proposition tagline is, "Coke®: *'The Real Thing'*." In real estate, it could be "John Sales Realty, *'The Success Team'*." The proposition can be a statement in a few words or a sentence. The shorter the proposition, the more likely the consumer will remember it. The idea is to differentiate yourself or your office from the rest of the real estate community. A unique USP can be remarkably successful. Take a look at media advertising the next time you go shopping. It is everywhere. Reeves' definition of USP has the following three parts:

1. Each advertisement must make a proposition to the consumer, not just words, product puffery, or show-window advertising. Each advertisement must say "Buy this product, and you will receive *this specific benefit.*"
2. The proposition must be one that your competition cannot or does not offer. It must be unique, either a uniqueness of the brand or a claim not otherwise made in that particular market.
3. The proposition must be strong enough so it can move the masses (i.e., new customers who will be drawn to buy your product).

How can you use your skills to be different? What tagline can you develop to differentiate yourself? As Reeves states, *"It is not just product puffery; you are making a promise now, and you must deliver on your promise."*

For your USP to be effective, you must know what your competition is doing, and know what your customers want. For example, if you are working with first-time homebuyers, does your competition have a USP which addresses first-time buyers? What promise is your competition making to first-time homebuyers? Can you make a better promise? What promises can you make that your competition is unable to offer? What benefits are important to first-time homebuyers? Your marketing message should also be unique. Focus your efforts on a niche, such as a location or working with first-time homebuyers. Again, you must be comfortable and knowledgeable about the niche you select.

Going to the Front of the Line as a Real Estate Agent

Buyers and sellers always think about whether or not hiring a real estate agent is worth the money. Saving 6-10% of the sales price is a legitimate reason that many homeowners think is a valid reason for not using an agent. Sellers also decide whether or not to hire you based on the services you offer that your competitor does not.

Before you meet with prospects, you should have a clear understanding of why any prospect would consider using your professional services. You should be ready to answer common questions, and your response should be clear and concise. Below are ten reasons that prospects should use your services. You may decide to use these or write your own. You should clearly understand your duties, and have a definite plan. In order to convey this message, practice saying your duties with an associate until you feel comfortable, and sound convincing. Some prospects may understand what you are saying while others may need it in writing in order to believe you and the information you give. Remember the old adage, *"If it is in writing, it must be true!"*

Duties I Owe to My Buyers

1. I will use all means to find you the right home for your family.
2. I am here to help you through the entire process of buying your home.
3. I will use all of my professional negotiation skills to get you the best value for your money.
4. I will give you my professional opinion on all real estate matters within my legal limit.
5. I am here to protect you and to make sure that you have all of the information and disclosures you need to make an important decision.
6. I am here to help you understand mortgage and real estate language.
7. I will be here to guide you through your real estate contract.
8. I will communicate with lenders, appraisers, surveyors, inspectors, and title companies to resolve any problems.
9. I promise to keep you informed and updated on any important matters.
10. I will help with closing and title problems.

_____Date_____

Duty of Professionalism

Start looking into professional designations. Statistics from Chapter One show that selecting an agent for his/her professional designations was 1% from buyers and 0% from sellers. You owe your clients the duty of knowing your craft. If you decide to work with buyers, what designations would best show your professionalism? The National Association of Realtors® is an excellent place to start looking for designations. For a complete list of designations, go to www.realtor.org.

The NATIONAL ASSOCIATION OF REALTORS® has nine affiliated institutes, societies, and councils that provide a wide array menu of programs and services to help members increase their skills, productivity, and knowledge. Designations acknowledging experience and expertise in various real estate sectors are awarded by each affiliated group upon completion of the required courses. In addition, NAR offers five certification programs to its members. Other types of certifications include the following:

- ABR, Accredited Buyer Representative
- REBAC, (Real Estate Buyer's Agent Council
- ABRM, Accredited Buyer Representative Manager
- ALC, Accredited Land Consultant
- REALTORS® Land Institute (RLI)
- CCIM, Certified Commercial Investment Member®
- CIPS, Certified International Property Specialist
- NATIONAL ASSOCIATION OF REALTORS®

- CRB, Certified Real Estate Brokerage Manager
- CRS®, Certified Residential Specialist®
- CRE, Counselor of Real Estate
- GAA, General Accredited Appraiser
- Green Designation
- GRI Graduate REALTOR® Institute
- PMN, Performance Management Network
- RCE, REALTOR® Association Certified Executive
- RAA, Residential Accredited Appraiser
- SRES®, Seniors Real Estate Specialist
- SIOR, Society of Industrial and Office REALTORS®
- At Home with Diversity Certification
- e-PRO®
- REPA, Real Estate Professional Assistants Certificate Course
- Resort & Second-Home Property Specialist Certification

Several private schools, public schools, and colleges provide other designations as well. While there are hundreds of designations available to show your professionalism, you should carefully pick designations that will improve your basic knowledge in the field of your choice. Simply buying several designations for your business cards is not going to improve your knowledge needed to support your clients and customers.

Differentiating Yourself with Personal Assets

Not all real estate agents are the same. We all have unique personal assets or skills and things we enjoy doing. If you are adept at a certain skill, use it in real estate. For example, if you like writing, then write monthly newsletters, on-line writing columns, or blog for the people on your mailing list and website. If it is fun for you, you are more likely to be consistent with your writing. Think about what you like doing and how you are different. Whether it is gardening, taking photos, writing, baking, open houses, being a member of an association, family, art, teaching, or other talents, try to incorporate what you like to do into your marketing ideas. If you like baking, then try baking pies. We will discuss this in more detail in Chapter 6, *Marketing*. You can write tips on what you like to do, have seminars, or host special events. If you cannot connect marketing to what you like to do, then select a marketing idea that you can commit to for years. If you like the color red, then always wear a red coat or something red, like a small red pin. If you like hats, then always wear one when showing and selling real estate.

Design and develop your own 'signature'. You need to start thinking about how to differentiate yourself from the rest of the real estate community.

Nearly all marketing ideas will work if you are committed, and you are more likely to be committed if it is fun. Compare yourself to your competition. What makes them good? Do not be afraid to be different. There is the old saying, *"To be good at your craft, you must find yourself."* This is a good saying, but take it a step further; be more aggressive. Think of it this way: *"Why find yourself when you have the opportunity to create yourself?"*

Marketing Gimmicks

While wearing a bold tie, a red coat, or a large name tag may get you noticed, it is still a gimmick. Gimmicks may get you recognized and even remembered, but you still have to win your prospects' confidence. The way to gain your prospects' confidence is by making career improvements.

Career Improvements

While it is important to increase your earnings per year, it is your duty to increase your job knowledge. Think about this rule: *"The more you learn, the more you will earn."* The Japanese word for continuous improvement is *"kaizen."* Talk to your broker about assisting you in formulating a list to execute your plan. Think about what your ten weakest areas are. For example, you may need to know how to fill out a contract, how to develop phone skills, how to present an offer, or how to effectively market yourself. Formulating a timetable that is aimed at working on improving your list, such as one year for difficult items or one month for easy-to-overcome items is a good idea. Your timetable should be challenging as well. The list of ten should be ongoing. As you complete one list, start a new list. Oliver Wendell Holmes (1809-1894) says, *"The mind, once expanded to the dimensions of larger ideas, never returns to its original size."* A quote by Ray Kroc (Mc Donald's) is *"As long as you're green, you're growing. As soon as you're ripe, you start to rot."*

As time progresses and you master each list, identifying enough items to make a complete list of ten may be difficult. This is alright, because in five years or so, you will have emerged as a true professional. The kaizen concept of developing the "list of ten" should be an integral part of your business life. Most real estate agents need to improve their sales skills. Your goal is to become a professional expert; after all, *"An expert is nothing more than a person who has mastered the simple basics."* In this business, the object is to grow out of your routine comfort zone. Only those agents who are serious and commit to yearly self-improvement will continue to grow as responsible salespeople.

Personal Assistants

It is your duty to service your clients. Would using a personal assistant be profitable and help better service your client base? Personal assistants can do much of the agent's or office's workload, thus leaving time for the company or the agents to concentrate on selling. Non-licensed assistants can help with daily office chores, manage files, design flyers, letters, keep flyer boxes filled, help with open houses, be in charge of mailouts, manage property signs, search for expired listings and FSBOs, update contact lists, update files, answer phone calls, take messages, help prepare marketing material, and prepare buyer/seller packets.

Conversely, they can also create liability and be a tax burden. The IRS has specific rules for employee status under which most non-licensed assistants qualify. It is important when using assistants to check with the IRS on employee status and requirements. Unlicensed assistants also must follow state requirements. Oftentimes, rookie real estate agents make the best assistants. This type of agreement escapes federal and state license requirements. This relationship, however, is more of a trade-off, involving working for experience in trade for mentorship.

Overcoming Fears

Chapter One introduced the subject, *"What other agents won't do."* There are many reasons why agents *"won't do,"* but the three biggest are fear of the unknown, rejection, and not being prepared to handle opportunity. To overcome fear, having a partner helps, there is strength in numbers. Letters, post cards, and emails can also help to overcome the fear of knocking on doors or cold calling, but the best way is implementing the following rule, *"For the right reasons or needs, you will always overcome your worst fears."* People will conquer their greatest fear if the need is great enough. If you have a fear of knocking on doors and engaging homeowners, try this trick. Write three checks of $3,000 each to yourself. Drive until you find a FSBO and park. Look at the front door and look at your three checks totaling $9,000. For the first check, if you win the listing, you will make at least the check amount. For the second check, that listing will bring you more listings and buyers. The third check is as good as money in your bank because it will be the first step to conquering your fears. Once you are able to see, smell, feel, and emotionally connect to the three checks of $9,000, knocking on a stranger's door is not going to stop you from earning your $9,000, especially when you are well prepared.

Being Prepared

Being prepared will enhance your chances of success. Below are three ways to be prepared:

Know your office inventory.
Know how to reply to the most common questions.
Keep your presentations ready.

Office Inventory

When it comes to floor duty, it is a good idea to review your entire office inventory before starting to answer phone calls. Be aware of any advertisements by other agents. If you have placed any ads, be sure all other agents and office staff are aware of your advertisements. Call your loan officer early for updates, or better yet, train your lenders to prepare daily updates on all of your files so you will have them early in the morning. Make it a habit to prepare for the next day as much as possible before leaving the office.

Effective Power Scripts

"Opportunity is being prepared by having the best answers for the most common questions, called **scripts**.*"* As discussed in Chapter 1, in your entire real estate career, you will be asked the same questions, but in a thousand different ways. Nevertheless, your answer is the same, the singularly best answer: knowing how to reply with effective power scripts takes practice. Opportunity starts with knowing your **power scripts** and repeating them until they are said with confidence. At that point, you can add your personality to it by changing the words and tone so it sounds like a natural dialogue. Another reason that you need to study scripts is that the people whom you will be contacting (homeowners, buyers, investors, FSBOs, and expired listings) have good scripts themselves and are waiting to use them on you. Below are tips that are effective power scripts:

- Prepare several scripts for different situations: for people you would generally meet, sellers, buyers, FSBOs, expired listings, those asking for referrals, and past clients.
- Always know exactly what you will say at the initial meeting. You must sound confident and not fumble through your greetings.
- Be direct; prospects will respect you for it.
- Keep the focus on your prospects. *"Prospects will find you interesting if you are interested in what they have to say and find you fascinating if you're fascinated in what they are saying."*

- Demonstrate a sincere appreciation for your prospects. Prospects want to feel appreciated.
- To practice, set a time period without distractions.
- Record and evaluate your voice and the speed of your dialogue.

Preparing for Common Questions

During your career, you will be asked several expected questions. For these questions, you should have carefully thought-out answers. Respond as if your answers are worth $1,000,000. Having the best answers will not always work, but it will substantially increase your chances of success. For example, for each of the questions below, rewrite your own answers to accommodate your personal style and confidence level.

Scripts for the Most Common Public Questions/Remarks

1. So, *how is the real estate business? Is it a good time to sell? What do you do?*

Reply: *"Real estate sales are great; it's an exciting time. Interest rates are at a historical low; there is a surplus of finer homes, and there are plenty of opportunities for great investments. You should consider taking advantage of this opportunity."* (Luck is being prepared with the best answer when opportunity presents itself. Your success will start by impressing people by the services you offer.)

2. *How long have you been selling real estate?* or *Have you sold very many houses?*

Reply: *You have a legitimate question. At ABC Realty, our managers are the best in the industry. They double check our work. Because our work is double checked and we are constantly being interviewed on how we can improve, we make fewer mistakes than season agents. Quality control is one of the reasons I decided to work here."*

3. *Go away. You're bothering us.*

Reply: *"I understand how you feel. Would you at least allow me a brief moment of your time to explain how I can help you?"*

Scripts for the Most Common Sellers' Questions/Remarks

1. *"No thanks. We decided to sell ourselves."*

Reply-1: *"I understand, I just wanted to say that we have qualified buyers in your area and wanted to know if I could preview your property to see if we have a match. If I bring you a buyer, would you be willing to pay a fee?"* They may say, *"Do you have a buyer for my house?"* REMARK: *"More than likely, but I won't know until I preview your home."*

Reply-2: *"Yes, I understand. Have you considered a backup plan?"* *(Keep a dialogue as long as you can; it's the fastest way to overcome an objection.)*

2. *" We don't need a real estate agent."* *(FSBOs)*

Reply: *"I understand. Would you be willing to give me the opportunity to show you how I can help you save money by getting the greatest return for your home?"* (Sellers may not understand that there are two types of buyers, home and investment buyers, and they are ready for neither. When a homebuyer cannot mentally move into the house, they will quickly turn into investment buyers. Homebuyers make better offers with fewer objections.)

3. *"My house is not ready. or We want to make repairs first."*

Reply: *"Wonderful, I'm glad I caught you in time. Getting your home ready may seem like endless work. I'd like to share some of my staging tips. It would save you a considerable amount of money and time."*

4. *"We will think about it. or We are not sure if we are ready to sell."*

Reply: *"Yes, that is a big decision. To facilitate the process, let me prepare a presentation package so when you do decide, it will be ready for you. I will call you in a couple of days in case you make an early decision."* or you can say, *"To help you make an important decision, may I offer you a free CMA, for comparison?"* (You need to give something they need and the fact that you will call back soon. If your prospect knows that you will call back, there is less chance they will use another agent.)

5. *"Why should I use you?"*

Reply: *"Yes, you have a valid question and I would like to help. Can you give me a few minutes, so I can show you recent statistics? In your area, my sales/listing ratio is at 92% of getting you what you're asking for while my competition is at 84%.* (Your clients want to know the facts and to clearly know their benefits.)

6. *"I'm looking for a discount broker or You guys charge too much!"*

Reply: *"I understand your concerns. To give you more options, XYZ Real Estate is a TRUE full service real estate company. We take great pride in being the number 1 real estate company in America in servicing our sellers. Give me a moment, and I'll tell you how you will benefit by saving your money."* or *"Would you want to save a few hundred or make a few thousand?"* (Start a dialogue and watch how soon your prospects will forget their objections.)

7. *"Will you reduce your commission?"*

Reply: *"Great, sounds like you have decided to use my services. Allow me to explain how commissions work. (shake hands) My commission is ½ of what my company's share is and the other 3% is paid to the other company."* (Explain the services that they will gain. Be able to list those services in a 1-2-3 fashion.)

8. **"What commission do you charge?"**

Reply: *"Good question, first, let me explain how the process works, and then I will give you the commission."* Explain all that you will do and the money you will spend to help sell the property and if the property does not sell after you have worked very hard, what the cost will be to them. Next, break the fees into two parts. Explain that ½ of fees are to list the property, and the other ½ of fees are to pay the other broker for bringing a buyer.

9. **"May I have your card? We are interviewing several agents."**

Reply: *"That is a smart decision. May I ask you a few questions? I want to be the first in line and be fully prepared to save YOU time, money, and frustration."* (Your goal is to be the first agent to set an appointment, 72% of sellers will pick the first agent they interview.)

10. **"Mail me your information and we'll think about it."**

Reply: "It's wonderful that you are trying to make the best decision. Because it's such an important decision, I would like to personally explain it to you." (Keep a dialogue as long as you can.)

11. **"ABC broker gave us a higher price."**

Reply: *"Great, it's important that we get the highest possible price for you. Since the market determines price and the amount of time for that price, let me do some more research to see how long it will take to sell for that price."* (Explain the price vs. time factor, and that the price is set by the market, not by agents or buyers.)

Scripts for the Most Common Buyers' Questions/Remarks

1. **"Hello, what is the price on _____?"** or **"Hello, can you give me information on _____?"**

Reply: *"This is a impressive looking property. Let me see if it is still available. It has been getting a considerable amount of activity.* (People want what they can't have.) or
Reply: *"Nice choice, you have excellent taste."*

2. **"We are just looking and weighing our options."**

Reply: *"That is a smart decision, and I would like to help make your search more effective. I will be happy to meet with you to discuss your goals, so may I help you find the right home?" (Always compliment and follow with benefits.)*

3. *"I have an apartment lease."*

Reply: *"Have you talked to your apartment manager about an early vacancy release, which is very common?"*

4. *"I'm not sure about my credit score."*

Reply: *"I have a very knowledgeable loan officer who can answer all of your credit concerns. It will take only a few minutes."*

5. *"I'm not ready to make an offer,"* or *"let me think about it."*

Reply: *"I understand your concerns. Tomorrow I will call to see if the property is still available."*

6. *"I am not sure about my job status."*

Reply: *"Since your house payments should be less than rent, where would you live if the worst were to happen?"*

7. *"I will not offer a penny more."*

Reply: *"I totally agree. I like people who base their decisions on market facts. Let me start the paperwork."*

8. *"We are too busy with the holidays."*

Reply: *"Holidays are the best time to sell. Research indicates the best prices are during the holidays when homes are warm and cozy, your home is already staged for warmness."*

9. *"I don't want to sign your exclusive agency agreement form."*

Reply: *"Yes, This is a good form designed to protect you, based on its provisions. I am able to offer you the best service possible and fully devote my time and energy to helping you find your home."* (Prospects will never sign unless there is a benefit.)

10. *"I do not like the location, price, color, etc."*

Reply: *"I understand your concerns. Those are cosmetic and they can be easily changed to suit your taste after you buy the house. Let us focus on key problems concerning the location or the house structure and see what we come up with."*

Your next step is to build rapport, "to be on their team." Once you have the homeowner's attention, start a dialogue. The longer the dialogue, the better the chances they will forget their objections. Try to find their biggest concerns with using a real estate agent. For expired listings, you can say/ask:

"You have a nice home. Do you know why it didn't sell?"
"You are in a nice neighborhood with great schools, so why do you think it didn't sell?"
"Why were you selling?"
"How was your past experience selling your home?"
"Can you tell me what attracted you to your home?"
"Did your past agent give you any buyers' absolute deal breakers?"

Your goal is to collect data which will intrigue them on your return visit; you want to find out more information. For your second trip, have a CMA, educational material, an attractive presentation, and your best opinions and advice ready for your prospects.

Listing and Buyers' Presentations

To win prospective clients, buyers, or sellers, you will need to have some form of presentation ready. Presentations are guides that will help you do the following:

- Organize your thoughts
- Control the conversation
- Make sure valuable information is not omitted
- Leave an impression by using visual and participation ads

People learn from and remember what they see, touch, and participate in far more than what they hear from presentations. Many studies show an 80% higher retention rate when they are able to see, feel and participate in presentations. Prospects will forget the verbal presentation more quickly than a visual presentation in which they participated. Two weeks later, when sellers/buyers are ready for real estate services, you want to be the person they will remember. For more information on how to prepare presentation packages, see Chapters 8, *Prospecting for Sellers* and Chapter 10, *Prospecting for Buyers*.

Having Files Available

Have copies of your active files with accurate information readily available. Buyers or sellers will usually call all hours of the day while they have loan processors or title companies wanting to be updated. They will usually call the person with whom they are most comfortable. As a general practice, be sure you have the latest information for all files that are active or in the closing process. At the end of each day, take time to update any active files.

Business Cards

Keep an ample supply of business cards. Never leave home without them. Your goal is to find and talk to at least five new people every day for the rest of your career. You should think every day you will meet five new people, and every day you will come home with five fewer cards. This means you are going to be a very sociable person. Every morning, be sure to carry a stack of business cards. At the end of the day, count how many cards you gave away and if you obtained their names and phone numbers. The idea is to develop this into a habit of looking for opportunities to distribute business cards. Your goal is to develop a habit of always looking for business opportunities. By giving away business cards, you will keep reminding yourself how being in sales means you are always marketing yourself.

The Card Trick

Once you have your business cards, the first thing you will need to do is visit all of your relatives or mail your card to them. I suggest at least five cards per relative and three cards for everyone else. Have them carry your cards in their wallets or purses, so when the opportunity presents itself, they will have your card at the tip of their fingers and first in mind. For example, *"Uncle John, it's very important that the public knows what I can do for them. Referrals are very important. If you can do me a great big favor, put those cards in your wallet so that when you hear of someone who needs real estate help, you will be able to pass along my card with a little bit of an introduction. This would help me immensely."* Going back to the real estate rule, *"Everyone knows someone who needs real estate services."* Your cards in the hands of hundreds of people who know you and are willing to say nice things about you will keep you busy for years. People always have their wallets or purses in their possession. Every time they look into their purses or wallets, they will be constantly reminded of marketing your services. Don't expect your family and friends to help you, but you need to ask for their help and let them know how valuable their help is. For more information on how to design business cards, refer to Chapter 6, *Real Estate Marketing*.

Having a Direct Approach

A **direct approach** is to ask prospective customers for their business and to let them know that you will work hard to earn and keep their business. In this business, you must take the direct approach when asking for referrals. Below are four rules to remember when asking clients for referrals:

1.   Ask for referrals during the transaction.

2. Ask several times in different formats for referrals.
3. Ask for their help in getting referrals.
4. Ask as part of your on-going work ethics.

Asking for Referrals

For some reason, many talented agents are intimidated when it comes to asking for a buyer's or seller's business or for a referral. Remind prospective customers that you are always ready to assist with their housing needs. Do not be intimidated; clients will respect you for being direct. Reluctance to ask for business tends to show that you are unsure of your services. After all, asking for referrals is one of the important steps that lead to your goal. When asking for referrals, you must reassure your client that you have their family member's or friend's best interest at heart. You might approach the matter by saying, *"Mr. and Mrs. _____, you are great clients, and I would appreciate your telling your friends and family about the quality services that I offer. I assure you that I will help your friends and family sell their home for the highest price, as quickly as possible. I will protect their interest, and I promise to give the highest quality service possible."*

Scheduling Meetings

Although you need your client's business, do not appear to be too eager and hungry for it when scheduling meetings. Pause a minute to relay to your clients a sense of how busy you are, so when you respond to them, they will appreciate your time. For example, if buyers or sellers ask you how soon they can meet with you, your answer should be, *"Give me a minute,"* pause, look in your pocket calendar, and maybe even count to ten before you reply. This indicates that you must be good at what you do—why else would you have such a busy schedule? Have you ever been to a restaurant during peak hours when you could not find a parking space? This indicates that the food must be good because there are many people who agree. What if your car is the only one in the parking lot? This may indicate that the food is terrible. The same is true for you; your volume of business is indicative of your services. You must be good at what you service because everyone else thinks you are.

Incidentally, on the first meeting, address your clients as "Mr., Mrs., Ms., or Miss" and ask what they prefer for you to call them. Learn to pronounce their names before your meeting. No one likes it when you mispronounce his/her name.

Creating a Sense of Importance

When a caller asks for information on one of your listings, convey to him/her the sense that the property is valuable and in demand by saying,

"Can you please hold while I check the status of that property" or *"Yes, let me check the current status for you. May I have your number and I will call you back, or would you like to hold for a minute?"* Doing so gives the caller a sense of urgency and in some cases, shifts the caller's attitude from one of aggression to passivity. Based on your response, it is most likely that the caller will want additional information. At this point, you want the caller to set an appointment and come into your office for a personal meeting. Usually, you can accomplish this by offering a tip-staging sheet or other free information, *"Would you like to come by the office for our company's free guide called...?"* If your callers are hesitant, you should offer to snail mail or email the information to them. Below are examples of free information you can give callers:

- Powerful Tips for Buyers
- What Every Buyer Needs to Know
- The 10 Most Powerful Tips Sellers Need to Know
- What are My Rights as a Home Buyer?
- Who Qualifies for Grant Money?
- How to Stage your Home to get Highest Price.
- What I Wish My Agent Would Have Told Me

Offering exclusive information booklets serves as a starting point to building a sense of trust and confidence towards you in the mind of the caller, especially if you ask, *"Has anyone offered, Know Your Rights by HUD or Powerful Buying tips for Buyers to you ?"* Buyers and sellers want real estate educational information on how to improve their economic position. You can also tell them that a good website for homeowner's information is hud.com as well as the websites for local, state, and national real estate associations.

Establishing Your Professional Services

Professional Services

The three services that your clients and customers will expect from you are the following:

1. Solutions
2. Value
3. Benefits

Providing Solutions

Sellers and buyers often come to you with the task of either finding a house or selling their house. For many sellers and buyers, doing this on their own is a problem. Solving these problems for your clients is what real estate sales is all about. The last thing your clients need to know are your problems. It does not matter if you have countless chores to do or if you are neck-high in paperwork. They do not want to hear it and could care less about your problems. *"We live in a world of "me," but sales is the business of "you."* When you meet with your prospects, try to not talk about yourself, your family, or your hobbies. Instead, focus on your prospect's 'problem' and their family or their hobbies. They expect nothing less than 100% of your attention. Neither do they need to know about the many degrees you have unless those college degrees will help them with their needs. The only reason they are talking to you is they believe you can provide a solution to their needs. Give yourself plenty of time to prepare for your prospects, put away all other files, freshen up, and focus solely on your clients. Do not forget that million-dollar smile.

Hidden Objections

After you show some buyers several houses that meet their expectations, the buyer may be unable to make a decision. This may be the case of early-buyers' remorse or buyers' confusion. If they are confused, chances are they will not go forward. Ask them if there are any hidden objections or if you made some sort of mistake. Perhaps they do not understand the buying process. If you find you made a mistake, figure out how to clear up the discrepancy. The hidden objections could be that the buyers heard there may be a layoff where they work, or they no longer have the down-payment money. If hidden objections are present learning what they are early-on is best.

Getting Down to Business

Your business is to find the right home for your buyer. In order for you to reach your goals, you need to perform your business as efficiently as possible. You do not have time to waste showing homes to your client that they are not prepared to buy. If you set standards of being candid and honest, your prospects will most likely do the same with you. Ask your buyers the following questions:

- Have you talked to a lender?
- Is there anything that you are concerned with?
- If you are ready to start looking, don't forget to bring your checkbook.
- If we find the right home, how soon will you be able to purchase?
- Is there another decision maker?
- Before we search, are there any deal breakers?

The sum of all of parts is equal to the sale. This is explained in more detail in Chapter 10. Ask your buyers for small agreements, such as *"Are the bedrooms large enough for you? Is the property in the right location?* or *Does the property layout work for you?"* These small parts will add-up to the total, which is the sale. As a selling point, small commitments will add to the overall weight of which property to purchase.

Meticulous buyers do not have a problem with small commitments. It is the big final commitment they are afraid to make. One small commitment at a time will help the client when it is time to make the final decision. In this area, your job is to keep a record and help the buyers separate what each property has.

In your notes on pros and cons, divide the pros into the buyers' needs, wants, and desires. As your buyers visit other properties, they will forget detailed information about each house, such as which house had the large back yard or which one had the dark carpet. The buyer does not realize that after a few houses, he/she will become confused about which house had what items (This is known as being house drunk.)

On your note sheet, enter what your buyer liked about each house and whether it is a must-have item, a needed item, a wanted item, or even a hate deal-breaker. This way, when your buyer is deciding on which house to purchase, you have the comparison notes. Your notes will also aid in retrieving small commitment responses from your client.

The Rule of Benefits

Decision making is part of our lives, and we make thousands of decisions daily. The basis of making a decision is whether or not the results end in a benefit to the decision maker. The **rule of benefit** is that decisions made will depend on the benefits or rewards the decision maker will receive. We are mostly unaware of the smaller, less significant decisions. However, we remember the more important decisions and weigh them heavily. Nevertheless, the rule of benefit remains the same: *"The greater the benefits, the faster the decision will be made."* In real estate, to gain positive responses, you need to learn how to use benefit words and statements. **Benefit words** are words like "free" in a sentence to attract the listeners' attention.

The same holds true for buyers, sellers, or any shopper. Their decision to buy is based on personal improvements. Their decision to select a particular agent or to read and act on a certain advertisement largely depends on the benefit. They are not going to read an advertisement

Professionalism and Salesmanship

or choose you as their agent if there are no real benefits involved. The advertisement rule is, *"You should lead with benefits and follow it with features."* For example: you may have stated that you have been selling real estate for 20 years, but how will your prospects benefit from your experience? By disclosing you have sold hundreds of homes in the Clear Lake area during your 20-year career, your benefit to the reader is the fact that you have the knowledge and experience needed to sell his/her home.

Sometimes while deciding whether there are benefits in buying a house, buyers and sellers need assurance. To help with processing their decision, write down the pros and cons, and have facts available. If buyers are not sure if they are getting a good deal, show them the CMA or the appraisal. If the pros outweigh the cons, they will quickly make a positive decision. Have a notepad and camera ready for every showing. Take pictures of what they like and make a list. All "pro" items that buyers like are the same as asking for small commitments. The same notes you took to solicit a small commitment will also help you solicit a decision from your client. Writing notes is a way for buyers to acknowledge their likes and dislikes. Most of our daily decisions are partially based on likes and dislikes. If they like the house, they will point out all of the "pros," and the house will soon sell itself; thus, a decision to buy that house.

If you are writing an ad, instead of saying *"Beautiful home in Clear Lake,"* write about benefits to the reader. *"Enjoy relaxing in this beautiful lake-front home."* The advertising rule is to make it personal and include the readers' benefits.

Keeping Decisions Objective

Sellers and buyers often become subjective and make emotional decisions. Try to remain objective by reducing negotiations to dollars and cents. For example, after viewing many houses, the buyer(s) may be trying to decide which house to buy. Go through your notes, and if the buyer(s) hate the color of a bedroom, put a dollar amount on it. If the seller(s) must keep the fireplace mantle, put a price on it.

The ABC Rules of Real Estate Sales

Real estate has several 'ABC Rules.' The first mnemonic is "Always Be Closing," which not only means being physically presence at the closing table, but always thinking forward to making the next sale as well. Another ABC is "Always Be in Control." In order to close a deal, you must always be in control. One thing to remember is that once you lose control, the closing will not happen.

Keep this in mind: most consumers will want to take control. Before they walk into your office, they have thought in advance how to gain control and will be waiting to reply with an objection. The meet/greet technique will help agents maintain control by not asking for an objection. Be assured that once an objection is stated, it becomes difficult for the agent to overcome it. It is much easier to avoid an objection than to overcome one. The logic is to never ask close-ended questions where an objection can be made because you will surely get one. Here are the steps:

- Always greet with a friendly smile.
- Avoid asking close-ended questions.
- Always agree with the prospect and then redirect the conversation. After the redirection, the prospect will have forgotten about giving an objection or he/she has decided to accept your invitation.

Often, you, the agent, are not in control because you allow the client or consumer to take control of the situation. For example, in an open house, the agent may say, "May I help you?" Of course, the consumer will most likely say, *"I'm just looking, I have an agent, or I'm not buying."* Untrained agents are asking for the consumer to take control and to be left alone, which would be all right if the agent did it on purpose and was ready with a reply to set the stage and quickly disarm the prospects' objections. Agents need to study their power scripts to the point that they sound natural when repeating them. *"Overcome prospects' scripts with better scripts."*

Power scripts are designed to keep the agent in control and to disarm the prospects' objections. An example of a power script for an open house is *"Hello, welcome to our open house. My name is _____. Please make yourself at home,"* or *"I am here to give you the information you need."* The consumer may say, *"I'm just looking."* The reply should be, *"That is great that you are looking. My job is to answer any of your concerns and provide you with all the information you need to make a well-informed decision."*

Voice Mail

Listen to your voice mail or answering service. Does it portray a sense of being business-like, being organized, and of being conservative? Is there unwanted music or noise in the background? Practice voicing your message multiple times until it sounds professional. If for some reason you do not feel comfortable, you may consider hiring a professional to record your message.

Business Etiquette

Business etiquette is a set of manners or social conduct in a business situation, a set of rules that govern the way people socially interact with one another in business. There are hundreds of different types of etiquette, such as dining, telephone, email, greetings, introductions, showing gratitude, meetings, and social gatherings. The list of formal manners is also endless. Spend time researching these etiquette styles, since it covers many topics of real estate.

Business Websites

Keep your website and email address business-like. All too often, young agents may decide to use their old personal email address or website for information, which is suitable for family or friends, but may not be suitable for business. Most brokerage firms have standard email addresses available for those who link to web pages. Pictures of your kids, home, or family activities should not be a part of your business website. While your readers may enjoy reading about your summer trip to Paris, France, they are more concerned about their housing needs. You need to keep the information on your website related to your business. While your family activities may not be appropriate for your website, community service by your family could help build your professional image. For example, if you are a community board member and farming in the same community, you may want to add a link to recent news or even include a blog on your website.

Training Courses and Real Estate Coaches

Attend as many sales skills training, product seminars, and professional speaking engagements as possible, and always search for new marketing techniques, products or new laws. Consider enrolling in courses on etiquette; how to improve your image, communicating more effectively, and educating yourself in your field of study. Sign up with local presentation training associations, such as Toastmasters, and learn to think and communicate in an organized manner.

Nearly all competitive industries have some form of personal coaching or strength training. In every sport, athletes decide whether to hire a personal coach, and if only one will help them get the edge over their competition. Real estate agents have the same options. There are many types of personal coaches, each one focusing on different areas of real estate. Before you decide to employ a real estate coach, ask about the coach's specialties. Ask about records of accomplishment, reference letters, and prices. Most coaches are good with developing goals and plans, deadlines for goals, and motivational techniques for agents.

Character

First Impressions

This cliché is true: *"You never get another chance to make a first impression,"* and, first impressions are very important, especially in the real estate business. It is paramount that your first impression be a good one. Remember, when you personally meet buyers and sellers, you will never have a second chance to make a first impression. Learn to smile and always be pleasant. Practice your opening lines, *"Hello, I'm John Ross with ABC Realtor®,"* or *"Good morning, I'm John. How may I help you?"* In this case, when the prospect walks into your office or calls your office, asking an open-ended question is preferred. Carefully select and pronounce your words so that the listener may clearly hear every word and remember to smile. You will be amazed what a smiling face will get you. Your prospects will also judge you by what you wear and if you are prepared for an interview.

Stand in front of a mirror and take a fresh look at yourself. Be honest with yourself and think about what impressions you think you convey in the first ten seconds. Ask your co-workers, friends, and relatives about their first impressions of you. Make a list of ten things about you that are vital for your success. This list can include qualities your friends admire about you, or self-improvements you think you need to make. Be open to constructive criticism. Although hearing negative comments about one's self is difficult, understand that these negative comments will only help you attain your goal of success. Ask your friends and loved ones for an honest opinion.

Remember the sports-saying, *"No pain, no gain."* The saying in the sales arena is *"No tension, no improvement, and no money."* You cannot improve without some degree of tension. Overcoming tension is beyond the scope of this book. However, you can consult a book store or professional counselor if you need help with overcoming tension.

Evaluations

Another way to help improve your quality of services is to have your clients evaluate your services after every transaction. Design evaluation forms for sellers, buyers, and renters. Mail your evaluation forms to your clients. Keep evaluations short by limiting them to one page or less. Ask for permission to use evaluations for training purposes and to quote your source. Large national brokerage firms may use **CSIRs**, Customer Service Index Reports. Refer to Chapter 6, *Marketing* for more information on designing evaluations and surveys.

Rules for Real Estate Success

Showing Empathy

One of the most valuable personal qualities you can have is to be **empathetic** toward your clients. Being empathetic means not just understanding how the other person feels but actually feeling those feelings.

Prospects must feel that you care about them and their needs and that you want the best for them. Buyers and sellers are looking for an agent because they have a problem and they need help. The last thing they want is to be taken advantage of or be looked as a meal ticket. To prove this point, walk into a car dealership and look at the salesperson's eyes. As the salesperson views you, what do you think he/she is thinking? Are you viewed as fresh meat, or are viewed as a deserving person in need of sincere, honest help? Do you view the salesperson as someone who is going to help you with your need; does he/she show empathy toward you? If your client(s) feel you lack this quality, chances are your prospect(s) will remain prospect(s) and never become a client(s). Ask questions to find out why your prospects want to buy or sell. Maybe they need to sell their old home, find a home in a different school district, or they are downsizing and need a smaller home since the children have grown-up and moved out. Always show caring, concern, and understanding. The person who can listen to what prospects have to say and what prospects' needs are will probably get a head-start in getting the sale

BuildingTrust

People will refer their friends and family to you *only* if they trust you and believe you are the best person for the job. Agents will often make the mistake of telling their clients what they want to hear and then end-up losing their trust. For example, the buyer may say, *"So, what do you think about the house?"* In trying to please the buyer, the agent may say, *"It is a great looking home."* After the buyer views the house and decides he/she did not like it, he/she will realize their agent is simply saying what he/she believes the buyer wants to hear. The agent should have been honest and said, *"As we look at the house, let us see if it has some of the details you stated you like and dislike, and then you can decide if it meets your needs."*

Showing Thankfulness

Be thankful. Learn to accept praise in a professional manner. For example, *"John, thank you for the kind words. I was happy to be of assistance."* Do not attempt to go overboard in trying to make an impression.

Avoiding Criticism

Be a professional, and never criticize another agent. Not criticizing another agent is part of the real estate professional code of ethics; people actually do not like the idea of criticism. *"One who criticizes another will surely criticize me."* Criticizing another agent shows poor character.

Finding a Winning Way

Find a way that works best for you. This textbook offers several scripts and hundreds of suggestions, but you need to determine which ones will work for you. **Find a Winning Way** is how you will fine tune your scripts or think how you can perfect them. If you cannot find what works for you, be creative; try something different, something new. You should always search for good scripts, but at some point, you need to be original and start designing your own scripts. This will give you an enormous advantage. Take notes of successful statements you have made. Listen to how successful agents win over their clients. Keep records and keep track of which types of mail-outs and emails have proven better results. Determine why and how you will gain referrals. You may have gained referrals because you gave quality services, but which services were essential to your clients? Whatever you find you are good at, use those skills to gain an edge in this business.

Keeping Promises

Be careful when making promises. Make sure you keep all of your promises, and maintain notes in order to conduct a follow-up. (For note taking, invest in handheld devices, electronic date calendars, or keep a supply of note pads handy.) If you have a 5:00 p.m. appointment, never be more than one-five minutes early or late. This will translate into how much you care about your prospects. A trustworthy person is only as good as his/her last word

Being Genuine

Be genuine, enthusiastic, and down-to-earth, but stay on a professional level. Be careful about fake smiles. The only person you are deceiving is yourself. While you cannot see your own facial expressions, others can.

Although you may accomplish showing a genuine interest by smiling, your body language may indicate something different.

Dressing Professionally

Dressing for Success

Some image-building coaches would say that forming an image is 90% show and 10% knowledge. Simply put, dress professionally. While attire has become more casual in recent years, it is still in a real estate agent's best interest to dress in a highly professional manner. Chances are good that you will often meet someone who knows you as a real estate professional.

Visit some of the upscale clothing department stores to do research on types of clothing that gives you a professional look and think conservatively. Your clients, customers, and co-workers will judge you every day by what you wear. Learn how to mix colors, what colors are used with the different seasons, and how much jewelry to wear. The list of how to dress professionally is almost endless. As you build your wardrobe, start discarding older worn clothing. It can become expensive to dress professionally, so do your planning and shopping, and remember, clothing does not have to be expensive, but it does need to look fresh. Below are tips for dressing professionally:

- Shop for the conservative look; conservative clothing communicates trust while bold, bright colors, 'sleezy' clothing and outdated clothing may communicate a shadowy character.
- While many suit colors will do, think about dark blue or black business suits for both men and women. Charcoal grey should be your second option, followed by green and brown tinted suits.
- For an informal setting, a khaki suit or slacks is acceptable.
- Women can wear red attire as long as it is in a business suit. Wearing too much red is a powerful statement; your intent is not to overpower your clients.
- Clothing should fit properly. The front of your pants should touch the top of your shoes while the back of the pants should be just above the heel.
- In a formal meeting, suits are buttoned while standing and unbuttoned in a sitting position.
- Dark blue or red ties with white or light blue shirts work best. Have you ever witnessed the President of the United States with any color tie except for red and blue in a formal meeting? For the last 100 years, presidents in formal meetings usually wore two colors of ties and two colors of shirts and sometimes a dark grey suit, which is rare.

- Ties should end at the middle of the belt.
- Shoes and socks should be a dark color. In a formal setting, shoes should to be darker than the suit. Shoes should be polished.
- For women's shoes, formal dress calls for closed toes. Avoid high heels that are over two inches. Shoes with heels less than one inch are business formal.
- For women, skirt suits are acceptable if there is a business jacket to go with it. Business skirts are recommended to be just below the knee level. Avoid low necklines on blouses.
- Do not forget to avoid wearing too much jewelry. Remove all rings except for wedding and college rings during the first meeting. During regular workdays, keep earrings to one set and avoid wearing anything too flashy.

Perfumes and Colognes

Be cautious about using strong perfumes and colognes. A bloodhound is not needed to track the person wearing too strong of a perfume. Whenever trying new perfumes, try measuring the right amount, ask a friend for help. Strong smells tend to be distracting, especially when there is close contact between the agent and prospect. Also, many people are allergic to perfume and cologne. How much is too much cologne? When a person leaves the room, and the scent of their perfume/cologne lingers, it is too much. Buyers are already nervous about a 30-year commitment without adding a distracting scent.

Keeping Clean and Neat

Keep your car and office neat and clean. If you need gas or need to check the oil, do it on the way home, not on the way to work. The scent of gasoline tends to linger on your clothes or hands.

Keep your office, desk, files, and briefcase clean and well organized. When customers come to your office for the first time and see a messy desk with paper everywhere, what are they going to think? Take pictures of other desks and mail them to other agents. Agents will not like this trick, but it works. This way, everyone in the office will have an idea of what looks professional and what does not when it comes to the work area.

- Keep facial hair neat and trimmed, no long side burns.
- Keep pockets free of clinking coins since they tend to make unnecessary noise.
- Keep all clothing freshly laundered and pressed.
- Before meeting clients, do not drink a lot of coffee and smoke cigarettes; the smell of tobacco breath is disgusting.

- Refresh your breath by using peppermints instead of gum; listening to someone chew gum is annoying. Keep fingernails neat and trimmed; women should use traditional nailpolish colors.
- Hide body piercings and tattoos.
- Refrain from unusual hair colors and wild hairstyles.

Communication Skills

Word Choices

Consider your choice of words carefully and practice how you would present a real estate Buyer Representation Agreement. Would you say, *"This form is to protect me so if you decide to use another real estate agent, I'll still get paid,"* or would you say; *"This is a good form designed to protect both of us; based on its provisions, I'm able to offer you the best service possible and fully devote my time and energy to helping you find your home."* From a psychological standpoint, if the consumer realizes that he/she will benefit from the service agreement, then he/she will agree to sign. In the first example, only the real estate agent receives any benefit, whereas, the second example illustrates mutual benefit.

You should practice your choice of words in as many different situations as possible. Ask a friend or co-worker to role-play with you. The situations you might encounter could be: meeting your sellers/buyers, presenting an offer, asking buyers and sellers to sign contracts, meeting For-Sale-by-Owners or greeting prospects at an open house. What you will find is that the more you practice choosing and using words carefully, the more likely that will become your standard way of communicating. Several textbooks on the market offer information that contains pre-designed letters and opening remarks for most possible situations. The basic rule is to add benefit clues to your choice of words. As previously discussed, benfits are extremely important to the consumer. Therefore, your use of benefit clues when speaking to your prospect(s) or your client(s) is critical. Benefit clues are words or statements that act as a positive signal for your audience. The statement has been previously mentioned: *"This is a good form designed to protect us; based on its provisions, I'm able to offer you the best service possible and fully devote my time and energy to helping you find your home"* is filled with benefit clues.

Words you may want to avoid are as follows:

- The words cost, selling price, deal or list price, can be replaced with 'investment opportunity', or 'investment amount.'
- Down payment or deposit may be replaced with 'your initial investment.'
- The word contract may be replaced with 'agreement.'

- Payment may be replaced with 'investment.'
- The word nice may be replaced with the word 'character.'

Communication

Sellers and buyers expect to be informed as a part of the service that you offer. Sellers want feedback about properties, and they want to know about market conditions. Set a communication schedule. For example, make it a rule to personally call your clients at least once a week, email at least twice a week, or mail a card once a month.

Communication Skills

Several barriers need to be removed to effectively communicate with prospects. Your prospects are counting on you to set the stage. It is up to you to clear any communication barriers. Try to be a good listener and focus on what your clients/customers have to say, "Smart people are skilled listeners and "talk" very little." Be patient; you can try counting before a reply. When buyers ask you a question, try counting to three before giving your answer. This minor span of time gives you an opportunity to process your thoughts and what you feel is important. A good training tool for this skill-building is videotaping yourself, which will give you the "outside view" on how you are expressing yourself.

Sound Enthusiastic

The energy in your voice is equally important. Add passion to your voice; show that you are excited about what you are doing. Interest and excitement shows you have a genuine concern in your prospects. After all, salesmanship is more about the presentation than the information itself.

Hearing and Listening: Two Different Things

Have you ever engaged in a conversation where you could not wait for the person to finish what he/she was saying so you could start talking? Have you ever had a conversation where the other party started talking before you were finished? In this case, do you believe the other person was hearing or listening? Did he/she understand the message? Hearing is to hear the words while listening is to understand what the speaker is saying. Developing the skill of being a good listener takes hard work, patience, and practice. You can start practicing today. Try listening all the way through, and give yourself a few seconds before you reply when you are engaged in your next conversation.

Hearing Speakers

Do not interrupt speakers. Allow them time to complete their sentences. Show genuine interest in what your speakers believe. *"People will find you interesting when you are interested in what they have to say."* Don't be concerned about whether or not you will forget to ask questions. This is why note taking is valuable.

If you believe the information is important, ask the speaker if you may take notes. You might say, *"Wow, this is interesting. Do you mind if I write some of this down?"* Ask speakers to slow down so you can write questions. This shows you are professional, organized, and you care about what your speaker has to say. The more intensely you write, the more encouraged your speaker becomes. The more the speaker talks, the more important information you are able to gather. When the speaker is finished, review some of the questions you have written down for further clarification. As you read your notes, you will probably find that your speaker most likely covered the majority of your concerns.

Keep Your Presentations Simple

Keep your presentations simple. What you say may not always be what the other party understands, or your choice of words may not be interpreted accurately. After all, *"Noise is a conversation that is meaningless to the listener."* Be specific and to the point in your presentations. By being specific, the client is better able to understand what you are trying to explain. You can say, *"The sales price is $120,500"* instead of saying, *"The price is somewhere around $120,000."* Try to not use phrases, acronyms, abbreviations, or initials. If your prospects cannot understand what you are saying, you are not communicating. *"If you are not communicating, you are not selling."* Real estate and mortgage lending professionals often use a language of their own. Although this language is understood in the industry, the general public may not understand the meaning of such words. For example, a loan officer may say, *"The loan type is an 80/20 combo, paying thirty-two bits on first with a total yield of 1.4 % on 3-2-1 pre-paid on the back side."* This type of jargon may be annoying to the buyer(s) because they do not understand it; it is not simple. Be sure to use complete sentences and common terms. If you must use a term that is specific to the real estate industry, be sure you explain it right after you say it. Remember, some people may be sensitive about having terms explained to them. The best practice is to avoid professional jargon as much as possible. House hunting is confusing enough without your adding more confusion to it.

Also, keep your presentation simple by keeping your personal opinions to yourself; your clientele want professional advice, not opinions. The rule is *"People don't care what you think; they want to hear what you know."*

Be Careful with Body Language

Body language is also a fundamental aspect of image building. **Body language** is nonverbal communication. Body language includes eye movement, voice tone, gestures, posture, and greeting. Walk confidently, sit straight, and use a firm handshake. Your voice should be friendly and you should clearly enunciate the words in your sentence. Practice by standing in front of a mirror. Say a few words to test your hand language. Often, we do not realize how much we use our hands and eye movement. Overusing our hands as a form of communication is an aggressive form of body language. People also have a need for personal space. Try to keep your hands below your chest and less than a foot from your body. How close can a stranger speaking to you get before it becomes uncomfortable to you? We all have a limit for personal space; a safe rule is at least two feet or the distance it takes to shake hands with arms bent at a 45 degree angle.

Developing eye contact is particularly important. Remaining focused on what the speaker is saying and keeping your mind from wandering is helpful in maintaining your body language. Looking away while the speaker is talking, may send the false message that you are not interested in what he/she has to say; it may send the wrong body language. You may also miss important nonverbal communication cues. Do not forget that body language is over 90% of what you are communicating. The following are suggestions that can be helpful with body language:

- In your next conversation, force yourself to listen, make eye contact, and closely hear every word the speaker is saying (try to keep your mind from wandering), do not interrupt, and wait three seconds before you reply. This exercise will demonstrate how hard listening really is.
- Whenever you meet someone for the first time, the first thing he or she will do is make a judgment call. He/she will be on overdrive, reading everybody's language cues. We all do this, but some people are more discrete than others when reading body language.
- Keep communications clear by removing distractions. Put things away to give prospects your full attention. Choose a quiet meeting space away from noise, other agents, or children.
- Make your prospects a part of the conversation. Instead of talking, ask your prospects open-ended questions. For example, ask, *"What do you think about the neighborhood?"* or *"How do you feel about the bedroom sizes?"* This way, the prospects are enthusiastic because it is their idea.

Good phone skills are certainly important. Most of your new sales calls will be over the phone. Buyers and sellers are going to call, and during the conversation, they will build a mental picture of you. These basic phone skills can make the difference in callers being your client or someone else's. Here are some suggestions to help you with developing your phone skills:

- Practice your phone skills by having a friend role-play with you, videotape yourself, or use a mirror. When using a mirror, place it next to your phone so every time you answer, you will remember to smile and relax when speaking. Even a smile can be "heard" over the phone line.
- Have phone scripts ready. For example, *"Hello, USA Realty, may I help you?"* or *"USA Realty, John speaking. May I help you?"* While most brokerages have scripts for agents to use, you should have some of your own as well. Practice saying your scripts until they sound natural.
- After your opening statement, the next step is to establish rapport. Once the caller asks for information, your response should be clear, calm, yet enthusiastic. The tone of your voice will let callers know the importance of their call.
- Encourage your prospects by asking open-ended questions. The goal is to get the callers to open-up as much as possible, which means that you need to listen more and talk less. When you do this, they will usually feel more comfortable revealing personal information.
- Keep your emotions under control. Getting excited about a property is one thing, but sounding like a five-year old who just walked into a candy store is another. Let your client be the one to show emotions while you continue to show professionalism.
- Before you start answering phone calls, be sure you are aware of any new listings, new advertising, or changes. If you have floor time, review listing information before your shift starts, and be prepared to share it with clients when asked.
- Return phone calls as soon as possible. Develop a return call policy, such as returning all calls within 15 minutes.
- Do not try to sell yourself over the phone; whenever possible, you should try to meet your customers in person. *"All sales are done in person."* Phone calls are the means to set-up the sale. One of the biggest reasons buyers refuse to leave their phone number or call about a property is the pressure they feel the agent will apply. They are afraid the agent(s) will constantly call or even plead for their business. Selecting a home is frustrating enough without agents constantly calling. The best way to get the caller's phone number is not to apply pressure during the phone call. Give the information

that is requested, and ask if he/she would like other educational information.

- Do not give too much information over the phone. The idea is to try to have callers come into your office by setting an appointment; however, you should set the time and date. *"Mr. Briggs, I am available Friday at 1:00 p.m."* This shows the caller you are busy, and your time is limited. Proposing a set time when setting an appointment will do one of two things: the caller will ask for a new time, or the caller will have the chance to terminate the call. Either way is an advantage for you. 1) If the caller agrees to a new time, you have a winner, and you have won their respect. 2) If not, then the caller was probably just looking and not serious about the real estate process. If the prospect wants the property, he/she will call back to set-up a meeting. The important thing is that you did not have to convince the caller that you are a good agent; he/she will realize this.
- You can always sweeten the call by saying. *"Thank you, Mr. Briggs. May I send you a free information kit for homeowners?"* Once again, people like to receive benefits.
- Try to answer the phone without too much delay. Your phone scripts should overcome the image of eagerness.
- When making calls, use the three-part rule, identify yourself, the reason for the call, and ask your questions.

For information on how to cold call, see Chapter 7, *Prospecting for Sellers.*

Phone Messages

If anyone else, such as your children or co-workers plan to take your messages, be sure you have a list of what you expect from the message taker. Message pads usually have most of the vital information, but you should be sure that your message taker understands the importance of asking for complete information and being friendly while taking your messages.

Rules for Real Estate Success

1. Visit your local Association of Realtors®, ask for pricing and course description of the different designations, and make a list of the designations in which you are interested.

2. Design an evaluation sheet. Make a list of ten things you feel are important to you. Have a few friends or co-workers write ten things they like about you and then ten things they think you can improve. Ask your friends for their honesty.

3. Write ten things you enjoy and how you will use them in your real estate marketing.

4. Make a timeline for improving the ten areas you hope to improve.

5. Plan how you will visit your family and friends who agree to help you pass out your business cards. Write your script for this marketing idea.

6. Write a unique selling proposition for your business.

7. Download a copy of Realtors Ethics as part of your presentations.

8. Practice your listing scripts, and have a partner role-play with you. In your conversation, count to two or three before replying. Work on eye contact in this exercise.

9. Practice your introduction scripts in front of a mirror while you videotape yourself.

10. Ask your broker for the office's how-to-answer phone calls scripts.

11. Study how top producers build their image.

12. Study your scripts for overcoming the fear of door-to-door sales.

1. Being knowledgeable, developing social skills, having empathy, and having accomplished listening skills are the start of building
   A. A professional image.
   B. Ethics.
   C. Advertising.
   D. First impressions.

2. Advertising material should include which of your purposes?
   A. To promote the property
   B. To promote your public image
   C. To brand your name
   D. To promote the company's professionalism
   E. All of the above

3. A unique Selling Proposition is
   A. To differentiate the individual person or an entire office from the rest of the real estate community.
   B. A marketing concept introduced by Rosser Reeves of Ted Bates and Company during the 1940s.
   C. A proposition that the competition either cannot or does not offer. It must be unique—either a uniqueness of the brand or a claim not otherwise made in that field of advertising.
   D. All of the above.

4. In a formal meeting, male ties should be worn
   A. Two inches above the belt.
   B. At the belt level.
   C. Two inches below the belt.
   D. Without any regard for level, as long as it is clean.

5. Body language is
   A. Verbal communication.
   B. Being specific in a conversation.
   C. Understanding how the other person feels.
   D. Nonverbal communication.

6. From the list below, what is the most important personal quality a real estate agent can have?
   A. Being grateful.
   B. Dressing professionally.
   C. Displaying a professional image.
   D. Being empathetic.

7. Business etiquette is
   A. Selling real estate.
   B. A set of manners or social conduct in a business situation.
   C. Making decisions, depending on the benefits or rewards.
   D. Helping with updating contact lists.

8. Being empathetic means
   A. Being prepared.
   B. Understanding how the other person feels.
   C. Being thankful.
   D. Having a sense of importance.

9. Having a direct approach means
   A. Understanding how the other person feels.
   B. Directly asking prospects for their business.
   C. Using the Unique Selling Proposition.
   D. All of the above.

10. The rule of benefits means
    A. Government health plan for real estate agents.
    B. Decisions are based on improvement.
    C. First impressions are Important.
    D. Agents know how to dress professionally.

11. One way to keep decisions objective is to
    A. Clearly convey what services you offer that your competitor is unable to offer.
    B. Limit the showing list of homes to fewer than ten homes.
    C. Be empathetic.
    D. Reduce negotiations to dollars and cents.

12. The sum of all parts is equal to the sale means
    A. To ask for small commitments; the sum of all small commitments would equal the sale.
    B. To convey clearly what services you offer, that your competitor is unable to offer.
    C. To find hidden objectives.
    D. To be able to give clients 100% of your attention.

13. Being prepared by having the best answers for the most common questions is by having
    A. Kaizen
    B. Presentations
    C. Prospecting
    D. Power scripts

14. The ABCs of real estate means
    A. Learning how to use new benefit words
    B. To close transactions you must always be in control
    C. A set of manners for social conduct
    D. To understand you must show empathy

CHAPTER 6
Real Estate Marketing

Objectives:

Understand

- The marketing process and marketing costs
- The importance of selecting the right marketing ideas and designing effective ads
- The importance of testing ads
- The importance of using pictures.

Know how to

- Design and use personal surveys
- Find, qualify and categorize prospects
- Design business cards
- Host special events
- Keep in contact with hundreds of people
- Work with real estate investors

Terms:

- Marketing
- Prospect contact list
- 666-Prospecting rule
- Testimonial scrap book
- Sphere of influence

- Marketing niche
- Name badges
- Contact management software
- Magnetic car signs
- Photo-books

Planning for Marketing and Sales

As a real estate agent, you may find yourself thinking, "Decisions, decisions, decisions when it comes to real estate marketing!" because you will have to make many of them. Some of the most common marketing decisions facing new real estate agents are listed in the table below.

Rules for Real Estate Success

Marketing Decisions You Will Face as a Real Estate Agent

- How will my marketing strategy work?
- How will I make the time to promote my business?
- How will I select the right marketing ideas?
- How much money do I expect my marketing strategy to cost?
- How will I meet new people?
- How can I use software to contact hundreds of prospects?
- How will I categorize my marketing prospects?
- How will I design effective business cards?
- How will I use my marketing ideas to find prospects?
- How will I host special events?
- How will I work with investors?

How Will My Marketing Strategy Work?

Marketing Plans

Marketing is generating leads for your business. The purpose of a **marketing plan** is to generate leads that will turn into commissions. You should view marketing as a daily activity similar to exercising and eating healthy. If you go to the gym on a regular basis and eat nutritious foods, you will be healthier. Marketing works the same; if you continually work at it, it will work for you. A successful marketing strategy requires a long-term marketing plan, and accurate records of your marketing activities.

Time to Promote Business

Scheduling Time to Promote Your Business

Each day, schedule time to promote your new business, regardless of how much present business you have, and take advantage of every opportunity you have to do so. Don't make the mistake that many agents make: neglecting marketing activities because they have enough business for the time being. Always plan for a rainy day; all businesses will dry-up unless they are constantly promoted. In this business, you are your own promoter; therefore, always include time to promote your business when planning your day.

Select the Right Marketing Ideas

The following chapters include hundreds of sales and marketing strategies that work. Your objective is to select those marketing ideas that YOU are comfortable with, thus creating a customized marketing plan that will work for you. This marketing plan doesn't mean using one type of marketing only, but rather using the RIGHT combination from a number of marketing tools. A **marketing niche** is a unique marketing plan, a type of marketing that you enjoy, one that is uniquely yours. Before deciding on the marketing strategies that you will use, you must have a plan of action. For example, a good plan will incorporate your introductory newspaper article, followed by direct mail (postcards or letters) by the third business day, cold calls by the end of the week, emails, and lastly, your door-to-door visits, all in a 30-day period. Before you even start your campaign, you will need your presentation packages, letters, research, videos, and a well-designed website. Next, you need to develop a database of prospects, and find a management contact software program to organize your prospects. Once your database of prospects is ready, you can start applying different marketing techniques.

How Much Will My Marketing Strategy Cost?

Marketing Strategies

Plan to spend at least 20% of your time and money on marketing. Again, marketing works only when it's done regularly and consistently. When making your daily plans, set aside time for marketing, and stay faithful in your endeavors. During the first few years of your career, advertising may use as much as 50% of your income. Once you have determined the greatest return for your marketing dollars and you have increased your income, you may want to devote a smaller percentage of your income to marketing. For example, you may use 40% of your income in your first year (in which you only made $20,000), but you may use only 10% of your income two years later (when your income has grown to $180,000 per year). Be sure to keep careful records of which ideas work, which ones you enjoy the most, and how you can improve those ideas. If your marketing ideas work, you will have an inexpensive rate of investment (ROI), on your money, but if you do not market, it will be very expensive. Marketing is an investment; a two dollar investment should yield a twenty-dollar return.

Testing Your Marketing Plan- One Variable at a Time

Before investing large sums of money on your marketing plan, test your material on a small sample. For example, if your area has 500 homes, test one of your marketing strategies on 50 of those homes. Then, try testing another strategy on another 50 homes. Then, compare the results to see which marketing strategy works best for your area. Test what happens when you use business cards, letters, door-to-door sales, door hangers, or cold calling in your farm area, and then analyze your results.

Meeting People

Prospecting

Once you have an action plan, your next step is to create a list of prospects. Real estate rule: *"Real estate is the business of being known for the services that you offer."* The best tool for creating a database of prospects is going out and meeting people, including old and new friends. When you look for prospects, think about this rule: *"Almost every person you meet knows someone who has a housing need."* First, you need to build rapport and then ask: ask in a different way, and ask in a thoughtful way. There are many ways to create leads, but the very best lead generator is your personal effort to meet people. Think of it this way: *"Every stranger is an opportunity for business, but your friends are twice the opportunity and your relatives are endless opportunities."* It's much easier and less expensive to work with old customers than to find new customers. In your daily life, with how many strangers do you actually have direct contact? If all of these people could bring you referrals, how many referrals could you gain daily?

Six-Six-Six Prospecting Rule

The **Six-Six-Six prospecting rule** was designed for new agents to start prospecting for six months, six days a week, making six new contacts per day. The way you let people know you are in business may be through having open houses, emailing old friends, visiting co-workers, mailing school friends, or simply meeting new people. You can try Internet blogging.

When meeting people for the first time, don't impose your services and products; instead, be a professional and think about your image. An aggressive approach is often perceived as unprofessional, and depicts images of greed, selfishness, or desperation. Whenever possible, the first meeting should merely establish trust and confidence.

Starting a Prospect Contact List

Creating a **prospect contact list** will help you find and keep track of prospects. Once you have a list of prospects, your next step is to organize your list. A good starting point is to make a list of 100 people you know. This contact list should be the beginning of your sphere of influence. Divide the list into two or three groups, and then determine which groups you will email, snail mail, fax, or contact by phone. Also, decide the frequency with which you will contact each group. Adding new contacts, keeping your contact list updated, and sending out mail regularly is crucial. Each year, your sphere of influence should grow by at least 100 new contacts. Conduct research on various types of data and e-mail software that you can use to do mass mail-outs or broadcasting, and try mailing or e-mailing monthly or quarterly newsletters. Don't forget this common rule in sales: *"If you forget your customers, they will surely forget you."* Don't let people around you forget what services you provide. You can do this by using Christmas cards, birthday cards, and/ or newsletters. If your friends, or **sphere of influence** (people who know the services you offer), are at a party, wouldn't you want your name to come up whenever the subject of housing is discussed? The rule is, *"It's not what you know or even who you know, but who knows what you do."* You may know thousands of people, but how many know that you sell real estate and are aware of the services you offer? Your potential sphere of influence list can be based on the following:

- Relatives and all of their contacts
- Community and social groups
- Past clients, customers, and all of their contacts
- Neighbors, friends, and co-workers
- Classmates and former teachers
- Business contacts, retail stores, and professional people
- Current customers who can refer new potential customers to you
- Neighborhoods
- Church groups

A secondary group of sources may include

- Nosy neighbors
- Builders
- Car sign magnets
- Sponsoring sports teams
- High school yearbook ads
- Supermarket postings and shopping carts
- Local papers
- Radio ads
- Just sold/just listed post cards and letters
- Wearing apparel with your name and company name

Make a separate list of your relatives. They may not have a housing need, but they know people who do. Ask relatives for assistance in supplying a list of their friends who may need a house, a loan, or your services. You can even start an email chain; design a flyer for your relatives to send to their friends and relatives or co-workers and their friends. Three tips when working with relatives are below:

- Ask your relatives for advice. Relatives are usually more willing to give advice than they are to use your services.
- Always be thankful for the advice and support that you get.
- Take every opportunity to mail "Thank-You" notes.

Management Contact Software

Contact Software

Once you have your list of prospects, the next step is to find software that meets your marketing needs. As you meet people, you will need a database that categorizes the people you know. You can use old-fashioned index cards, notebooks, or what most people use today, software. You can send post cards, letters, or emails to this list of people. As you meet new people, your list will grow, and as your list grows, you will need to develop sub-categories. The more sub-categories you have, the more valuable your list becomes. For example, the category of sphere of influence groups will eventually include "buyers." Using buyers' sub-categories, you can decide to whom to send mail, newsletters, emails, thank you letters, holiday cards, and other forms of communications. Many of the popular contact management software packages, such as Microsoft Outlook, Top Producer, Gold Mine, and Act, can sort your list by any sub-category you choose. If you choose to email birthday cards to buyers in a particular week in a particular area, the software will help you sort those buyers. Here are the types of sub-categories you can include in your contact lists:

Categorizing Prospects

Category Groups

- Relatives
- Buyers
- Sellers
- Previous clients
- Credit scores over 620/credit
- Scores under 620
- Email addresses
- Phone numbers
- Friends
- Referrals

- First-time buyers
- FSBO
- Commercial
- One-four family
- Financial information
- Date of closing
- Product rate, and term
- Luxury homebuyers
- Commercial buyers
- Group 1 – wants to buy soon (must have)
- Group 2 – wants to buy or will buy later (need)
- Group 3 – would like to buy someday (wants)
- Kids' names, ages, and birthdays
- Anniversary dates
- Hobbies
- Senior citizens military
- International clients
- New home
- Co-workers
- Single parents
- Condo/town houses
- Investment buyers
- Farm and Ranch sellers/buyers

Marketing software is fairly inexpensive; ask your local computer store or someone who understands software for assistance in this area. Contacting the person you know who can best advise you about the different software programs available is advisable.

How often you send emails depends on your relationship with your contacts and the type of information being sent. Contacting past customers and future prospects, four times per year is usually plenty enough to maintain a viable business relationship; do not overdo it. Next, you should plan distribution timetables for special occasions. Decide if you will send correspondence for birthdays, special events, holidays, or at other times.

Designing Effective Business Cards

Designing Effective Ads

Ads should capture the readers' attention. When designing the headline, write about any important property features. You might even have them in a bold or larger font. Readers want to know how they will benefit from your ads. State the features followed by the buyer's benefits. Are there any top-ranked schools nearby, world-class eateries, or shopping centers? What unique features does the property have, and how will the reader benefit from that feature? Pictures also portray benefits; in fact, pictures often capture some reader's attention sooner than words alone do. Ads have to be clear and easy to read. Lastly, keep statements as short as possible; do not use abbreviations, and mention specific facts. For example:

- Make a list of all of the features of the property.
- Next, reorganize your list by the greatest benefit to the reader.
- The one feature with the greatest benefit should be the headline.
- Headlines should be matched with corresponding graphics or pictures.

Designing Business Cards

Well-designed business cards are essential since they are the most inexpensive form of advertisement. Below are some general guidelines for designing business cards:

- The front of the cards should be simple, easy to read, consistent with the office theme, and color.
- Try the billboard effect—readers need to be able to read the entire card at a glance.
- Avoid having more than one profession listed on a business card.
- Avoid dark backgrounds; while they may be exciting, they can distract readers - light, warm colors work well.
- Include designations, as these can attest to the fact that you are a professional.
- In real estate, designations are fairly easy to acquire; a few following your name gives some credence.
- *Never* leave home without your business cards. An agent without business cards is like a carpenter without tools or a banker without money.
- As you design your business cards, ask your broker for suggestions on the types of photographs that will work best for you. Your photographer will need to know what you are trying to accomplish; he or she may even have ideas of his or her own. For photos, a dark blue suit with a white shirt works best for both men and women. (See Chapter 5 for dressing professionally).

Using Pictures

Pictures work; they give business cards a personal touch, but remember to keep it professional. Well-prepared photos can extend the shelf life of your card. By the end of the day, consumers decide which cards to keep and which ones to toss. Generally, real estate shoppers discard most cards but retain the cards that appeal to them the most. Consumers must be able to identify your card at a glance.

There are two types of business card readers: visual readers and word readers. For this reason, instructions on how to put an item together usually has both step-by-step visual instructions on what the products should look like and word instructions for putting the item together. Many people read the pictures first and try to put the item together; whereas, non-visual learners follow the word instructions. Business cards work the same way that instructions work. Some people read the picture first while others read the wording. Why do people read pictures first? They find pictures much easier to read. These readers are more visual; they will infer what they want from the picture and then decide whether to finish reading the rest. Remember the analogy of 'judging a book by its cover.'

For this reason, getting a professional photographer to take your photos is your best option. Let the photographer know what image you're trying to convey. Real estate shoppers are looking for an honest, friendly, caring professional. How can you convey these attributes in a photograph? Tips for taking pictures are as follows:

- *Visit your hair stylist a few days before taking pictures.*
- *Wear bright colors; for example, a navy blue coat over a white shirt. Bright colors will make your picture stand out and give a healthier complexion. An all-white shirt will give you a pasty pale look.*
- *Try to get comfortable. This will convey a warm friendly look.*

On the way home, look at billboards. How many capture your attention with a picture? After they get your attention with the picture, they follow with a few words to hold your attention. Advertisers know that the old cliché is true: *"A good picture is worth a thousand words."*

If you plan to use photos on your business card, make sure they are recent. Using business cards with a twenty-year old photo may appear deceptive to the public. After finally meeting, who are you fooling? Yourself! If you use a 20-year old photo, all you are going to get is a good laugh with some possible trust issues. Keep your photos clean and professional. When taking photos, keep your business attire professional looking as well. Cheap-looking glamour photos are not advisable. Using sexy-looking pictures may be attention grabbers for certain audiences, but not for potential real estate consumers and you may be causing yourself a bigger problem.

The back of the business cards can be used to target a particular type of sales. Give your prospects something they want. If you decide to farm for For-Sale-by-Owners, the back of your cards should include a statement for For-Sale-by-Owners. For example, "For a free copy of *How to Sell Your Property.*" or "*How to Save Thousands by Selling your Own Property, call 1-888-000-0000 toll-free.*" or "*For more information on all our free articles, go to: www.freeabc Realtyinformation.com.*" The point is to have your prospects call you or visit your website.

Another item you may consider putting on the back of your business card is your mission statement, which is your promise on the quality of services you offer. You can also print the 12 items required to originate loans. Real estate agents may want to add a calendar or a professional statement to the back of their business card. As discussed in Chapter 5, the back of the card can be a good spot for your Unique Selling Proposition. This USP statement is the promise you are making to the reader.

Marketing Ideas for Finding Prospects

Making Business and Mailing Labels

You can also use business mailing labels following the same image and theme as your business cards, but in a smaller version. Business labels are self-sticking for letters, cards, packages, water bottles, or for mailing lists. Your labels can also be used for books, CDs, items in your office, or for information that you are giving to your clients and customers. You can use photographs from your own photo collection or even your clients' new home, pets, or family. A distributing label is generally more appropriate to share than a business card at seminars, educational conferences, or meetings.

An example of a simple but effective use of labels is on water bottles; original labels can be easily replaced with your own label. You can include four items: your picture, a picture of the house, the company logo, and your information on a 2X4 label. You don't have to worry about anybody getting sick; the ingredients are simple. If someone spills, it is easy to clean up. You can make labels for open house water bottles or to give away at your office. For your closings, you can add labels to wine bottles. Avery produces several label sizes. The software, available from Avery, Microsoft Office Publisher, or many other publishing software and websites, such as VistaPrint.com or Avery.com, can help you create labels from thousands of designs which can include photos or logos.

Placing an Announcement in a Local Paper

If you are new or transferring to a new office, place an announcement in your local paper. Plan your marketing campaign a few days after the announcement is to be released. Start your campaign by introducing yourself and the needs of your community; later, you can concentrate on your sales pitch. In your letter, refer to the announcement so the receiver can double-check the new celebrity. Check for announcement prices, select a farm area, and have your letters or postcards ready. If your farm is attracting younger clientele, consider social marketing instead of old-fashioned newspaper ads.

Advertising Discounts

Discount coupons are a good way to start a listing campaign; however, you should not make it a permanent part of your business. Consider this rule, *"Pricing will bring you business; service will keep your business."*

Designing Name Badges

Your **name badge** is important. There are three simple pieces of information you must include on your badge: your first and last name, company information, and your profession. Because of the limited space, don't try to include all of your designations. If space permits, include your most important designations, but only if you have the extra space. Keep your name badge in line with the theme of the office. If the office uses red lettering on a white background, do the same. Most offices allow agents to choose their own name badge. Most agents select gold or silver badges with black lettering. By using bold lettering with a standard font, you ensure that your name badge is easy for your prospects to read. The proper business etiquette is to wear your name badge on your right side. You can wear your name badge just about anywhere—meetings, sports events, and social activities. Use your discretion when choosing to wear your name badge outside of the office. For example, wearing your name badge at a place of worship is inappropriate.

Using Magnetic Car Signs

Many agents like using **magnetic car signs** to attract business. You can take them off during off hours or use them on different cars. Soon, all your neighbors will know you as the neighborhood professional.

Before choosing to use a magnetic car sign, think about the overall impression that you are making. Will the sign bring in business, or will it make your prospects think you are so desperate for a sale that you are willing to drive around with your face on your vehicle?

Using car signs is debatable. If you choose to use magnetic car signs, be sure that the information is up-to-date and the picture is professional and current. When using magnetic car signs, make sure that your vehicle is always clean and presentable. Nothing is funnier than parking next to a dirty old car with a twenty-year-old glamour picture of a smiling agent who no longer looks anything like the picture he/she is using to advertise.

Providing Post-Sale Service

While providing quality pre-sale service is important, the services that you provide AFTER closing are what will have a far more lasting impact and set you apart from the rest. Your **post-sale services** are what will help you build long-term relationships. Many agents don't take this part seriously. That is one of the reasons that an estimated 80% of agents make only 20% of the income. Most agents get their money and run to the next deal, if you have such a "get-the-money-and-run" attitude, your customers will notice it quickly. Nobody likes that approach. It is not difficult to email or mail four-six letters per year to past clients. You can even take small and inexpensive housewarming gifts to the new homeowners after closing. Before giving any gifts, be sure to familiarize yourself with Section 8 of RESPA and state law on giving and receiving gifts. Gifts that you can give right after closing include the following:

- Information packages with phone numbers of local police, fire departments, city and town offices, trash pickup services, utility sources, moving companies, restaurants, county tax agencies, cleaning services, lawn care, and schools
- A list of home energy saving tips
- Calendars filled with pictures of buyers' new home, kids, and pets. There is an abundance of software that can do this; you just need an inexpensive digital camera and some patience.
- Order take-out food for buyers when they are moving into their home. They will greatly appreciate this gesture. Ask when they will be moving, who will be helping, and show up with some pizza.
- Hire a one-time maid service to clean up. No one likes cleaning up someone else's mess.
- Order flowers, plants, or wine with an accompanying thank-you card to add a personal touch. Be sure to choose the appropriate type of flowers, and stay away from red roses to avoid conveying the wrong message.
- Show up personally with a simple thank-you card. It doesn't take much money to show someone that you care. It's the time you're willing to give after the sale that counts.

Keeping in Touch

Keep in constant touch with your sphere of influence, and make it a part of your work ethic. Keep your contact files updated; people may change their phone numbers, place of employment, or address. You should look for every opportunity to contact your past customers. You can also use mail-outs or emails for anniversaries, birthday cards, or letters. You can use several dates for an anniversary: the date they bought their property, a wedding anniversary, or a special holiday. People sometimes forget about special days. If cards are mailed early enough, they can serve as a reminder for husbands to pick-up flowers on the way home or to make dinner arrangements. You can always hire a private marketing company to do automatic follow-ups with your customers or clients, or you can learn to do your own automatic follow-ups.

Start a **scrapbook** of ads, cards, and letters that you like, or ask your friends to look for real estate postcards or letters, which you may add to your scrapbook; this way, you will always have fresh ideas to choose from when you need them. Another type of **scrapbook** is **testimonial**. These are the letters that your clients write wonderful things about you. There are several real estate compilations of pre-designed letters. Ask bookstores or your broker for help with identifying good marketing books. The Internet can also provide a good source of marketing and sales training material. Try Half Price Book Stores for used material. Use letters or post cards as often as you can. Be sure that you spell check your work before distributing your information. Have a friend or co-worker proofread your letters. Examples of letters/documents may include the following:

- Photo-books
- Surveys
- Anniversary cards
- Current real estate or mortgage news
- Community news
- Your introduction into business
- Letters to your sphere of influence
- Letters to other real estate agents or loan officers
- Post cards or letters about how to showcase your property (Staging)
- How to prepare your property for best showing
- Letters to For Sale by Owners on how to sell their homes
- Thinking of you letters
- Birthday cards
- Just Listed, Just Sold, and Open House door hangers, post cards, or letters
- Thank you letters for after closing and for referrals
- Letters to buyers or borrowers
- Holiday letters and cards
- Letters to relatives
- Letters to sellers
- Follow-up letters
- Referral letters
- Moving tips

- Gardening tips
- Children's coloring contests
- Halloween costume contests
- The winner of yard of the month
- Information tips, such preparing a garage sale or spring cleaning
- Important information or newsletters
- A list of all your listings
- Questionnaires and other miscellaneous documents

Using Photo-books

A photo-book is the latest marketing tool for agents. A **photographic book,** or **coffee table book,** is a collection of photographs made into a professional quality book. The images are printed on heavy stock paper with 30–100 pages per book. There are several companies such as Shutterfly™, Apple™, Kodak gallery, Picaboo, Mypubisher, Lulu.com, and many others that can create these books at a reasonable starting cost: $18-$30 per book; for more internet options, browse photo books. The agent can take pictures of his/her clients, pets, properties, or closing, and have it made into a high quality custom coffee table book for his/her clients' entertainment. Make sure to include yourself in front of the home with your sold sign and other information. Agents can also make their buyer/seller presentation packages into photo-books. A reasonable time for delivery is about two weeks.

Mailing Postcards/e-cards

Be sure to include your name, phone number, address, slogan, and maybe a professional photograph of yourself on all of your marketing postcards or letters. The information on postcards or e-cards, however, is different from letters. Postcards should be simple, like a billboard. The recipient should be able to read the post cards or e-cards in seconds, whereas letters are designed to capture the reader's attention for further reading. Postcards are designed with pictures and a few words to leave a message in the readers' mind. Most homeowners will sort mail to eliminate junk mail prior to opening the envelopes, yet postcards, even if they are junk mail, will capture the recipients' attention with its simple words and colorful pictures. Postcards are also less expensive than mailing letters. Letters can be discarded without the readers' opening the letter. One way to prevent your letter from being discarded without being opened is to hand write and/or place a red sticker with the text, "Free inside" on front of the envelope. Everyone likes to get free gifts. The free item will depend on the type of letter. The free item may be entering a children's coloring contest at your office, a CMA, company pen, or just free information for FSBOs.

Working with Old Files

On average, most people move every seven years. If you are new to real estate, ask your broker if there are any files left behind by agents who no longer work for the company. Ask for permission to go into the old files to look for past clients who no longer have an office contact person. To remain ethical with other agents in the office, show your list of past clients to your broker for permission to contact each past client. When you have your list of approved contacts, first mail an introductory letter, then personally call each one and arrange a meeting if the client needs/wishes to speak with you in-person. At this point, your goal is to establish contact, not to make a sale. Ask for permission to email or to snail mail them with important news. Ask them if they are satisfied with their home and use the information to update old files.

Surveys

One way of keeping in touch after the closing is to offer a survey or questionnaire based on the services that you provide. Surveys can be designed with several goals in mind: you can ask about satisfaction with your services, the overall transaction, the financing, or details on how you can improve your business environment. Below is an example of a survey focusing on overall improvements:

ABC Real Estate Center
1313 Uvalde Houston TX 77723
Office 713-400-4000 Fax 713-400-4001

We wish to congratulate your family on the purchase of your new home.

At ABC Real Estate Center, we take great pride in providing our customers with the very best service possible. To achieve this end, one of our goals is to continuously seek to improve the services we offer. Your comments are valuable to us and will be greatly appreciated. Please take a few minutes to share your views on the recent service you received from our company.

Customer Satisfaction Survey

How would you rate the performance of the real estate agent and services provided based on the following categories/questions?

	Extremely Satisfied	Satisfied	Dissatisfied	No Opinion
Was your agent ethical and professional?				
Knowledgeable and competent?				
Was your agent courteous?				
Were you made to feel that your business was appreciated?				
Was your agent prepared?				
How likely are you to refer a friend/family member to ABC Real Estate Center?				
Was your agent enthusiastic about helping you?				
How satisfied are you with the purchase of your home?				
How satisfied are you with the overall performance?				

What can we do to improve our customer service?

May we share this information with your real estate agent? Yes __ No __
Would you like to speak to a company representative? Yes __ No __
Name_____ Your Phone _____

Surveys and gifts should never take the place of a Thank-You Letter. Instead, view surveys and gifts as an additional tool that you can use to leave a positive impression with your customers. People are often flattered when their opinions are used for improvement. The survey also demonstrates that you are a serious professional.

Here are some guidelines to follow when creating your surveys:

- You can use the list of items on your survey to develop either personal or sales skills. There are many ways to draft surveys. For example, divide your survey into two parts: (a) survey questions and (b) referrals.
- Surveys should be mailed promptly while the transaction is still fresh in the sellers' or buyers' mind.
- Emphasize the importance of referrals in your survey.
- Perfect your ideas.

There are hundreds of reasons why you should contact past clients. Read through them to see which ones would work best for you. These are only ideas; it's up to you to decide how to lay out your career, pick what works, and perfect whatever ideas you decide to use. Again, be sure you enjoy whatever ideas you decide to use.

- Start a testimonial scrapbook. Have your happy customers write testimonial letters about your services, and ask them for permission to use these testimonials.
- Bake pies or cookies. If you like baking, holiday baking always has special meaning for many people. Consider ordering pie boxes and pans from a restaurant supply store and personally baking the pies. Twenty pies may cost you approximately $80 (20 x $4 = $80). Additionally, print colorful holiday labels so that you can attach them to the boxes. When designing the labels, be sure to include

pictures and phone numbers. In the example below, you can attach a picture of yourself baking and at the same time you're letting customers know how important they are to you. Maybe you can have a baking party with other agents or family members who are good at this. This works best if you deliver the baked goods in person and make it a yearly event. If you don't like baking, you can always order pies and change the information below to your needs. The point here is to try to include your special skills into real estate marketing.

Rules for Real Estate Success

Example of a label for a pumpkin pie:

For Mr. & Mrs. Smith

I trust that you and your family are enjoying this wonderful holiday season in your newly purchased home.

I baked during the night to bring you the best pumpkin pie in the world, made with caring, loving hands. I hope you enjoy it as much as I enjoyed baking it for you.

Maggie J. Michaels
xxx-xx-xxxx
Your devoted Realtor®

Picture
of your baking

- Some brokers even have barbeques for clients and customers. Yearly barbeques are a good reason to call your past clients to show your appreciation, as well as to meet them in person once again.
- Toward the end of each year, start calling your past clients to see if they need copies of their closing cost statement or HUD-1 statement for tax purposes. You can even e-mail/mail tip sheets regarding when and how to protest their property taxes. The information on how to protest property taxes should be personal (in the first person). People don't care about how to protest property taxes in general; they want to know how to protest their property taxes. Remember that it's the "ME" factor that people are more concerned with in all of your correspondence. Make the tax information as personal as possible.
- There are ten federal holidays, which gives you ten additional reasons to communicate with your clients. Why not mail recipe cards, such as how to cook a turkey or baking tips for the holiday? The recipe cards can have pictures of you cooking, baking, or even gardening. The recipes can be from the Internet or even from grandma. This material should be gathered as soon as possible and ready to mail-out in time for the holiday season. Mark your dates

on your calendar; you can fine-tune your material as the date gets closer. Have the material printed months ahead of time.

- In the early spring, when people are thinking about gardening, try mailing a newsletter containing gardening tips. These tips can be for planting trees, plants, or even lawn care.
- Be sure to include a picture of yourself doing whatever your article is about. If you're going to be a star, you need to show yourself as a one.
- As you plan your marketing, plan your photo shoots as well. Consider the types of pictures you will use of yourself while baking, gardening, or other activates for all of your business cards and letters. Make a list of all the types of marketing you will use, and have a few photographs for each. As you adjust your marketing each year, include new ones, making sure they are fresh and updated.

Introductory Letter from an agent who just joined a new company

ABC Real Estate Center

Julia M. González, *Real Estate Agent*
1313 Uvalde Houston TX 77723

Office 713-400-4000 Fax 713-400-4001 (Date)

Photo

[Address Block]
<Greeting>

I recently began working for [Agency name]. I am truly excited about the recent training that I received, as well as the tools and facilities available to assist me in effectively serving my clients.

An integral part of my success in the real estate industry depends on my referral base, so I would appreciate it if you could consider referring to me anyone who may be interested in buying or selling property. Please contact me via telephone [at #] or email [email address], if I can be of assistance to you or any of your friends.

Our company also has a website [web address] which you may visit to obtain information on the services we offer. In addition, please bear in mind that we are members of the National Association of Realtors® and have access to the Multiple Listing Service (MLS), which provides information on properties that are currently on the market.

Indeed we are committed to providing excellent professional service to all our customers, and I look forward to serving you or anyone who you may refer in the near future.

Thank you

Sincerely,

[Agent's Name]
[Agent's Title]

Thank you letter to a client who referred a friend

(Date)
< Address Block>
< Greeting>

Photo

I want to thank you for referring [Mr. /MS or Company] to me for real estate services. Referrals are a significant part of the ongoing success of my business, and I am truly grateful for your taking the time to refer [Mr. /MS or Company].

Please be assured that I will endeavor to serve [Mr. /MS or Company] to the best of my ability in performing my duties and responsibilities as a professional Realtor.

Please do not hesitate to contact me if I can be of assistance in the future.

Sincerely,
[Agent's Name]
[Agent's Title]

Real Estate Marketing

Announcing new neighbors in the community

(Date)

<Address Block>

Photo

Hello, I'm [Name] with [Company]. I just wanted to let you know that you have new neighbors. [Name of Buyers] will be moving into the house located at [Property address] at the end of this month. They are a great family, and we would like you to feel free to pay them a visit and welcome them when they move in. You may mention my name to [Name of new neighbors] and refer to the letter if you so choose.

Many things are happening in the world of real estate, and if you or any of your friends have real estate needs or would like a free evaluation of what your/their home is worth, please do not hesitate to call me at [Telephone]. I am available for any questions/ assistance/ advice.

Have a great day

Sincerely,

[Agent's Name]
[Agent's Title]

Compliments on the condition of your home

(Date)
Picture of you
<Address Block>
< Greeting>

I trust that you are enjoying the luxuries of your newly purchased home.

First, I wish to thank you again for choosing me to represent you as your realtor when you purchased your home located on [address]. I must say that you have done a wonderful job of continuing to maintain the property, and I wish you many years of trouble-free enjoyment.

Please feel free to contact me at [telephone] or to send an email to me if you or any of your friends need my assistance in the future.

Again, thank you

Sincerely,

[Agent's Name]
[Agent's Title]

For Sale by Owner- Thank you letter

(Date)
[Address Block] Picture of you

<Greeting>

It was truly a pleasure speaking with you on the phone [or meeting with you at the office or at your home]. I want to reassure you that I am committed to helping you sell your home.

At [Agency name], our goal is to ensure that our customers receive excellent quality service in keeping with our company's mission [put in company motto or mission statement]. Our years of long dedicated service to our customers have taught us how valuable each customer is to the success of our company, so we thank you for using our agency to sell your home. Additionally, please note that I will be contacting you soon regarding the progress of the sale of your home, especially as it relates to potential buyers

If you have any marketing or real estate questions, you can reach me at [telephone # and or email].

Sincerely,

[Agent's Name]
[Agent's Title]

Hosting Special Events

Special Events

Try hosting special events at the office to market your business. You can also add video announcements to your website or link several videos to YouTube™ or any of the social networks. Items you can host are as follows:

- Free educational seminars on how to buy real estate for first-time homeowners
- Free educational seminars on forbearance
- Seminars on foreclosures
- Seminars on Loan Modification Agreements
- Information on how to get a real estate license
- Office seminar on "How to Sell Your Home Without Hiring a Real Estate Agent and Save, Save, Save"
- Understanding mortgage lending and how to pick the right loan or identify "junk fees"
- Free credit score improvement seminars or understanding how to improve credit scores
- Home improvements or do-it-yourself seminars
- Working with local supply companies on lawn care and landscaping during the different seasons
- How to find grant money for home ownership or rules relating to housing grant money and how grant money works
- Home safety tips, such as "Does Your House have Mold? or How to Protect Your Home"
- Family and child protection seminars hosted by local law enforcement
- How to use software classes
- How to take the perfect picture with digital cameras
- How to prepare your home for the real estate market
- How to showcase your property, (staging)
- Low cost tips to get the best price for your home
- How to save for retirement and other financial services
- Tips to Reduce Property Taxes
- What sellers should expect from their agent

The list of free seminars is endless, and there are usually local experts who are willing to donate their knowledge and time to worthwhile ventures. Start planning your hosting events as early as possible during the off-season to make them work. Try having seminars at the office; the prospects will know the location and feel more comfortable knowing they have been there before. Larger seminars can be held at local community

Real Estate Marketing

colleges. Most community colleges will be interested if it's a community event. Colleges are also marketing to gain student enrollment.

Plan your seminar with the information your audience is seeking. All too often, agents use seminars for a chance to grandstand, to talk about how great they are, or to communicate what services they offer. This is known as the typical "bait-and-switch." If the seminar is about grant money, then fully present the program, not about what a great real estate agent you are. If the audience is first-time homebuyers, then 100% of the subject matter should be information the buyers can use. If you conduct your seminar as if you are fully concerned about the buyers' interests, then the rest will take care of itself. You can always end the seminar with remarks like, *"If you would like more information about grant money, my business cards are located in front of your package."* or similar words. Don't forget about the rule of benefit. If the audience believes the benefit is greater for the agent, more than likely, trust will be missing, and referrals are a result of trust.

Plan to video your educational seminars and get permission to use them later. With Microsoft™ Movie Maker or other video software, you can start your library of educational videos for your website. Your videos can be posted on YouTube™ and linked to your website.

If you plan to use outside vendors, make sure to include a disclaimer for the originality as well as accuracy of their information.

Working with Private Real Estate Investors

Private Investors

There is usually some type of real estate investment seminar or a "get rich quick" scheme and investment clubs in most cities. You can attend these seminars to obtain additional information and establish new contacts.

These investors are always looking for homebuyers and someone to sell their real estate. One important point about investment properties is that lenders often require the property title to be seasoned from six months to one year. A seasoned title means that the investor has held the property in his/her name for a long term, which is six months or more. Property held less than six months will require additional documentation from the appraiser and sellers. Wholesale lenders are normally concerned about illegal flips. This refers to the purchase of property at a low price and its sale at a substantially higher price. However, there are lenders who will finance unseasoned property, as long as the appraisal holds up in today's market.

Rules for Real Estate Success

*Note

Agents should beware of investors or sellers who try to sell the property at a value greater than 100% CLTV, (combine-loan-to-value). For example, investor John wants $120,000 for his property and the property appraises at $115,000. Investor John writes up the contract, and the buyers are willing to pay 80% of the appraised price ($92,000) while John owner finances the difference of $28,000. The common rule is that lenders will not accept a loan over 100% CLTV or LTV (loan-to-value). If sellers and buyers pre-agree to additional terms without the lender's knowledge, such an agreement is considered fraudulent by most lenders. In the world of finance, however, there will always be a lender who is willing to finance such a transaction. To avoid problems, disclose all current or potential transactions to the lender.

Real Estate Marketing

Rules for Real Estate Success

1. Start a contact list of people who you know. Include the following categories:
   - Names
   - Cell phone
   - Work phone
   - Address
   - Relation to you
   - Personal remarks

2. Research management contact software that has the required options that you will be comfortable using. Examples are as follows:
   - Microsoft Outlook
   - Top Producer
   - Gold Mine
   - Act
   - Others

3. Use the Internet and book stores to research information on designing letters. You will need to develop a database of several types of letters. Below are categories:
   - Introduction letter
   - Thank-you for the referral letter
   - Announcement of a new neighbor letter
   - Letters to sellers or buyers
   - For Sale by Owner letters
   - Expired listing letters

4. Start a collection of real estate business cards and a scrapbook of advertisements.

5. Make a list of the types of seminars you are willing to give at your office, or at a Community college, or a church.

6. Design a survey for door-to-door sales.

7. Make an introductory announcement for a local newspaper.

8. Check the Internet for hosting sites for on-line articles presentations.

9. Find and visit where foreclosures are being held to make contact with real estate investors.

10. From your list of family and friends, make it a practice to meet at least five people every day or thirty people in thirty days.

11. Find a professional photographer who has experience with real estate agents.

12. Check for cost and design of name badges.

1. The purpose of marketing is
   A. To generate the type of leads that will not waste time or money.
   B. To promote business.
   C. To build a professional image.
   D. All of the above.

2. Marketing works best when
   A. Researching the target area.
   B. Organizing ideas.
   C. It is done regularly and consistently.
   D. Testing small samples before spending large sums of money.
   E. All of the above.

3. The best tool to generate business is
   A. To sit behind a desk and wait for the phone to ring.
   B. To borrow money to advertise heavily.
   C. To personally meet people.
   D. To do nothing since prospects will come to your market.

4. When meeting prospects for the first time, it is best to
   A. Try to sell the property before someone else does.
   B. Give business cards, and ask prospects to call you when they are ready to buy.
   C. Ask for their phone number.
   D. Establish trust, rapport, and confidence.

5. A good way for new agents to get started is
   A. To build a contact list of all the people they know.
   B. To sit behind a desk and wait for the phone to ring.
   C. To use management contact software to categorize prospects.
   D. Both A and C.

6. The best way to create a contact list is
   A. Use the phone book.
   B. Use management contact software to categorize prospects.
   C. Save business cards.
   D. Avoid making a contact list, since it is time consuming and not worth the trouble.

7. The best way to capture the readers' attention is
   A. Having long detailed letters.
   B. Using as many abbreviations as possible.
   C. Using effective headlines.
   D. Focusing on the body of the ad.

Rules for Real Estate Success

8. Business cards
   A. Should include as many professions as possible.
   B. Are not an effective form of advertisement.
   C. Are the most expensive form of advertisement.
   D. Are the most inexpensive form of advertisement.

9. Using pictures on business cards is
   A. Effective because it gives the card a personal touch.
   B. Ineffective because photos take-up too much valuable space.
   C. Unprofessional.
   D. Necessary, so agents should use their best photo, regardless of the age of the photo.

10. What types of readers are there?
    A. Word readers
    B. Picture readers
    C. Clairvoyant readers
    D. Both A and B

11. Providing post-services is
    A. Just as important as pre-services.
    B. Not important, since buyers are unlikely to buy another house anytime soon.
    C. Too much for the unlikely return of investments.
    D. Illegal under RESPA Section 8.

12. Placing an announcement in a local paper is
    A. Useful for announcing your recent transfer to a new office.
    B. A good way to start a farming system in a particular area.
    C. A way to give yourself accreditation.
    D. All of the above

CHAPTER 7
Prospecting for Sellers, Part I

Objectives:

Understand the Importance of

- The advantages of working with sellers
- How to start a listing plan
- The importance of building an inventory of listings and buyers
- The CPS rule
- How to farm open houses
- How to develop a listing campaign
- How short sales and REOs work

- How to select and conduct open houses
- The importance of farming
- How to find and work with expired listings
- What buyers expect
- How to prospect for sellers
- How to contact absentees
- The importance of signage

Terms:

- Absentee property owner
- CAP
- Comparative market analysis
- Broker open house
- Expired listings
- Listing pipeline
- Open house signage
- Prospects
- Sign riders
- GEM
- Selling rules

- Area Comfort zone
- Cold calling
- CPS selling rule
- Exclusive listing agreement
- Geographic farming
- Open house
- Perpetual sales
- Real estate prospecting
- REO
- Short sale

Real Estate Prospecting

Real estate prospecting is searching for potentially new customers, clients, or purchasers for the possibility of a desirable real estate transaction outcome. A **prospect** is a possible or future client/customer that will yield a favorable result. Real estate sales work the same way as other types of sales do, as far as prospecting is concerned. Without prospects, you can't make a sale. The greater the number of the right types of prospects, the greater the number of sales you can make. This chapter and Chapter 8, teaches the process of finding prospects to working and closing the transaction. Think of prospecting for sellers as a six-part process:

Prospecting for Sellers – Part One

1. Understanding the importance of prospecting for sellers
2. How to find prospective sellers

Prospecting for Sellers – Part Two

1. For sale by owners (Ch.8)
2. How to build rapport and win over sellers (Ch. 8)
3. Overcoming sellers' objections (Ch. 8)
4. Serving your listings (Ch. 8)

Part One - Understanding the Importance of Prospecting

Specializing

As mentioned in Chapter 1, in this industry, you will have many choices: you can work with buyers, sellers, or specialize as a seller's agent, a buyer's agent, or be a generalist, working with everyone. However, to attain success, you should consider focusing on being a specialist, such as an agent who represents sellers only. To represent the seller or serve as a listing agent, you would work with only sellers/listings unless your sellers become buyers or have a need to take a short break.

Sometimes, working with buyers is advantageous because it allows you to stay in tune with what's new in the industry. However, you may want to spend as much as 90% or more of your time on listings and 10% or less of your time working with buyers. If a caller wants to look at your listings, show him/her, if you have the time. Once the caller decides to look at homes other than those featured by you, refer or sell the caller to someone else, and stay focused on gaining more listings. As a listing specialist, your sole job is to find listings and to service those sellers. Agents usually think they can earn a few easy dollars and will try to sell their own listing or show their new prospects other listings. If you show homes other than those on your listings, your focus will be withdrawn from finding other listings. Soon your listings that generate leads will dry up, and you will have to start all over, which will be difficult.

Working with Sellers Offers Fifteen Advantages

1. Once you have an inventory of homes, buyers will come looking for you, not you looking for buyers.
2. You can sell your inventory to buyers.
3. Sellers will usually become buyers.
4. Sellers require less preparation time.
5. Listings are perpetual.
6. Listings provide more opportunity for growth.
7. As a listing agent, you will have better control of your personal life.
8. There are more qualified sellers than there are qualified buyers.
9. Working with listings is a numbers game. You can work with ten times more sellers than buyers.
10. Sellers are committed to paying a commission, regardless of who sells the property.
11. Listings generate steady income.
12. Sellers are easier to find.
13. It is less expensive to work with sellers.
14. The fastest way to create a professional image is to work with sellers.
15. Life is simpler when focusing on one goal—finding sellers.

Building an Inventory of Buyers and Sellers

Inventory is very important; without it, you're out of business. Building an inventory of listings is like having a savings account. Once you learn how to price and market your inventory, you can count on it to close. In the movie "Field of Dreams," Kevin Costner famously says, *"If you build it, they will come."* There are no better words to describe building a real estate career. It starts with building an inventory of listings (properties for sale). Building your inventory requires a substantial amount of work, but once you have it, buyers will come looking for you.

Selling Buyer Inventory

Once you have buyers looking for housing, you need to decide how to best use your leads. You can keep and work your buyers or sell your new inventory of referrals to other agents. Sharing referrals is determined by office policy, but remember the golden rule, *"He who holds the gold makes the rules."* Referral lists can also be priced according to categories. If you're an exclusive seller agent after you determine that a particular buyer does not want any of your inventory, refer him/her to other agents in your office or an agent who works exclusively with buyers. Chapter 10 details how to categorize and sell buyer inventory.

Sellers Who Become Buyers

All too often after you have sold your listings, your sellers will become buyers and will want to use your services. They will usually refer other buyers; however, if they require housing in another location, make them part of your inventory. If they are searching for real estate in your area, take the required time to fully service their needs, and after you have met their requirements, get back to your focus as soon as possible. Remember, the better you service your clients, the more they will refer prospects to you.

Preparation Time for Buyers and Sellers

Another matter about deciding whether to work with either buyers or sellers is the preparation time that is involved for each. Because working with buyers initially takes less preparation time, most new agents start-out working with buyers, and consequently, never become solid listing agents. Being a strong listing agent requires more up-front preparation. If you are willing to pay the price to do the work up-front, and, if you can wait for the results, then being a sellers' agent may be the better option for you. In the long-term, though, it's less work and pays more to work exclusively with sellers.

An effective listing plan includes the following seven steps:

1. The first step is to find your area comfort zone. **Area Comfort Zone** is the area in which you feel comfortable talking to homeowners. It may be where you live or work, maybe an area where you enjoy visiting. Your next step is to research the area to find the number of houses, phone numbers, addresses, competition, and listings. Phone numbers are on the Internet, cross indexes, and many companies sell information by zip codes, address, or phone numbers. You can find your competition by searching MLS listings. Most subdivisions or county records have maps, bylaws, and numbers of houses. Research MLS for houses that have been sold, expired, or terminated. Before you decide on your farm area, make sure there is enough business in it for you.
2. Cold calling. Decide how many calls to make per day, what time of the day to make them, and the type of scripts that you will use.
3. Send a mail-out. The type of mail-out that you send will depend on the conversation that you had. You can start by sending a card, letter, or introduction letter.
4. Personally visit each house in your area. Determine how many houses you will visit per day, what material you will pass out, and what you will say to

each homeowner. Remember, right now your job is not to sell yourself, but to make contact. Moreover, you can update your contact lists and ask for phone numbers and email addresses.

5. Make sure you have something to give your prospects. Give literature on your business and a way for your prospect to retrieve more information. For example, in your introduction letter, outline how to prepare his/her home for the greatest dollar while adding a web link of videos of you (the star, the expert, the go-to person) staging a home. In your video you can add, "To Stage Your Home to sell for the greatest dollars, call ..."
6. Every day run an expired sheet from your local *MLS®*.
7. Use your local papers and Internet to find for sale by owners.

Perpetual Sales

Listing is **perpetual**. As you list more properties for sale, more homeowners will call you to have their homes listed. Now you will have buyers and sellers calling you, and not you calling prospects. As you put more signs in more yards, more people will start noticing your name. Signage leads to success, and signage is the best way to be recognized in any area. As you have more signs in an area, people will start recognizing and trusting you. Your mission is to capitalize on every listing. Each one provides you with the opportunity to gain two more listings, and five listings should yield ten listings. The more listings you produce, the more buyers will call you.

For each new listing, have open houses, and mail out information about your listing to every home in that area, especially absentee owners. The importance of absentee marketing will be discussed later. The idea is to flood homeowners with your constant listing letters, post cards and open house signs. Plan how you will visit the first fifty homes. If your farm is too large of an area, your signage becomes ineffective.

As you build a listing bank, the phone will start ringing, and you will be so busy that you will no longer have to concentrate so hard on searching for new listings. However, what will usually happen is the agent becomes distracted by buyers and will lose the momentum of gaining listings. In perpetual sales, you must always stay focused on gaining momentum and continue to search for more listings.

Listings Provide a Better Opportunity for Growth

The only opportunity buyers provide is if they buy the house, and you hope they will refer business to you. In fact, buyers create very little business opportunities compared to working with sellers. While working with sellers is a better investment, you can use the listings to gain leads by having open houses, farming absentees, signage, mail-outs, placing ads in newspapers, and Internet marking. Listings are lead generators, which will bring you more sellers and buyers.

More Control

Being focused on gaining listings rather than focusing on buyers or being a generalist gives you better control of your personal life. Let's say that you want to take some time off to go on vacation. If you are primarily a listing agent, your broker or another agent in the office can take over your listings. Your listings will continue to bring in calls, and the office staff or servicing company addresses them while you are away on vacation.

More Qualified Sellers

The economy dictates whether we are in a sellers' market or buyers' market. When there are fewer employment opportunities or lenders requirements are tightened, it creates fewer qualified buyers. Fewer buyers denote a surplus of homes. Because our economy is usually in a positive state, sellers control the market over buyers. What this means in real estate is buyers will more likely compete for housing rather than sellers competing for buyers. Seller agents understand if three conditions are met, the property will always sell, and they will get paid. The property will sell if the following three conditions are met:

- The agent has the sellers' cooperation
- The property is priced correctly
- The property is properly serviced, which will be discussed in more detail later in this chapter

Numbers Game

Working with listings is also a numbers game. If you work with buyers, you can work with only a few prospects at a time; however, if you work with sellers, you can work with a greater number at a time. Not all buyers will be able to close, but nearly all sellers will close, and you will get paid. With the power of the Internet and computer programs, making and maintaining contact with hundreds of sellers is now possible. Personally working with up to three buyers at a time is difficult, expensive, and you place a cap on your potential earned income. Buyers demand more personal attention, especially first-time buyers. It costs time and money to drive buyers to properties and show them. Do yourself a favor; ask any agent at any office this question, *"What are the most buyers you can work with?"* When you do the mathematics, what you will find is that you will limit your income. If you decide to specialize, you have a choice: you can work with three-five buyers or work with 20-30 sellers, with a good assistant and software you can include an additional 100 sellers, now do your math. Your assistant will also be limited on the services they can provide to buyers. Buyers require you to sell to them, (a license is required). Sellers require you to service their needs. Here is a good rule to remember, "Buyers, you sell and sellers, you service." Working with and how to control buyers is discussed in Chapter 10, *Prospecting for Buyers*.

Commitment to Paying a Commission

If you work with sellers, you have a greater chance of getting paid. Not all buyers will yield a commission. If buyers are unable to get a loan, decide to postpone buying a house because of employment issues, or find another agent, you won't get paid for all of your hard work. We're in a time where lenders are becoming very strict with mortgage guidelines. When working with buyers, you can spend hundreds of hours showing properties, but if they decide to not buy, not only will you not get paid, you will also lose the opportunity to work with other qualified buyers. Remember, buyers are concerned with their needs, not yours. Therefore, you will occasionally encounter buyers who are uncommitted and will try to use several agents to fulfill their needs. Buyers often get frustrated and tend to disappear unless there is a standing agreement you will not get paid. With seller, no matter who buys the property you will get paid for your hard work.

Listing Agreements

An **exclusive listing agreement** is a legal contract that stipulates the conditions of the listing between a seller and your broker. A seller who is using an agency commits to using one agent for a certain period of time. The time span can last for a few days or a few years. It doesn't matter who brings the buyers; the sellers' agent and broker will get paid. While there are contracts for buyers as well, buyers can be reluctant to have only one agent representing them, but in listings, it's common to have one agent. Inexperienced agents are reluctant to ask buyers for an exclusive agreement. Don't be shy about asking for an exclusive agreement, as a new agent; if you don't, you can spend your valuable time and money showing properties while another agent will obtain an agreement and will benefit from all of your hard work by writing the contract. Keep in mind real estate is a business. See Chapter 10 on how to obtain an exclusive agreement.

Generating Steady Income

When you work with buyers, you are showing and trying to sell other agents' listings or helping other agents get paid and look amazing. Turning this around, means getting hundreds of agents to sell your properties, thus helping you get a steady paycheck. Here, you can focus your energy on serving your clients while the rest of the real estate community will be trying to sell your listings.

Cost of Working with Buyers vs. Sellers

As previously discussed, buyers require more time and money to work with, and there are more qualified sellers. To check if you have a qualified seller, have a title company check the title. Sellers who want to sell usually can; however, qualified buyers are a different story. For a buyer, have a mortgage lender/bank qualify your prospect. Once you have determined you have a qualifying buyer, showing is the next big step. Here, you are going to spend your time and gas money driving your prospects around, which also means a better grade of auto and insurance. A simile by an unknown agent is called "The Shoe Salesman."

> A real estate salesperson is like a shoe salesman. If you have ample inventory of color, style, sizes and shoe brands, customers will be eager to bring you business.
>
> A shoe salesperson without inventory will be driving customers all over town just to find that one pair of shoes, which is unprofitable.

Part Two - Finding Prospective Sellers

Finding Prospective Sellers

You may be convinced that the way to start a real estate career is to work with sellers, but how will you find them? Where are they? How will you work with them, and how will you convince them to use you instead of another agent? Sellers are everywhere. Below are a few suggestions on how to find them; Chapter 8 discusses how to find sellers by using the following:

- Farming for prospects
- Geographic farming
- Expired listings
- Open Houses
- Meeting home owners
- For-Sale-By-Owners
- Absentee Home owners
- Floor duty
- Virtual farming (Chapter 4)
- Farming for buyers (Chapter 10)
- Old office accounts (Chapter 10)
- Listing signage/open house signs/yard signs

- Estate sales
- Door-to-door sales
- Cold calling
- Out of town property owners/absentees
- Hosting special events (Open House) at the property that is for sale
- Working with builders
- Apartment renters
- Family law/probate attorneys
- Social and internet networking
- Over 30 Internet sites, such as craigtslist.com, Internet ads (Chapter 4)
- Editorial writing
- Advertising discounts
- Drip marketing- Newsletters
- Post cards/e-cards
- Human resources
- Bank short sales, foreclosures/REO
- Referrals
- Family/neighbors
- Friends and co-workers
- Telemarketing, cold calling, and cross directories
- Giving free information
- Newspaper ads
- Publication ads
- Website development
- Blogging
- Purchasing leads
- Weddings
- Meetings
- Associations, local unions
- Letters, business cards, flyers
- Legal professions, divorce attorneys
- Classmates and past teachers
- Community memberships
- Church members
- Barbers and hair stylists
- Builders
- Seminars
- Schools
- Car sign magnets
- Sponsoring sport teams
- High school year book ads
- Supermarket postings and shopping carts
- Magazine advertising
- Yellow pages
- Local papers
- Radio ads
- Direct mail, promotions

- Just sold/just listed post cards and letters
- Wearing apparel with your name and company name
- Obituary postings for estates

Farming for Prospects (Buyers/Sellers)

Farming for prospects is focusing on a particular group of people or a geographic area. You can farm for buyers or sellers, apartments or houses. You can also farm for certain prices of homes or for military personnel. You can farm virtually using today's technology or farm using the tried and true old-fashioned methods. Physical farming, distinguished from virtual farming, is picking a physical area to cultivate prospects. In order for physical or virtual farming to work, it must have boundaries, and you must be consistent. The boundaries for a physical farm may be the number of houses in a subdivision, whereas, boundaries for virtual farming can be the number of contacts or type of prospects; for example, renters, recent college graduates, or someone new to the area. Essentially, farming is a long term marketing plan in which you select an area to plant seeds and cultivate until you're ready to harvest your crops. In this case, the seed is your reputation, and the crops are your monetary rewards. The old reliable methods of farming by mail, walking door-to-door, cold calling by phone, or advertising in a certain area or for a certain group still works beautifully.

You can start farming by having a library of predesigned letters. See Chapter 6, *Marketing*. Establish a plan for contacting each home by door knocking, mail-outs, or special events.

Geographic Farming

Geographic farming is when agents farm in a particular physical location; they farm for sellers to acquire listings. In this type of farm method, agents are better able to concentrate on being known as an expert in their particular area. Their signage is concentrated in a smaller area. Agents can find how well schools are performing, the latest community news, crime rates, tax rates, new improvements, and the most up-to-date information on property prices. Prospects are more comfortable knowing that the agent is familiar with the area. Prospects will see the agent's signage throughout the community. This will make cold- calling and door-to-door sales much easier. If you are comfortable in that area, chances are you will be comfortable making cold-calls, or walking door-to-door. After all, you're the local expert who most homeowners have heard about or have seen your picture somewhere. As noted earlier, if you have listings, buyers will be looking for you, like bees and honey. Should you decide to farm in a particular area, here are some suggestions that will be helpful:

- Pick a location in which you are comfortable. Many agents farm near their home or workplace.
- Check to see who else is farming the neighborhood you are considering, and know your competition. How strong is your competition?
- Can you legally do door-to-door marketing or door canvassing in your area of choice?
- Can you place door hangers or advertising material in your area?
- How many properties are in your area? You should keep your farm area under 500 homes. That is why it's important that you select an active area. The narrower the focus, the easier it is to become an expert in that area. While some communities are larger than 500 homes, it is possible to effectively farm as long as the information you gather will be from the same area, such as civic, worship centers, schools, police, retail centers, or fire departments.
- What is the average value of homes in your selected area?
- What is the real estate activity rate in your area of choice? To find activity rate, *MLS®* will have all sold, and active files on record, and county records will provide the number of homes per area. Most county records are online. Make sure there is enough activity to justify farming the selected area.
- How close is the farm area to your work and home? The closer the farm area, the better results you can expect.
- Are there any apartment units in the area?
- What will be your total cost of farming?
- What is the expected cost per return?
- How much labor is involved? What is the time factor per return of dollar?
- Can you have yearly promotions in your area?
- How do you plan to keep detailed records of your area? Realtor® website is a good start point for information.
- How do you plan to study the area, schools, retail stores, public recreation centers, churches, government services, tax rate, and future development?
- Within the year, can you personally visit every home in your community?
- How often will you make contact?
- What community leadership role will you play?
- What is the crime rate in your area?
- Would you enjoy this type of farming, and what other types of farming would create a greater rate of return?
- Will the competition, cost of marketing, activity rate, average home price and the number of homes justify your annual income? Are there any areas that will produce a greater return?

Farming Techniques

There are many ways agents can start reaching out to homeowners. The first thing is to design a long-term plan with a budget in your area comfort zone. Second, plan an introductory postcard or letter. Third, examine each listing method, fourth, decide which to use, and fifth, follow up. The top five farm methods which work well together are the following:

- Expired Listings
- For Sale by Owners (See Chapter 9)
- Open Houses
- Absentee Property Owners
- Signage

Expired MLS Listings

Finding expired listings is an effective way of building your inventory. **Expired listings** are property listings that were for sale on the *MLS®* system, but the contract period has expired.

How to Farm Expired Listings

Real estate agents should have a mail-out system in place for expired listings. For example, every morning, assign someone to check the *MLS®* for expired listings, followed by a visit or phone call, if possible. Every morning have marketing material ready for mail-outs. There are hundreds of expired listings; these properties were on the market for several months, but for some reason they didn't sell. Expired listings have their own set of problems. There can be several reasons, but the most common reason that the property did not sell is overpricing. To overcome this objective, see Chapter 8. The biggest reason that agents lose their listings is a lack of communication, (Chapter 5). Usually, the second biggest reason the property did not sell is lack of cooperation by the seller (Chapter 9).

The "CPS" Selling Rule

The *"CPS"* **selling rule** is *that all properties will sell for the highest dollar if the following three items are met:*

- *Cooperation – by the sellers*
- *Priced – correctly for the seller with the help of the agent*
- *Service - properly by agent*

Cooperation by the Owner

Owner cooperation falls into three areas:

1. The property has to be available for showing seven days a week from 8 a.m.- 8 p.m.
2. The property has to be staged for showing.
3. The inside/outside of the property has to be maintained during the selling period.

Available for Showing

Having the property available for showing is important. Thousands of homes are on the market for sale; therefore, buyers will try to eliminate as many properties as they can before searching for an agent and making appointments. Most viewings are between 10 a.m. until 6 p.m. Most real estate agents will use a centralized showing service or train in-office personnel to collect valuable data to protect homeowners.

Staged for Showing

Staging a property helps buyers emotionally connect to the property by enabling them to envision themselves enjoying living there. With the right staging, they will see themselves playing with their children in the family room, cooking in the kitchen, or having a cookout in the backyard. Before a buyer decides to buy, he/she expects three things from the property, the **GEM**:

1. Good value for one's money
2. Emotional connection
3. Move-in condition, clean, with few, if any repairs

For more information on staging, see Chapter 9.

Contacting Expired Listings

Mail those expired listing letters, and make personal contact as soon as possible before someone else does. A good rule is to mail the letter the day the listing expires and wait three days before visiting. You can call the property owners once you have cleared their phone number on the Do-Not-Call-List. Selling expired listings will show your community that you are an excellent real estate agent. Developing a working expired listing program to properly market and sell other agents' expired listings provides an excellent opportunity for you to be recognized as a true professional. Doing so would place you leaps ahead of your competition.

You will establish yourself as a listing/selling specialist, one who does what other agents can't do.

Be selective with expired listings; stay away from top producers. If their listings have expired, there is probably a good reason. Top producers work hard to keep their better listings. What you will find is that in the more expensive or the more exclusive subdivisions, the more agents will aggressively mine or farm these areas. The less expensive areas usually have fewer agents farming. If the owners are too demanding and expect a ridiculous price, walk away and save yourself a headache.

Meeting the Homeowner

Don't be intimidated; schedule a meeting with the homeowners as soon as possible. Don't take any negative remarks personally; the remarks are not directed at you, but to the last real estate agent who failed to sell their property. Property owners will usually be frustrated and unhappy with their past agent.

If you are still uncomfortable with visiting expired listings, try teaming up with another agent. There is strength in numbers. Keep this in mind: mailing letters will get you a 1-2% response, but with a follow up visit, it will yield you a 5-15% return. As you learn to overcome the fear of knocking on doors, your sales skills will improve; thus, your ratio will increase.

For every expired listing, there will be several agents who will try to win over the owners, but this is no problem because most agents will mail a letter and never follow-up with a visit. It's the personal visit that agents cannot manage to overcome because of the fear of not knowing what to ask, how to say it, and when to say it. If you have a program in-place with which you are consistent, you know what to say and are ready to overcome any objections, chances are you will win the majority of listings. Keep your interview short; never say negative remarks about the other agent.

When you approach a stranger's door, you must know exactly what you will say and how you will say it. Here is a four-part approach, which is helpful in designing your own approach for expired listings:

1. Identify yourself.

    *   *"Hello, I'm _____with ABC Real Estate."*

2. State your purpose.

    *   *"I noticed you were trying to sell your home."*

3. Ask questions.

- *"May I ask you a question? Are you still interested in selling your home for the highest price?"*
- *"Would you be open-minded to a second opinion?"*
- *"What price would you be comfortable with?"*

4. If sellers refuse your services, ask for permission to follow-up. Try to get emails.

- *"May I contact you in a few weeks?"*
- *"Would you mind if I call you in a week?"*
- *"Would you like me to email information on what properties are selling?"*
- *"May I mail you information on how to prepare your home to sell for the highest dollar?"*

To help with your visit, your goal is to get an appointment to make the presentation. Plan to make it a two-part visit; in the first visit, introduce yourself, state your purpose, ask questions, and ask permission to follow-up. Always try to get email addresses; this way you can keep in constant contact because an expired listing homeowner will usually try selling again, but this time you will be first in their mind. On your second trip, be prepared. The first meeting is to gather information, establish rapport, and "NEVER" to give advice or an opinion. Listen carefully to what sellers have to say. Find common ground to *agree.* There are common remarks sellers will say, your job is to role play with your best responses.

Listing Campaign

Attaining success with real estate listings involves maintaining a pipeline of 20 or more listings per month. The first 20 listings are the hardest to get. Afterward, if you sell four or five per month, your goal is to replace the sold listings with four-five new listings, thus developing a **listing pipeline**. Keeping a large pipeline may sound difficult, but it is not. If you know your scripts, have plenty of signage and are consistent by sending out your expired letters in your comfort zone, letters to absentee property owners, hold open houses, and make sure to knock on those doors, you will get more than your four-five listings per month. At the same time, while driving, you will find For-Sale-by-Owners and use the same system with FSBO as expired listings. Again, the more signage you have in your farm area, the more buyers and sellers will be looking for you. Another interesting point is if you share your listing ideas with other agents, they will also acquire listings. The office goal for all agents is to maintain a good size pipeline. For example, an office of twenty agents may have 200 listings. Two hundred listings will keep the phones ringing non-stop. What this means for you is every time you have floor-time, you should pick-up a few buyers and new listings. One floor duty should yield four good leads. After adding your referrals from past contacts and their friends plus your FSBO, expired listings, open houses, and business card campaign, maintaining a pipeline of 20 listings is not difficult. "Yes, this is hard work, but again you do the math on selling four-five listings per month for one year, and ask yourself what other profession pays this well?"

On your return visit, when you talk to prospects about their expired listings, try to pinpoint why the property did not sell. Was it staged properly, was it overpriced, or was there a lack of communication by the agent?

Remember the CPS rule. Does the property have curb appeal, and was the property available for showing? Did the property have good exposure? Was there a lack of advertisement or any open houses? Act as Sherlock Holmes; your job is to find why it didn't sell, so when you list it, it will sell. The next thing is to assure the homeowners, based on a set of promises and a written game plan, that you will put forth your best effort to sell their home. The promises are things that you will do, such as how you will interact with the owner to sell his/her property. If the owners are the cause of the property's failure to sell, it is best to walk away and protect your reputation. Your goal is to take only workable listings; unworkable listings with demanding owners are a distraction and will expend your limited time.

Keeping it Ethical with Expired Listings

When farming expired listings, keep communications ethical. Ask the sellers if their listing agreement is still intact. Some sellers may not even know that their agreement has expired. In your conversation, be honest and direct. Sellers have already lost valuable time. Don't ask for the listing in hopes that the sellers will later drop the price or that you will later be able to lower the seller's price or that a buyer will take it as is. After you have stated your opinion of the list price and the owners still want a greater price, list it and assure your clients you will do your best. Later, when the property hasn't sold yet, you can suggest a lower price. Always be honest and upfront; let the sellers know where they stand. You will perform a great deal of research the first time you work with expired listings. However, the longer you work with expired listings, the easier and more enjoyable it will become. Before long, you will become an expert at knowing how to list and sell expired listings. You will notice that most expired listings are homeowners who have an unrealistic value of their property and in time, you will learn how to work with that type of seller.

Rules for Real Estate Success

There are absentee property owners in all areas. **Absentees** are property owners who do not live on the property. These once homeowners are prime candidates for leads. The farther the absentee lives from the property, the more likely they are to list for sale. In most cases, homeowners were transferred or found employment somewhere else or simply inherited the property. They decided to rent in case they return to their home. What they soon experience is that being a landlord in another state is challenging.

The problem is finding absentee property owners. County tax rolls and your MLS are good sources for finding homeowners' forwarding addresses. Many agents farm absentees with letters to list their property. What works even better, however, is contacting absentees with handwritten letters about your company and your personal listings. In your short letter, ask them if they are interested in buying investment properties, and tell them how successful you have been in selling properties near their property. What you will find is that a high percentage of absentees will also want you to also sell their property.

Working with Builders

One way for builders to expose their inventory is to have a real estate agent list their properties on the MLS. It's a trade-off. You list the builders' properties in the MLS, and you get calls from buyers. Whether the properties' listings truly belong to the broker will depend on the agreement between the broker and the builder. Some builders will allow the broker to place signs on their properties as well. Make sure to view state law for advertising requirements by a real estate brokerage.

Builders have an inventory of homes, so they receive several calls per day on their properties. Some of these prospects are first-time homebuyers, while others want to sell their present home to buy a new one. Homeowners who are thinking about selling their homes are an excellent referral source. Visit each builder and all of their sales employees to make contact. Builders want results just like you do. Builders will refer business to you if they think you are the best qualified person to sell for them. Sales people who work directly for builders are usually not allowed to list or sell properties other than those that belong to the builder.

Many real estate companies will list properties non-exclusively at discount fees, such as $300, for placing it on *MLS®;* usually there is a fee to pay the selling agent. The small fee pays for the paperwork, and they hope that sellers will list low enough to attract buyers. This type of agreement allows sellers to sell the property themselves to save the commission.

Since over 58% of buyers will find the property before they search for an agent, this type of listing campaign works well if you are able to get the sellers to a saleable price. The problem with this listing method is that the do-it-yourself seller(s) usually wants a ridiculous price, and as discussed in the For-Sale-by-Owner chapter, this type of seller(s) is the main mental block for most buyers.

Farming with Open Houses

Open house is a form of prospecting for buyers and sellers, a powerful lead generator. The concept of **open house** is having the property available, or open, for the public to view. The National Association of Realtors® has several articles and much research for conducting successful open houses. Whether or not an open house is successful will largely depend on how the real estate agent conducts the process; this should be a planned system. With open houses, you are doing several things at once:

- First, you are trying to sell your listing.
- You are showing the owners how serious you are in selling their property.
- You are prospecting for sellers.
- You are prospecting for buyers.
- You are winning trust from buyers and sellers.
- You are building your professional image and your company image in that community.
- You are building relationships with other agents; the same agents who will decide whether or not to push your listings. Respectable agents prefer not to work with rude or unprofessional agents.

Open House Campaign

How are you going to get the word out about an open house? Will you advertise in local newspapers or mail out letters? Will you send post cards or place a notice *on MLS®*? Will your flyers be balanced with pictures and description? How many open house signs will you use? What will your signs look like? What time and date will be most effective for open houses? Will the property be staged and ready? Conducting weekly or bi-monthly open houses consistently provides your best chances of finding new prospects, but most importantly, letting the community know about your services.

Open House Signs

Open house signage is a good way to establish yourself in your farm area. Most agents will use simple signs that read Open House with an address. This type of sign promotes the property for only a few hours.

To take advantage of open houses, agents should have custom designed signs to promote all three or **"CAP"** the following.

- Company
- Agent
- Property

Try to be consistent; have as many open houses as possible, and try to keep them in one area. Use open house signs as a catalyst to promote your career. For example, with ten open houses, you should have 100 open house signs in your area, a ten-to-one ratio. These signs should complement office color and design. Match the For Sale sign design with that of your office. You should be consistent on every weekend, especially during March, April, May, June, and July. These are the months people are thinking about real estate. Your signs should have balloon colors that match your signs. Red balloons just a few inches above the sign work best. Balloons moving with the wind will capture the eye and draw attention to the sign. You need only a balloon or two per sign. Balloons should be placed close to eye level. The idea is to flood your area with your presence. People in your area will see your signs everywhere, and anyone going or leaving your area will notice your signs and your name. The goal in conducting open houses is not only to sell the property, but also to get your name out to the public. This identifies you as the only agent, which is the same concept a politician would use running for public office. Make sure to post your sign early, be respectful of property owners, and pick them up every day. Start a few days early to make sure you get permission from homeowners to place signs on corner lots. The next week, select different homes to place signage.

If you're going to farm open houses, then an open house system gives you a reason to contact homeowners, such as cold-calls or door-to-door sales. Door-to-door sales will give you the opportunity to personally meet homeowners. If you have had several open houses, homeowners have most likely noticed your signs and will be more receptive to you. Homeowners will probably say, "*I noticed your signs.*" When they are ready to sell their home, more often than not, you will be the first or the only one they will call. This is called creating *"first awareness."* When the homeowner decides to sell, you will be the first person in their mind. As discussed earlier, maintaining a pipeline of 20 houses is not difficult when the community recognizes you as the only professional.

People want to hear what you have to say only if the information you have will benefit them. Having an open house in your farm area creates the perfect opportunity to call or meet homeowners, which now allows you to have a good reason to call. Community members are always interested in their property value and education material. In the old days, before technology was available, farm areas were kept under 400 homes. Now, agents are successfully farming larger areas, even whole communities. In your data base, keep track of which homes you have visited, and use open houses to cover the rest of your area.

If your listings are skillfully staged with beautiful looking yards and are reasonably priced, won't it be valuable to your professional image? Don't you think neighbors want to know about a good value? Homeowners will start noticing three things: a property's curb appeal improves about the time your sign goes up, a property will sell faster when your sign is in the front yard, and your name is on every open house sign every weekend. This won't happen overnight; it will take time, which is why farming for listings is a long-term process. Homeowners will want to hear what you have to say because they have noticed that your listings quickly sell and for more money. Here is another rule: every homeowner will someday sell, and every homeowner knows at least three people who are now thinking about buying or selling.

Agents often use open houses as a means to find buyers, that's fine, but be more aggressive; think of open houses as a prospecting system to find new listings and an opportunity to build your reputation.

Selecting Open Houses

Not all properties make great open houses. If the property is an investment property and priced to sell, market it as such. Sellers usually want top dollar for their property. It's far better to have one successful open house that produces many quality buyers than to have many open houses that result in only a few quality buyers. Below are five rules for selecting the ideal open house site:

1. Be sure the property is fairly priced, and support the price with an accurate CMA.
2. Be sure the owner is able to keep the property in good condition and have it well staged.
3. Be sure the property is easily accessible; include signage, showing how to get to the property (the fewer turns, the better).
4. Pick a property that has not been on the market very long; over two months is a long time.
5. Pick a property that has not had many open houses in the past.

Conducting Open Houses

To present the property in the best possible light, offer advice on how to stage the property. Staging is discussed in more detail in Chapter 9, *Staging*. Consider the following:

- Post the property days in advance on *MLS®*.
- Make a pre-video of your open house, and be sure to link it to your social websites.
- Be sure you have plenty of help for the open house. Safety is important; ask a loan officer or another agent for help. If a non-licensee helps as a greeter, be sure he/she understands the rules for selling real estate. Have a greeter welcome all visitors.
- Have your cell phone fully charged.
- Be sure there is an escape route in case of fire or any other safety hazards.
- Bring a digital camera, notebook computer, and have a safe place to store these items while you are busy.
- Research your area, and have vital statistics available.
- Design an open house package with information, such as pictures, a list of other similar properties in the same area, flood elevation, CMA, appraisal, tax, school ranking, property inspection or termite reports, important community information, disclosures, and your success rate. Disclose the number of sales you have made up to the current date and the percent of sales price compared to the listing price. For example, your total volume of sales was 98% of listed price when the average is 89% of listed price; this gives sellers and buyers a good reason to use you.
- If you are a listing specialist and you are focused only on developing your listing inventory of homes, find someone who is a buyer specialist who wants to add a few hundred prospects to his/her inventory of buyers. Better yet, it's your listing, so sell your buyer inventory list for a referral fee.
- The number of signs you place will largely depend on the neighborhood. The rule is an average of ten signs per open house. Start placing signage a few hours before the open house. Drive around to find where to place key signage. If it's at a corner, ask the homeowner for permission to place your signs. After the open house, mail a thank you note to the neighbors who let you put signs in their yards. Be certain that every entrance way has directional signage. If there are four ways to enter the community, you may have as many as twelve signs. Make sure to number your signs so that all your signs are recovered at the end of the day. Think about having a sign painter custom design a large door opening sign or a sign for welcoming your guest. You can place these signs at the entry door or in the front yard. You will be able to reuse these signs many times over. Use balloons to indicate interest. Don't think more signs means more work, but rather more income.
- Call as many people as possible, friends and neighbors, and place ads as well. Be sure to advertise both online and offline.
- If possible, go door-to-door with door hangers or fliers at hand. Personally meet as many people as possible. If you are the new kid on the block, let them know.

- Mail out post cards to at least 100 people about the new listing and announce when the open house will be.
- While they are not part of the open house, hosting special events is useful. Ask sellers about having Tupperware or Amway parties, Mary Kay Cosmetics, Boy Scouts, PTA, or community meetings—any type of event that will bring guests to your unofficial open house.
- Be sure sellers are not present during the open house, as they can be a deal killer. They are the primary mental block for many buyers.
- Avoid holiday dates and community events. Saturdays around noon are usually the best time, but any day will work. Allow about two-four hours per open house.
- Show homeowners how to stage (Chapter 8, *Staging*). Use your technology, have videos on YouTube, or better, your website. As discussed earlier, you can't be afraid to be the movie star. Try making 'how to' videos for your customers/clients to view. This will show your expertise.
- Have sellers put away all valuables and jewelry. The property should be very clean.
- Have sellers remove all pets.
- Open all of the window blinds or drapes and turn on the lights. If it's cold outside, turn on the fireplace. If it's warm outside, turn on the air conditioner. On a hot summer day, have the prospect walk into a cold comfortable house.
- Leave the entrance door slightly open with a welcome sign. This will help visitors feel welcome.
- The yard should be well kept; start early on lawn maintenance.
- Strong odors can be eliminated using air filters, odor eaters, odor-blocking paint, potpourri, scented candles, or airing out the property.
- Take out excessive furniture to make rooms appear to be larger and cleaner.
- Consider hiring a professional cleaning service.
- Use warm colors, flowers, vases, candles, pictures, towels, books, and magazines to make the buyer feel a sense of warmth and coziness. Design a photo book about the house.
- People will show-up if there is a benefit for them. Bake chocolate chip cookies to give away to adult guests. Never give food to kids, however, without a parent's permission.
- Have bottled water available; never give soda or any stainable drinks. A parent may have concerns with sugar drinks, nuts, or cheeses.
- Give away advertising items (this is not a staging item, but it is a good idea). Be sure all giveaways have some advertising on them to keep with RESPA section 8 rules.
- Line the front desk or kitchen countertop with sufficient educational material and your business letters, introduction letters, and business

cards. Make a DVD loop of your videos. You can even have a list of other properties that are for sale. HUD has several publications available for buyers. Lenders are required under federal law to pass out HUD's Special Information Booklet 1676-H. The booklet explains the process involved in purchasing real estate and the duties of real estate brokers, mortgage lenders, appraisers and other professionals associated with the transaction.

- Advertise your open house on your website. Take plenty of pictures or even design a virtual tour video with you in it. You may even add a second yard sign that says, *"Look at this beautiful home at abc-realty. com."*
- Wear a name badge; make sure everyone helping has a name badge. Be sure to personally greet and thank all of your visitors during the open house. Be careful not to talk too much.
- Show your guests where your community and property information is located.
- Ask your guests to sign your log book, which should have a place for names, phone numbers, and e-mail addresses with an option to send more information. Be sure to have a notepad for taking visitors' questions. Ask if they want information on new listings.
- Write notes about your conversation after each visitor leaves.

Not all of your visitors will be interested in buying; some are just curious or nosy. Start a conversation with each visitor. Determine the type of Visitor's needs. Ask all of your visitors if you can e-mail or snail mail more information to them, even the window shoppers. Build rapport with serious buyers, show the property, and ask if they have any questions. Keep your questions short and friendly. If you start a long dialogue, other potential buyers may come and go. You also want to remain ethical; always ask if they have an agent helping them. If they do have representation, limit any personal information, and have their agent call you.

Open house visitors (prospective buyers) hate aggressive sales agents. Don't forget the rule; *"Never try to sell on the first meeting; develop trust before you try to sell."* Instead, be friendly, helpful, and informative. If your visitors show interest, however, then be ready to give your best sales pitch. Have your presentation ready. If visitors are ready to sign, take their signatures. In most cases, visitors are seeking information about value. They are probably comparing properties to have an idea about value, or they may be thinking about buying or selling in the near future. Most visitors are not looking to buy the open house property. These prospects, however, can be excellent buyers in the future. Like other types of prospective buyers, you have to learn how to categorize buyers who attend open houses. We will discuss this more in Chapter 10, *Prospecting for Buyers*. Chapter 10 covers the type of questions to ask in order to separate real buyers from window shoppers.

Prospecting for Sellers, Part I

- 191 -

If the property is vacant, ask if prospective buyers would like a personal tour or if they would like to view the property alone. At the end of the tour, always thank your visitors and offer free items, such as water, marketing, or educational information. Some agents even give away balloons to children. The point is everyone wants to walk away with something free. Showing professionalism during the open house is a good way to win those prospects. Professionalism can be shown by:

- Being empathetic and a good listener.
- Knowing there are two rules for having closet and other doors open or closed. The old rule was to open all doors, making it easier for viewing. The problem with this rule is it's easy-in and easy-out. The newer rule is to keep doors closed, encouraging prospects to touch as much as possible. Let them have fun, feel, use their imagination, and discover on their own. This idea falls under the discovery rule.
- Have information about the house, community, mortgages, and other open houses or a list of all properties for sale in the area.
- Toward the end of the presentation, ask open-ended questions. For example, *"What do you think about the property?"*
- Be properly dressed.
- Never volunteer the price. Wait, so when prospects ask for the price, you can start building rapport and trust. Remember the rule: *"Never give price until you have established value."* Many agents give the price first and then try to support it with value. All too often, once you give the price, prospective buyers are not concerned with how the value was determined. You may not have their full attention at this point.
- Give visitors enough space to walk around and the opportunity to talk to one another.
- Many agents give visitors the option of a personal guided tour or let them walk through the property themselves.
- Never push the property to visitors; at this point, your job is to build an inventory of buyers.
- Prospects will want you to show them the house, not to sell them the house; after all, the outside sign says Open House.
- Try to determine who the decision maker is. Over 80% of the time, the wife will make the initial decision to buy. The final decision will usually be a joint agreement.

After the viewing, ask open ended questions such as, *"May I ask you a few questions? Can you me tell what you like and dislike about the house?"*

Broker/Pre-Open Houses for Sales Agents

The two main types of open houses are open houses for the public and pre-open houses for other agents. Plan accordingly for each type of open

Rules for Real Estate Success

house. Having a good business relationship with other agents is very important. Most real estate agents have a list of buyers. Be sure to take time to show your **broker/pre-open houses** to other agents who are in the same area. You can even have a broker open house questionnaire and ask for advice from other real estate agents. Don't forget these agents can control what their buyers view. If others agents in your area believe that you are an ethical person and that the transaction will be pleasurable, they are more likely to want to show your listings. On the other hand, if you are confrontational, chances are other agents will avoid your listings.

An open house does not have to be your own listing; it can be any listing in your office or from a new homebuilder. Be sure to get your broker's approval. Try to form a liaison with new home builders. Smaller independent builders are normally better sources of business, while larger builders usually have their own source of agents. The person hosting the open house does not have to be a real estate agent, as long as the host does not try to sell real estate or act as a real estate agent. The host (non-agent) can only greet the public, must say that he/she is not a real estate agent, and can only talk about non-real estate matters; nonetheless, he/she is permitted to show the public where your information is. If the public asks for a sales price, the host can say, *"I'm not a real estate agent; however, the agent left information on the table."* You can also team-up with other agents or offices that have listings in the same area.

Open houses are a great place to give away educational information. Below is an example of free material you can offer your client.

The following publication is found on HUD.org website:

ATTENTION BORROWER!

This may be the largest and most important loan you get during your lifetime. You should be aware of certain rights before you enter into any loan agreement.

- You have the RIGHT to shop for the best loan for you and compare the charges of different mortgage brokers and lenders.
- You have the RIGHT to be informed about the total cost of your loan, including the interest rate, points, and other fees.
- You have the RIGHT to ask for a Good Faith Estimate of all loan and settlement charges before you agree to the loan and pay any fees.
- You have the RIGHT to know what fees are not refundable if you decide to cancel the loan agreement.
- You have the RIGHT to ask your mortgage broker to explain exactly what the mortgage broker will do for you.
- You have the RIGHT to know how much the mortgage broker is getting paid by you and the lender for your loan.
- You have the RIGHT to ask questions about charges and loan terms that you do not understand.
- You have the RIGHT to a credit decision that is not based on your race, color, religion, national origin, sex, marital status, age, or whether any income is from public assistance.
- You have the RIGHT to know the reason if your loan was turned down. You have the RIGHT to ask for the HUD settlement costs booklet, "Buying Your Home."

Listing Yard Signs

The more homes you can list for sale, the more recognizable your name will be. Every yard sign you have in place is free advertisement for you. In a tight community, your signs reflect how busy you are. **Sign-riders** are the smaller signs with your name, personal phone number, and web site address that are placed on top of or below the office sign. These riders are very effective. Most people call the number on the rider before calling the office phone number. Buyers want to talk with the person who knows the property best, not with someone from the agency who has to look-up the information. Be sure to add a sign rider to all of your yard signs and open house signs. While your loyalty is to the sellers, first-time buyers often believe that working with the listing agent is more beneficial than searching for an outside agent.

Yard-of-the-Month signs

Start by selecting a panel of homeowners who understand that the purpose of the yard-of-the-month program is to improve the overall value of their neighborhood. Set the rules; you can even have two or three categories. This is a good way to build your professional image. Now you have a good reason to start calling homeowners, go door knocking or post results on your website. Talk to your broker before you decide to place your office logo with office color on yard-of-the month signs. Having your company logo, depending on the area, may diminish the value of what you are trying to achieve. A yard-of-the-month program is one way to improve property value, bring a sense of pride to the neighborhood, and increase your listing base.

You can start by checking to see if anyone from your farm area is promoting yard-of-the-month in that area. If your neighborhood does not have such a program, ask local officials if you can start one.

Free Estate and Garage Sale Yard Signs

A good way to pick up listings is to offer free estate or garage sale signs. Place a link on your website for free signs, or mention them in your mail-outs. If you find an estate or garage sale in a newspaper ad or on the way home, offer free signage; you can get your signs back after the event is over. Garage sale signs are a good way of getting your name and logo in front of the public. Nearly all estate sales are selling the property, and most are looking for a real estate agent. Nearly every city has estate sale specialists who enjoy partnering with a real estate agent. However, there cannot be any commission splits unless all parties have real estate licenses.

Specializing in Estate Sales

Working with estate sales is another specialization. Estate sales are recorded as part of probate court records. There are attorneys who specialize in this field, and many estate sales are advertised in newspapers and websites. For example, on www.craigslist.org, type-in estate sales on the search option box and you put up a list of estate sales in your city. Usually, the person in charge of selling the estate items does not realize that many of those items/chattel items that they are preparing to sell were purchased to enhance the property and can play a key role in selling the property for a greater amount. A staging expert will need to select which items are to be saved that can showcase the property. Chapter 9 discusses how staging improves the chances of selling the property in a shorter time and receiving greater offers with fewer objections. County on-line records will usually give you the contact person's name and address. Design letters that will address the importance of saving certain items and your specialization in this area to send to homeowners and attorneys.

Like cold-calls, most agents dislike door-to-door sales and are not successful at this type of sales. When you approach a stranger's door, you must believe you have a valid reason to be there, know exactly what you will say, what the homeowner is going to say, and how you will reply. Here is a three-part approach to a For Sale by Owner:

- *Identify* yourself;
  "*Hello, I'm _____with ABC Real Estate.*"
- State your purpose;
  "*I noticed you are trying to sell your home.*"
- Ask your three questions;
  "*May I ask you a few questions?*"

  1. "*What price are you asking?*"
  2. "*Would you be interested if I bring you buyers?*"
  3. "*Are you willing to co-op if I could sell your home?*"

- Be prepared to overcome objections. Homeowners are waiting for the opportunity to say, "*No, thank you, what do you want? I'm just looking, or I'm not buying.*" Chapter 5 addresses the ABCs (**A**lways **B**e in **C**ontrol) of real estate, how to overcome the "NO" objections. You must know what you will say, the services you offer and the value homeowners will gain by using those services. You can never be vague about what you offer. Overcoming objections is discussed in Chapter 5.
- Mention how your presence at their doorstep will benefit them. For example, "*Mr. Jones, I have free ...*" "*I have good news. I would like to help.*" The word "free" is a powerful word. You can also say, "*I'm a Realtor® who specializes in this area, and I would like to share some useful information.*" In this case, the free object can be any number of topics. Getting buyers is what they really want to hear. The three-part approach works well if you're at a loss for words; the main reason is to start a dialogue as quickly as possible and keep it going as long as possible.
- Door-to-door sales will never work unless you feel that you have a good reason to knock on a stranger's door.
- Understand that this will take planning and several visits. Make it a habit to routinely visit homeowners in your farm area. A real estate rule that is applicable here is, "*Real estate success is to follow up, never give up, and be the first one there.*"

Knocking on doors may be the result of many reasons. One may be that you have buyers who have certain requirements. (See Chapter 10 for more information on what to say). Many people are uneasy about a stranger at their front door. To ease the owner's fears, here are a few tips for meeting homeowners for the first time:

- Dress in conservative business attire.
- Have a name badge visible.
- After knocking on the door or ringing the doorbell, give the homeowner space. Stand back a few feet, but not more than five feet, and look sideways down the block and to the right. This will give the homeowner time to examine who is at their front door. The owner will have time to read your face, look over what you are carrying, and read your name badge. Ninety percent of the homeowner's attitude towards you is made before he/she opens the door; the remaining ten percent is based on what you have to say.
- Have something official looking in your hands, such as a clipboard available with a crisscross or tax roll directory of all homeowners. Now is a good time to update information. If homeowners are still a little uneasy, however, thank them and let them know how valuable their comments will be.
- While it may be a sunny day, do not wear sunglasses.
- Have business cards ready, smile, and reply in a warm, soft tone.
- Be sure to give owners space to open the door and be able to greet you.
- Have your opening script prepared and ready to recite. Homeowners will want to know why you are at their door.
- Write several scripts and rehearse them until you are comfortable; don't forget homeowners have common questions, so it will be helpful if you are prepared.
- There are hundreds of reasons why you are visiting. For example, if you decide to survey your new farm area, have your survey ready with stamped return envelopes. Your survey can have information about asking permission for future calls or even your introduction to the community.
- Plan what information you will give verbally and what written information you will hand to homeowners. If you have marketing items, such as calendars or pens, ask if you may leave your marketing items.
- Try to keep smiling even when you are talking.

Cold-Calling for Listings

Cold-calling is making unsolicited phone calls. Usually, cold-calling doesn't work for many agents, and it is restricted by the National-Do-Not Call List. Because cold calls are associated with rejection, you may be apprehensive about calling. You don't want to sound like you are hungry for business or feel rejected. If you are eager and excited and follow a few rules about cold-calling, however, then it works beautifully. First, you have to believe you have a good reason for calling. You can use any number of reasons for your calls:

- Open house or permission for signage
- Help an FSBO or Estate Sale with staging
- A new listing
- News in your community
- A holiday gift, such as an American flag for special days
- A newsletter that you have designed
- An important announcement
- Community real estate research
- An article you have been writing
- Advice from outstanding community members

If you are still uncomfortable with cold-calling and door-to-door sales, try mailing postcards or letters, informing the recipient that you will be calling or making house visits in the future or within a few days, which will usually turn cold-calls into warm calls. Cold-calling and door-to-door sales don't work for most agents simply because they were never trained to view it as a process. The advantage of using this sales technique is that there aren't many agents using it. Below are suggestions for cold-calling:

- Make a long-term plan on how many mail-outs and phone numbers you will be calling.
- Do a weekly mail-out to the homes on which you will be calling. Allow a few days before you start calling. For each mail-out, be sure to follow-up with a phone call or you will be wasting advertising dollars. Plan smartly and follow-up.
- Keep a log book with a brief description of the conversation.
- Prepare your cold-calls. Keep your phone calls at a normal tone, clear, and be direct. Pick a location to call from, away from noise, such as phones ringing and other people talking. If possible, use a land line, avoid cell phones or Bluetooth headsets. Focus on your calls; don't multitask. Do not chew gum or eat during cold-calls.
- Have an opening line ready, such as, "*Good morning, I'm Steve Marks from ABC Realty. I have wonderful information for you.*" Try to stay away from saying, "*Hello, I'm Steve Marks from ABC Reality. Is this a good time for you to talk?*" The second statement leaves room for the homeowner to close unwanted solicitation.
- Keep your scripts brief and friendly. Discuss the benefits to the homeowners. Practice your scripts before you call. You may even use a recorder for practicing, or you can practice by calling close friends.
- Describe yourself as your company's representative for the area.
- After all favorable calls, be sure to follow up with a handwritten thank you letter.
- Include a few business cards with follow-up letters.

- Thank the homeowner for his/her time.
- Be persistent. A majority of successful sales result from making several calls.

For more information on developing phone skills, refer to Chapter 5, *Building a Professional Image*.

Hosting Special Events

For market exposure, you can link your listing to social gatherings. If sellers are interested in Tupperware™, Amway™, candles parties, or selling Mary Kay Cosmetics™, have them host those parties. If they know a friend who sells candle products, schedule a candle party. Boy Scouts or football parties work as well. Nearly all sellers know someone who needs a place to host an event. Before hosting any events, make sure the property is well staged and have all your literature ready for display. You can even give a small presentation before the event. Give visitors property information, and encourage them to tell their friends and family. Some agents have credit or staging seminars.

Contacting Renters

Be careful about contacting renters. While it's legal to mail information to renters or to call them, it may be trespassing if you enter the apartment complex without being invited. Depending on your area, landlords will often consider real estate agents physically doing door-to-door canvassing or leaving door hangers as trespassing. Do your mail-outs and cold-calls before you visit renters. Be careful in selecting which apartments to market. Renters can be good buyers, but many have credit or employment issues.

Networking

Try networking with homeowners in your farm area. If you're at a social function, don't try to pass out business cards to every single person or try to meet every person in the room. Its quality leads, not quantity, you should be searching for. Walk around, be selective, spend time getting to know the right people, and build a relationship with a select few.

Editorial Writing (Local/International)

If you enjoy writing, think about contacting your local paper to start a weekly or monthly on-line column, or try using websites such as Go.articles.com to post real estate articles for an international market. Using social media to blog current real estate issues will show your expertise in real estate. For your local market, find what your farm community is concerned with, and do your research; however, stay away from political or religious views. Your local and international topics should remain within the real estate field. For example, write an article about "How to Prepare Your Home to Sell" or the "Importance of Staging." There are many topics to write about. You can always do follow-up articles or a question-and-answer editorial blog. The goal is to have readers want more information, so you can direct them to your website, which will also help your Internet ranking.

Newsletters

A monthly newsletter for your community will demonstrate knowledge in your field. Newsletters are a good way to keep your name in front of hundreds of people. You can include links to your newsletters on your website. If readers want more information, direct them to your website or let them voice their opinion on your blog.

Post Cards/E-cards

Post cards are not usually expensive. You can also use e-cards if you want to save the stamp on a traditional snail mail postcard. There are several companies that provide e-cards or provide a drip campaign. A **drip campaign** is when your prospects are placed on a list to receive cards, letters, emails, calendars and books with your information on it. For example, you can go to e-flyer.com, onletterhead.com or www.nhsprint. com for web space, letter headings, and a large selection of professional looking e-cards or post cards. Microsoft Office Publisher is software used for designing postcards.

After designing your post cards, the next step is to decide where you are going to mail them. When you list a property, mailing postcards is a good way to capitalize on your listing. Input a picture, property description, and information about your services for 50-100 postcards, and mail the cards to the closest neighbors.

Bank Short Sales

Short sales are another way agents can increase your inventory. A **short sale** happens when the lender agrees to sell the property for less than the amount owed. The proceeds from the sale of real estate are insufficient to satisfy the liens on the property. To avoid foreclosure, lien holders or lenders and insurance companies will agree to accept less than they are contractually owed. The lien holder forgives the homeowner of the remaining debt. In this type of arrangement, the homeowner provides evidence of financial hardship. Lenders try to avoid short sales, but working with the homeowner's agent is sometimes better than having the owner walk away from the property. If the lender believes that it's in his/her best interest to foreclose, then he/she will not approve a short sale. As in a forbearance agreement, the homeowner must show hardship, have no assets, and the property value must be far below the amount owned. The lender will also order an appraisal to verify the property value. For more information on short sales and forbearance, read Chapter 12.

Selling Short Sales

Working with lenders on short sales is a huge money maker. It's not a difficult area to get into, but it's time consuming. Lenders are slow to react to short sale contracts. Start contacting all of the loss mitigation departments of major lenders and ask for the contact person. Most departments are out of state, and there are no set standards in this area. Most departments will ask for a resume, financial statement, proof of E&O insurance, and want to know the amount of help staff.

Lenders will often ask you to accept a reduced commission rate. You are not obligated to accept a reduced commission rate if you have a listing agreement. Nevertheless, it's a good idea to disclose how commissions will be handled if the lender demands that you accept less commission to cooperating brokers.

The relationship between the brokerage company and the client doesn't change because a lender is involved. You must be careful with lenders. Ask for the conditions up front, since most are out of state and have little real estate knowledge. For example, the owners will agree to sell for the balance if the lender agrees to accept the short. After the property is listed and a full offer is on the table, the homeowners will sign, but the lender or investors may refuse. At this point, the seller is under contract to sell. To avoid this problem, you should always use the new short sale addendum or a similar form designed by real estate attorneys. This form will protect the homeowners or buyers if the lender withdraws or refuses to accept the short sale.

Be sure to use title companies on any short sale purchases because of possible second liens or unpaid taxes. Lenders usually have their own addendums and procedures on short sales and accepting offers. You should determine who the contact person is, phone numbers, and ask for lender's procedures and if there is a stacking order sheet. Real estate expenses are typically reimbursed in 30-45 days. Lenders are accustomed to having an organized system of documents or a stacking order. Below is an example of stacking order sheet.

Stacking Order
• Fully completed and signed hardship letter • Broker letter • Credit report • Derog. credit LOE • BK discharge documents • Two paycheck stubs • 60 day bank statements • P&L • VOD • VOE • 1040's • W-2's • Divorce decree • Original appraisal • Inspection reports • Survey

Working with Foreclosures

Most lenders report that a majority of foreclosures could have been avoided. Lenders really don't want the properties and are willing to work with homeowners and their agents to keep their homes. Many homeowners, however, do not know their options, so they walk away from their homes. What these people don't understand is on a foreclosure, the loss is still owed to the lender or mortgage insurance company, and any forgiveness of debt could be taxable income, depending on the Mortgage Forgiveness Debt Relief Act of 2007 (See Chapter 12).

If the owners have no choice but to sell, ask the lender for an extension and an agreement to sell the property. If the owners are in a true hardship, most lenders and mortgage insurance companies are more tolerant in a buyers' market.

Working with Bank Real Estate Own Properties (REO)

Working with banks selling banks' real estate own properties (REO) is another good way to build an inventory of listings. Banks, mortgage insurance companies, and investment trust companies often have real estate properties (**REO**) they have purchased at auction and will list those properties. See Chapter 12, Post Closing Services for more detail.

1. Research the farm area selected.
    *   Find and study your competition.
    *   Find what is unique to your farm area.
    *   Know what activities are in your farm area.
    *   Find the number of homes, names, addresses and phone numbers to homeowners.
    *   Use *MLS®* to find the activity rate.

2. Design a listing plan.
    *   Research for an area to farm.
    *   Design a mail-out plan.
    *   Discuss how you will personally visit every house in your farm area.

3. Study and prepare a listing agreement and presentation. Ask your broker or another agent for help on this project.

4. Design how you will make daily searches for expired listings and how you will contact each.

5. Make plans to search for open houses for ideas on how to better host your own open houses. Ask questions to discover what works, and take plenty of notes.

6. Research how you will contact homeowners in your farm area. Design scripts for communicating with them.

7. Research builders in your area, and make plans to visit them. Find out what builders offer and whether they work with real estate agents.

8. Ask a broker for a sample of a Seller's Presentations.

9. Learn how to prepare and present a CMA.

10. Research internet sites that are rich with sellers.

11. Meet with your office manager/broker on how you can start a listing pipeline and the number of properties it will take to fulfill your goal.

12. Study how you will research and work with absentees.

13. Ask your broker about designing open house signs and how many you will need.

14. Design your sign riders and know the number you will need.

15. Carefully study how you will host and greet prospects in open houses.

16. Research if your brokerage firm has the National Do-not-all clearance service.

17. You have many opportunities for finding sellers, but you need to narrow your list to a few which work well together, ask your manager or broker for help on this project.

18. Research if you want to be a generalist or specialist.

Prospecting for Sellers, Part I

Rules for Real Estate Success

1. The search for potential new customers, clients, or purchasers for the possibility of something happening soon, a desirable real estate transaction outcome is called
   A. Real estate prospecting.
   B. Exposure.
   C. The listing period.
   D. An inventory list.

2. A federal act which protects individuals from having their information disclosed is the
   A. Truth-in-Lending Act, TILA, Reg. Z
   B. Fair Credit Reporting
   C. Deceptive Trade Practice Act, DTPA
   D. Real Estate Settlement Procedures Act, RESPA

3. Having an inventory of property listings will bring you
   A. Buyers.
   B. Sellers.
   C. A and B.
   D. None of the above.

4. Listings give the agent
   A. More listings.
   B. An inventory of buyers.
   C. More exposure.
   D. All of the above.

5. An exclusive agency listing is between whom?
   A. The client and broker
   B. The buyer and seller
   C. An agreement between a mortgage broker and a real estate broker
   D. The real estate broker and agent

6. The concept of farming is
   A. Growing corn.
   B. Focusing on a particular group of people or in a geographic area.
   C. A system of crop growing.
   D. A form of advertisements.

7. Property listings that were for sale on the MLS system, but the contract period expired and the property did not sell are called
    A. Open houses.
    B. MLS active listings.
    C. Expired listings.
    D. An inventory list.

8. The concept of trying to sell a property by having the property available or open for the public for viewing is called what?
    A. Farming
    B. MLS listings
    C. Expired listings
    D. Open house

9. What are the two types of open houses?
    A. For public viewing and broker viewing
    B. Agent viewing and broker viewing
    B. A and B
    C. None of the above

10. Smaller signs with your name, personal phone number and a website that are placed on top or below the office sign are called
    A. Public signage.
    B. Sign-riders.
    C. Cold-calling.
    D. Door hangers.

11. Plans for the real estate agent to knock on every door and personally visit each homeowner in his/her farm area in hopes of listing his/her property are called
    A. REO.
    B. Short sale farming.
    C. Door-to-door farming.
    D. Cold-call farming.

12. When the agent makes unsolicited phone calls in a certain neighborhood from a data base, it is called
    A. REO.
    B. Short sale farming.
    C. Door-to-door farming.
    D. Cold-call farming.

13. When a lender agrees to sell the property for less than the amount owed, it is called
    A. Short sale.
    B. REO.
    C. Farming.
    D. Inventory listing.

14. Properties that lenders have purchased at auction, which are being listed for sale by real estate agents
    A. Short sale
    B. REOs
    C. Loan modification
    D. Forbearance

CHAPTER 8
Prospecting for Sellers, Part II

Objectives:

Understand how to

- Meet For Sale by Owners' expectations
- Find and work with For Sale by Owners
- Meet and respond to sellers
- Prepare a CMA
- Overcome sellers' objections
- Make contact with FSBOs and the FSBO process

- Sell For Sale by Owners
- Service your listings
- Prepare a presentation
- Meet sellers' expectations
- Overcome commission issues

Understand why

- Some homeowners try to sell their property themselves
- For Sale by Owners should use real estate agents
- FSBOs have a short life span
- You should be aware of Internet websites that promote FSBOs.
- It is beneficial to have dual licenses: one in real estate, and one in mortgage lending

Terms:

- A.C.R.E.S
- Comparative market analysis (CMA)
- Drip campaign
- Financial Modernization Bill
- Mnemonic strategies
- S.U.R.E.

- Buddy system
- Discount real estate broker
- Expired MLS listings
- For Sale by Owner
- Presentation package/kits

Rules for Real Estate Success

Prospecting for Sellers – Part Two

1. Working with For sale by owners
2. How to build rapport and win over sellers
3. Overcoming sellers' objections
4. Serving your listings

For Sale by Owners

Working with For Sale by Owners is another form of prospecting. Because it is such a powerful lead generator, it deserves a chapter to itself. A **For Sale by Owner** is a property that is being sold by the homeowner without the assistance of a real estate agent. While working with FSBOs does have its problems, the rewards are plentiful.

Should you decide to work with For-Sale-by-Owners, there are three areas with which you should be concerned:

1. What you and For-Sale-by-Owners should expect from each other
2. How to find For-Sale-by-Owners
3. How to work with For-Sale-by-Owners

Why Home Owners Want to Avoid Using Real Estate Agents

There are many reasons that a homeowner may choose to sell his/her home without an agent. The most common reason is to save money by avoiding paying a real estate commission. Other owners don't mind the commission so much, but believe that the value of service they receive from the real estate agent doesn't justify the amount they must pay in commissions. They'd rather sell the home themselves than pay for an unjustified cost. Some homeowners believe that the fees real estate agents charge is a form of equity stripping. It takes approximately 9-10% of the home value to sell a home, while real estate agents charge around 6-10% for their services. On the average, over 80% of sellers' closing costs are the real estate agent's commission. Some sellers think that all a real estate agent does is put a sign in the front yard, include the property in the MLS® database, and process a minimal amount of paperwork. Most homeowners, however, know little about real estate laws or the selling process. Real estate agents do much more. They are trained in real estate sales, contracts, and a knowledgeable agent is usually able to save homeowners' money and a large degree of frustration. Below are the pros and cons of using a real estate agent.

FSBO vs. Using Real Estate Agents	
Why you Should Not Use a Real Estate Agent	**Why you Should Use a Real Estate Agent**
Homeowners can save approximately 6-10% in real estate fees.	Buyers are aware of the cost savings of not using a real estate agent. They often expect a lower price or splitting the commission cost. Real estate agents know that there are two kinds of buyers: those looking for a home and those looking for an investment. Investment buyers find FSBOs easy prey because most FSBOs believe they know the real estate system, but they actually don't. They usually don't have representation and usually don't know the value of their home. These investors are skillful at obtaining the information they need to take advantage of the FSBO. This is why FSBOs should never talk to any buyers. Where FSBOs attract the wrong kind of buyers, (investment buyers) real estate agents attract more of the correct kind of buyers.

The biggest reason that FSBO properties are not sold is that the owners are not able to determine the accurate value. Most FSBOs are priced too high. To determine property value, homeowners can hire an independent certified appraiser (approximate cost $350 for a full appraisal or much less for a partial). Since the appraiser works for the homeowner, not the lender, the homeowner can point out important details of the house for a more accurate value. Homeowners know their property better than anyone else. How can a real estate agent or anyone else look at a property and determine value amount in two minutes? It is likely they will miss key details. More importantly, the certified appraisal helps make the sale price and negotiations more objective in the decision making process. Real estate agents use CMAs that are more subjective, which can cause problems in the negotiations.

Realtors® use CMAs to find values; if the homeowners were to order an appraisal for the cost of $350, that appraisal would be good for 60 days, depending on the lender. Lenders are able to accept an appraisal report for up to 90 days, but rarely will lenders do so. If the property is not sold during the 60 days, an updated appraisal report may have to be ordered.

If the lender orders the appraisal, the appraiser must be independent and cannot talk to the homeowners. If there is financing, the lender will expect an appraisal, which is usually paid for by the buyers. The real estate agent or the loan officer can ask for a review of the appraisal only after the value is determined and only with hard facts.

Most homeowners have yet to learn the importance of staging.

Under new federal law, lenders cannot accept a Realtor's® CMA or a certified appraisal, unless it comes from a pool of appraisers. Another rule: lenders will accept the lower of the certified appraisal or sales price, regardless what the sellers' want or buyers are willing to pay. If the seller believes his/her property is worth more than the appraisal, he/she will have to protest the value.

Presenting buyers with a certified appraisal would make negotiations much easier. It would also remove the fear of buyers thinking they are paying too much for the property. Most buyers don't understand lenders' rules on accepting property value. By knowing the appraised value, sellers can share the saving with buyers for a faster sale. In this case, it would be a win-win for buyers and sellers.

Using a loan officer to qualify prospects allows homeowners to save time and money showing the property. Homeowners can make pre-qualifications or pre-approve a requirement for all interested prospects, helping to avoid a violation of the fair housing laws. Prequalification is estimating the range of housing the buyers can afford. Pre-approval is verifying the buyer's income, credit scores, debt ratios, and the exact amount of housing loan buyers can afford.

Homeowners don't understand that they are the biggest mental block that buyers have to overcome. The rule is buyers should *NEVER* meet the sellers until closing. Buyers don't need any interruptions in emotionally connecting and mentally moving into the house.

Most homeowners will talk buyers out of making an offer. Buyers are mentally trying to move into the house, while sellers are talking about happy times and are creating a mental block for buyers.

More often than not, emotional decisions in business are poor decisions.

Using loan officers is an excellent way to screen-out candidates, such as serious buyers as opposed to onlookers. Loan officers are better able to screen prospects than real estate agents. Loan officers can order credit reports, tax returns, housing history, and check employment history. Where real estate agents lack the tools to carefully screen unwanted elements, loan officers are paid by buyers, not sellers.	Whenever homeowners decide to personally sell the property, they are exposing themselves to unknown elements. How would a homeowner know which person is 'puffing' or who will bring harm to his/her family? Agents are better able to pre-qualify buyers.
When should required disclosure forms be used? In this area, homeowners may seek a real estate professional in contracts, federal, and state-required disclosures. At this point, homeowners have already found qualified buyers and only need real estate agents to meet contract, federal, and state requirements. Since the seller has done most of the real estate agent's work, why not negotiate the commission. After all, there is much less work and only one agent to pay versus two brokerages.	When selling a house, there are federal and state disclosures and penalties for not making the required disclosures.
Homeowners can post flyers just as real estate agents do. They can also leave messages on time-rented phone numbers, hire answering services, post websites and have the loan officer pre-qualify borrowers.	Prospects will call all hours of the day, seven days a week. Agents sell 24 hours a day. Agents have a system of showing properties. How are sellers going to show their property when they are at work? How do sellers recognize serious buyers?
Most serious buyers already have mortgage funding sources. If not, homeowners can interview different mortgage lenders for rates, products, services, and helpful information.	Real estate agents have already found the best of the best in loan officers who can offer the best rates, products, and services.

Using technology to find buyers is becoming easier for sellers. Why pay a real estate company to find buyers when there are several tools available for sellers? There are companies that will market the property, list the property for sale, and even provide material and training for For Sale by Owners. These companies can have a real estate broker available who can give advice at a discount and write contracts for a fee. A **discount real estate broker** is a brokerage firm that offers services at a discount price or accepts a lower or no fee.

Realtors® have a powerful tool called MLS® which gives the property maximum exposure to other Realtors®. This is the biggest advantage Realtors® have. Most Realtors® will also list on other websites. The most commonly used website is MLS®, regardless of the hundreds of other websites.

Only a Realtor® can list property for sale in Multi-Listing Services (MLS). For a flat fee of $400-$500 a Realtor® can post the property for other Realtors® to view. In MLS, homeowners can post what, if any, commission they are willing to pay.

Agents are more objective negotiators. Real estate agents are trained to handle problems that often occur after the contract has been signed. How about property inspections and buyers not qualifying? How are possession issues, earnest money refunds and repairs being handled if the property does not appraise? The list of things that could prevent a closing is a long one. Here is where real estate agents earn their fees.

Prospecting for Sellers, Part II

Finding For Sale by Owners

Make finding FSBOs a part of your business plans, and schedule daily and weekly time slots to research new FSBOs in the area in which you plan to work. Personal visits are best during evenings.

Any home that has a FSBO sign in its yard must also disclose any ownership affiliation to a licensed real estate agent by stating Owner/Realtor®. Real estate agents must always disclose if they are the sellers or if they have an ownership interest in the property. Therefore, if the sign does not state any real estate ownership, go ahead and knock on the door and give the owners your best script.

Ask your friends and family to look for FSBOs, and call the homeowners as soon as possible. Explain to your friends and family how beneficial finding FSBOs is to your career. There is no monetary compensation of any kind for your friends or family for helping you find FSBOs, a RESPA rule. However, they should do it because they want you to reach your goals and to succeed. Of-course, you can always drive around looking for FSBOs. Gas is expensive, so every time you drive home or to a location, start early and take a different route.

Websites that Promote "For Sale by Owners"

Below is a partial list of websites that advertise "For Sale by Owners," and the list is growing. Today there are over 100 such sites. There isn't any reason why you can't develop your own For Sale by Owners website and link it your main web page. The cost to design a For Sale by Owners website and link it to your homepage is not expensive compared to other marketing ideas. Meet with web designers for price and services. You can even offer homeowners an FSBO space on your website for a fee. There isn't any reason why you can't have information links on your website for FSBOs. Real estate websites are as follows:

- owners.com
- trulia.com
- oodle.com
- cyberhomes.com
- therealestatebook.com
- featureyourlistings.com
- propsmart.com
- livedeal.com
- vast.com
- edgeio.com
- rentspider.com
- finehomerentals.com
- allspaces.com
- fsbocentral.com
- fsbofreedom.com
- buyowner.com
- 2buyhomes.net
- realestate.yahoo.com
- forsalebyowner.com
- byownersales.com
- 4salebyowner.com
- house.com
- abetterfsbo.com
- homes.com
- realtyfeeds.com
- ehouseads.com
- ahome4sale

- justlisted.com
- realpropdeals.com
- backpage.com
- local.com
- zillow.com

FSBOs in Newspapers

Newspapers are filled with For Sale by Owners. The rule for most states is that real estate agents must identify themselves in all advertisements; therefore, all ads that do not have the agent's name or the company's name are For Sale by Owners. To find FSBOs, look in your local newspaper (s) that list properties in your area. The ad will either have a phone number or address. You will find that there are hundreds of FSBOs available.

FSBO Process

Working with FSBOs is a process, and you will need an action plan. Like any process, it will take some time to work. Don't expect to knock on doors, give your best speech, and walk away with a listing. You must first build rapport and trust. Make several visits while not wearing-out your welcome.

Try introducing yourself by saying pleasant things about their property. Offer to give homeowners helpful educational information. Stay in contact with sellers. It may take several visits, letters, and post cards. Keep records on which letters, postcards, and educational information you have sent.

Keep notes on conversations. Keep dialogues positive. Never make negative remarks about what the sellers are doing. For example, if their property needs cleaning, don't say *"If your property were cleaner, it would sell"*, instead say, *"Property staging does take a lot of work, but it will bring better offers and a quicker sale."*

Never act as a salesperson with a bad out-of-date sales pitch but more of a real estate consultant for their real estate needs, using rich and engaging scripts. Ask homeowners if you can help sell their property by taking pictures, giving suggestions, and adding their property to your website to give your FSBO better exposure. After adding their property to your website, give the homeowners your web address. Explain how beneficial it is to pre-qualify all prospects before letting them into the house. If they sell their home without your listing their property, they will not forget your services. They will remember you and refer their contacts to you, but most likely, they will not sell the house on their own, and you will be the first on their list to call.

Making Contact with FSBOs

Many agents are unsuccessful with FSBOs. This is because they fail to realize that working with FSBOs is the same as working with listings. It is a process. It is rare that on the first visit, if you knock on a FSBO's door that you will have the chance to talk the seller(s) into letting you list their property. Usually, this type of prospecting will yield you a high rejection rate. If you desire to be a successful listing agent, remember it will take several letters, calls, emails and personal visits to win FSBOs. Nevertheless, usually they will eventually decide to use an agent, and you want to be there when opportunity presents itself. If you are driving in the neighborhood, and you see a For Sale by Owner sign, you cannot be afraid to knock on the door. Knocking on doors brings fear because most agents are not sure what to say, have fears of rejection, and they don't feel that they have a compelling reason to be there. As discussed in Chapter 1 and 5, if you plan to door knock, you must have scripts to the most commonly asked questions or objections and know what questions to ask.

FSBO Scripts

Below is a three-step example in making contact:

- Have preprinted letters for first, second, and third contacts
- Make your phone calls
- Wait a few days and knock on their door

Below is an example of a FSBO script:

"Hi, good afternoon, I'm Joe Smith with ABC Realty. I noticed your For Sale by Owner sign, and I would like to ask you a few questions."

The most common FSBO objections/remarks are

- *No, Thank You!*
- *We don't work with realtors!*
- *Are you MAD? Can't you read the sign? It reads, For Sale by Owner!*
- *We are not paying a commission.*
- *We don't need your help.*
- *Why would we use you?*
- *Go away; you're bothering us.*
- *We are selling it ourselves.*
- *We have a Realtor® friend that will help us.*
- *You guys charge too much.*
- *I'm looking for a company to list my property on MLS for a small fee.*

Rules for Real Estate Success

The second step is to try to preview the property by showing your concerns and telling FSBOs what they want to hear. At this point give no opinion, but ask questions to start a dialogue and get the information you need. If you can't get an appointment, get their email by offering to provide free marketing material, CMA, or a sellers' net sheet.

Examples on how to handle objections are as follows:

"I understand, I just wanted to say that we have qualified buyers in your area and wanted to know if I could preview your property to see if we have a match, and if I bring you a buyer, would you co-op?"

Most FSBOs are willing to pay a selling fee to the agent who brings a buyer, but are trying to save the listing fee. FSBOs usually don't understand the services they are losing just to save half of the commission. In your approach, first you must agree and next, clearly state the benefit to the homeowner. Ask open-ended questions to start an engaging dialogue.

"I understand, I'm only offering my card in case you need some quick, free information from a professional in your area."

"I just wanted to let you know that we have free homeowners' packages which consist of ..."

"I understand. Would you be open-minded and give me the opportunity to show you how I can help you get the greatest return for your home?"

"Good, yes, I agree. Have you considered a backup plan?"

"Yes, you have a valid reason, and I would like to help. If you can give me a few minutes, I will show the recent statistics to you."

Next, your prospect may ask:

"Do you have a buyer for my house?"
"When can you bring those buyers?"

Your response should be:

"I won't know until I preview your home."
or
"Great, I will be in your area tomorrow. How does 5:00 p.m. sound?"

The third step is to build rapport. Here, the sellers must know you are on their team, that you are joining forces. Depending on your response, the best way to start a dialogue is to ask questions. Asking questions works exceedingly well when you cannot think of any scripts/words to use. For example, once you have previewed the property and have the homeowners' attention, turn the conversation to the sellers' interest. Say, *"Nice home, why are you selling?"* If you are working with an expired listing, you can say, *"WOW, you have a nice home! Now I'm confused, so why do you think it didn't sell?"* Homeowners will recognize you are on their side. Go over standard rules, such as why sellers and buyers should never meet. Next, try to set-up a mail or e-mail follow-up system. They may not be ready to sell now, but when they do decide to use a real estate agent, by using your drip campaign, you will be the first in their mind. **Drip campaign** means to put your contacts on a regular mail-out list. Be honest about what you say to sellers. Most agents do know of several buyers or expect to have buyers, especially in their farm area.

Sellers' smaller objections are as follows:

"My house is not ready."
Your reply: *"Great that I caught you in time. Getting your home ready takes a considerable amount of work. To save you time, money, and frustration, I would like to share many of my short cuts."*

"We'll think about it."
Your reply: *"Yes, that is a big decision; I'll call you in two days in case you make an early decision."*

Questions to Start a Dialogue are as follows:

- *When you were looking at houses, what attracted you to your home?*
- *What are important factors in your home?*
- *Tell me what you like about this neighborhood.*
- *Have you selected a new home?*
- *What are decisive factors in selling your home?*
- *Is there a price you are looking for, and how did you determine the price?*
- *Is there a moving date?*
- *Have you spoken to other agents?*
- *How would you describe your home?*
- *Do you have a goal in mind?*
- *If I were to do an excellent job selling your home, would you refer me to your friends?*
- *Can I help with staging ideas?*

An example of the values you can offer to For Sale by Owners:

Values I Owe to My Client

- I know what it will take to sell your home, and I will do my best to sell your home for the highest possible price.
- I will place your property on MLS to give your property the greatest exposure possible.
- I will help you determine the highest value of your property by using a Realtors® CMA and/or assist the appraiser who will work with you and not the lender/buyer. In this way, you will be able to point out notable details for an accurate value. A lender's rule is that it will accept the lower of sales price or appraised value and not a penny more. An appraisal will also help buyers make realistic offers.
- I am trained to follow state and federal laws regarding real estate contracts and disclosures. I am a trained negotiator who will help you get the best possible price.
- I will be here to clearly explain the real estate process.
- I will open title as soon as possible. Title policies are paid at closings and will remove any buyer's doubt to the quality of your title.
- I will show you how to stage your property to sell it for the greatest amount of money. Property staging is preparing the property for the maximum appeal for the fewest dollars. The goal is to help buyers visualize themselves in family rooms: cooking, playing with their kids, having family moments or inviting guess for parties. A well-staged home suggests the property is well kept and free from repairs. There are many tricks and rules on staging, which I will show you. A well-staged home will bring greater offers and a quicker sale.
- I will advise you in attracting more buyers by using the best curb appeal, such as fertilizing and tidying the yard, trimming any bushes that may block natural lighting from entering rooms, and much more. Curb appeal is the first and only chance to make a first impression. Buyers are eliminating as many properties as they can, by judging a book by its cover.
- I will be here to help you avoid the biggest mistake homeowners make, and that is showing the property themselves. You know more about the property than anyone else, but that is the problem: giving too much unwanted information. Buyers meeting homeowners is the main distraction for buyers who are trying to mentally move into your home. A major mental block for many buyers is the presence of the homeowners.
- I am here to help with the most important rule, which is to keep your family safe. As a FSBO, you don't know who wants to bring your family harm. Real estate is showing your home to strangers. I will screen all my buyers, and I will expect the same from fellow agents.

- I will walk your neighborhood, doing door-to-door sales.
- I will design flyers and broadcast your flyers to all my buyer contacts.
- I will call people in your community about your beautiful home.
- I will spend my weekend promoting your home with open houses.
- I will mail out postcards to nearby communities about your home.
- I will place at least two advertising ads in the local newspaper.
- I will keep you updated on anything that pertains to your home.
- I will avoid the problem of buyers wanting to share the real estate commission.
- I will place real estate signs, lockboxes, and information boxes to help sell your home.
- I will follow-up with buyers to make sure we are closing.
- I will make sure we do not miss valuable calls about your home. We have a staff of people trained to answer phone calls.
- I will place your property on my company website. My company has advanced software technology to market your property.

The Seven Rules of Conduct I Owe You

Fidelity: I will always place your interest above my interest and all others.

Obedience: I will always be obedient to you within the law.

Loyalty: I will unconditionally be loyal to you at all times.

Disclosure: I promise never to share any of your information unless I have your permission.

Confidentiality: I promise to inform you of all relevant issues concerning your property, and I will protect all confidential information.

Accountability: I promise I will earn your trust with the handling and care of your home.

Reasonable Care and Diligence: I pledge to do my best to be informed on market conditions and to be knowledgeable of real estate matters and to communicate all important issues to you as soon as possible.

Name: Date:

FSBOs will have a difficult time selling their property because: 1. They lack the knowledge of how to qualify buyers. 2. Unable to handle the financial part of real estate. 3. Unable to correctly price the property. 4. Lack the marketing exposure to sell their property. 5. Fail to realize how buyers shop. 6. Most importantly, they fail to understand that using a professional agent is an investment.

The use of "For Sale by Owner" signs can create a steady stream of prospects. Agents should start looking for "For Sale by Owner" signs and ask friends and relatives to report any such signs. Developing flyers with loan information is a good marketing strategy. However, loan officers cannot advertise real estate property without a real estate license.

What many agents do is design letters for For Sale by Owners and have a constant stack of envelopes with letters available while driving, looking for FSBOs.

Should you decide to work with FSBOs, you must have a system in place to make daily mail-outs. Whenever you are driving and find a FSBO, write the address on the envelope. Place your letter on the door, if possible, or mail it. Keep records of which properties you mailed letters to. As previously mentioned, working with FSBOs is a process; it will take several letters, postcards, and personal meetings to win their trust. Remember the Benefit Rule — when the homeowner finally realizes that they will benefit more by using you over the money they could save, they will start calling, and you will be the first on their list. Depending on the neighborhood, these letters should be pre-designed and stamped so you need only to add the address. You can always have a second or third letter in case you don't get a reply. The second and third letters should have different information to catch the homeowners' attention.

Using Educational Information to Gain Trust

Sellers want help without having to pay for it or having to pay a reasonable price. The free information package you are willing to give to FSBOs can be titled the following:

- How to Stage their Property
- Sellers' Net Sheet
- Buyers' Net Sheet
- Tips for FSBOs
- HUD's Homebuyers' Information
- How to Know if Buyers are Ready
- How to Determine the Monthly Payments

Prospecting for Sellers, Part II

- Sellers' Disclosure Information
- How FSBOs can Protect Themselves
- Protecting Your Home from Bad People who Prey on FSBOs.
- Fair Housing Act
- How to Determine the Value of Your Home
- Comparative Market Analysis, CMA
- Your Contact Information

The free information that you can give FSBOs is almost endless. For the FSBO who is hard to get a response from, have a system in place, such as letter one, "The Intro Letter," letter two, letter three, and so on. You will also need to select what software you will use, such as Excel, and plan how you will keep-up with all of your FSBOs.

When You Should Walk Away

Be selective when working with FSBOs. While FSBOs can provide ample leads, be careful in deciding which FSBO to represent. In this business, your time is very important, so you will have to make a decision if you are willing to spend the time to work with FSBOs. After all, it's your name and career at stake. If the property is extremely overpriced and the homeowner is unrealistic about dropping the price, after you have made your best presentation, it is much better to walk away. Also, if the property has had a FSBO sign over eight months, and the owners are not willing to advertise, drop the price, or let you put it on MLS, walk away. If you don't, other prospects will start associating your name with unrealistically priced homes, which is not a smart career builder.

Working with FSBOs does work, but it has a limited shelf life. As soon as owners place a sign on their property, they will get several calls. If the property is at or below market value, they will have a sale. However, most are overpriced. After a while, the calls dry-up because most FSBOs lack the exposure. It's important to talk to homeowners who are selling their home as soon as possible. The longer the property is an FSBO, the harder the effort to sell becomes. Ask homeowners why they decided to sell. If they do not provide a valid reason, think about walking away.

FSBOs require the same or more attention than regular MLS listings. Bring out the signs, flags, open house signs, and flyers. Plan your open houses, have the property staged, and go all out. Build your inventory of prospects. There is no reason why you can't help FSBOs with open houses; however, have formal agreements before you help with any open houses.

A key note: There are five problems which can occur when dealing with "For Sale by Owners:" (1) the telemarketing sales rule, (2) selling real estate without a license, (3) limited property exposure to buyers, (4) the client-customer-broker relationship, and (5) the homeowner may not be motivated to sell.

Keeping it Ethical

Loan officers should be very careful when helping owners sell their property. Only real estate agents are allowed to sell real estate for another and for a fee or consideration. For example, in Texas under the Texas Real Estate License Act, (Sect 1, (b) it is unlawful for a person to act in the capacity of, engage in the business of, advertise or hold that person out as engaging in or conducting the business of a real estate broker or a real estate salesperson within this state without first obtaining a real estate license from the State Real Estate Commission. It is unlawful for a person licensed as a real estate salesperson to act or attempt to act as a real estate broker or salesperson unless that person is, at such time, associated with a licensed real estate broker and acting for the real estate broker.

A real estate broker is a person who, for *another person* and *for a fee*, commission, or other valuable consideration, or with the intention, the expectation or the promise of receiving or collecting a fee or commission and other valuable consideration from another person of the following:

- Sells, exchanges, purchases, rents, or leases real estate
- Offers to sell, exchange, purchase, rent, or lease real estate
- Negotiates or attempts to negotiate the listing, sale, exchange or purchase of real estate
- Lists, offers, attempts or agrees to list real estate
- Appraises, offers, attempts or agrees to appraise real estate
- Purchases, sells, offers to buy or sell, or otherwise deals in options on real estate
- Aids, attempts, or offers to aid in locating or obtaining for purchase, rent, or lease real estate
- Procures or assists in the procuring of prospects for the purpose of effecting the sale
- Exchange, lease, or rental of real estate procures or assists in the procuring of properties for the purpose of effecting the sale, exchange, lease, rental of real estate.

FSBO Limitations

Working with For Sale by Owners has its limits. The rule is, "*The greater the exposure, the greater the sale.*" For Sale by Owners lacks the exposure that Realtors® give to MLS properties. As a matter of fact, over 80% of buyers who use the MLS system have better results over For-sale-by-owner websites. When owners stop advertising and the neighbors have already called about the property, calls will soon dry up.

The Buddy System

The **Buddy System** has been around for hundreds of years. It has all kinds of names, but the basic principle is the same. For example, in real estate, two agents team up to work with FSBOs. Each partner makes a list of all their FSBOs, call them, keep careful notes, and then switch lists. Partner number two then calls the other partner's list. If the FSBO says that someone from your office already called, the partner says, "*That had to have been John. I'm sorry to have called. John is a true professional and you couldn't have a better agent. Would you like for John to give you a call?*" The partner's job is to reconfirm that they should use John. Well, this could be unethical; no one likes to be set-up. This is short of a con-game. If you are going to play the buddy game, do it honestly; don't set-up the homeowners just for a sale. Be honest. Say "*Yes, that was John who called you last week; John has asked me to follow-up to see if there is anything we may help you with.*"

Build a trusting relationship, and be honest so that when the owner decides to use a real estate agent, you will be the first and only person being considered for the job. FSBOs will tell other FSBOs, family, co-workers and friends, not to mention all of those prospects who called, about your services,. Soon, your FSBOs will start telling you that their next-door neighbor wants to talk to you or that their sister is looking for a house.

Working with FSBOs is a smart way for new agents to build an inventory of buyers. Below are tips you can pass on to your FSBOs.

Tips for Homeowners

1. Have the property appraised or get three CMAs by Realtors® before placing the property for sale. Since the appraiser works for you, the lender/ buyer, you will be able to point out important details for an accurate value. A lender's rule is that it will accept the lower of the sales price or appraise value and not a penny more. An appraisal will also help buyers make realistic offers.
2. Check with your state laws or a real estate agent for the required real estate contracts.
3. Have a real estate agent or attorney review all contracts. A badly written contract may have legal complications.
4. Open title as soon as possible. Title policies are paid at closings. Remove any buyer's doubt about the quality of the title.

5. Talk to a real estate agent or an interior decorator on how to stage the property to sell for the greatest dollars. Property staging is preparing the property for the maximum appeal for the fewest dollars. The goal is to help buyers visualize themselves relaxing in family rooms, cooking, playing with their kids, having family moments, or inviting guess for parties. A well-staged home suggests the property is well kept and free from repairs. There are many tricks and rules on staging; talk to a professional. A well-staged home will bring greater offers and a quicker sale.

6. Remove and pack anything that is personal, such as pictures, sport team logos, valuables, and medicines. A real estate rule when working with buyers is *"Buyers will never buy unless they can first mentally move in the property."* How can buyers mentally move into the property if personal items are blocking or distracting the buyers?

7. Start preparing for curb appeal. Fertilize and tidy the yard; trim any bushes that may block natural lighting from entering rooms. Curb appeal is the first and only chance to make a first favorable impression. Buyers are eliminating as many properties as they can by judging a book by its cover.

8. Start airing out your home. Another real estate rule is "If your buyers can smell it, you're not going to sell it." Pets are also a huge distraction. Some people may have allergies and may be intimidated by barking dogs. Think about finding a home for your pets until the property is sold.

9. Get a home inspection. Repair as many items as possible. Properties that need many repairs will lead buyers to think the property has other hidden problems. The number one reason for buyers' remorse is potential problems.

10. Get the facts, and have a list of all homes sold in your area so that buyers may compare.

11. Do not show the property yourself. Have a friend, neighbor or even a real estate agent show your property. You know more about the property than anyone else, but the problem is giving too much information, for example, how you and your family had wonderful holidays or how the kids decided to paint their rooms a certain color. You are the main distraction for buyers' mentally trying to move into your home. A major mental block for many buyers is the presence of the homeowner, this could be a deal killer. Often, when prospects are unable to mentally move in they will switch from a homebuyer to an investment buyer. They will search for reasons to pay a lower price. But, once prospects have mentally moved-in, the home becomes priceless. Now, the focus is more about their comfort and family happiness. They are not buying a house but a home.

12. The most important rule is protecting your family. You don't know who wants to bring harm to your family. Be careful about showing your home to strangers. Have buyers prequalified by a Realtor® or a mortgage lender.

Building Rapport and Winning Sellers

Meeting with Sellers

Rules for Real Estate Success

Meetings with sellers are usually conducted in two parts, sometimes three. If the sellers are ready to sign, however, take their signature. If sellers have heard about you or have noticed your listings or the massive amount of open house signs, you don't need to convince them of your performance. They are ready for you to put your sign in the front yard. If rapport and trust is missing, you should expect to have a two-part listing process: gathering information and building trust, followed by the presentation, to win your prospects and overcome their objections.

You will need to prepare a presentation package soon after you have scheduled an appointment with the sellers. Here is your last chance to win over the sellers. Like most people, sellers want complete honesty, but they also want assurance that you are capable of completing the job in the quickest amount of time and in the most profitable terms to them. They also want to understand how real estate works and the steps you will take to sell their property. Their judgment of you starts the moment you walk into the room.

Before meeting with prospective sellers, be aware of their biggest concerns so that you can prepare a custom package tailored to their major concerns. Few listings are gained with having one meeting; mostly it is a two-part process. The reason for two meetings is to find what sellers are concerned with and develop a plan to overcome their concerns. As discussed in Chapter 5, the presentation will help do the following:

- Organize your thoughts
- Control the conversation
- Overcome sellers' objections
- Meet the sellers' expectations
- Be sure valuable information is not omitted
- Interact with sellers so they will remember your presentation

Ask as many questions as possible to determine what concerns homeowners' have. Now you have the time to research solutions to overcome their objections, giving you the time you need to research and plan or to ask for guidance from your broker and office managers. Homeowners' biggest concerns are from the list below:

- Price
- The cost of selling their home
- Whether or not you can sell the property
- The length of time it will take to sell their home

- Market conditions
- Understanding real estate
- The marketing plan that you will use
- Whether or not you are the right person for the job
- Safety

Interactive Presentations

The more senses you can stimulate using your presentation, the more information your audience will remember for a longer period of time. School teachers use different mnemonic strategies, depending on the subject. **Mnemonic strategies** are employed to facilitate learning by creating connections where the connection is not immediately obvious to the learner. Teachers have a saying for young students, *"Tell me and I'll forget, show me and I'll remember, but involve me and I'll understand."* For the most common objections, have at least two analogies or metaphors to which a seller can identify or relate. A **metaphor** is a figure of speech using a word or phrase that denotes a certain object or idea that is applied to another word or phrase to imply some similarity between them. (An analogy is telling a story to show the similarity between two ideas that are different.) An example of a dollar analogy is to show the sellers two dollars, one old and dirty, and the other a fresh clean crisp dollar. Ask the sellers to pick one, and they will pick the new dollar bill. Why? They are worth the same. Well, buyers will do the same: pick the fresher home. The more interaction and stimulation you have with sellers using analogies or metaphors, the more they will remember your presentation.

Mastering the Presentation

Your **presentation package** should be as visual as possible, using pictures, graphs, and charts with the intent of stimulating the sellers' senses. The cover information should be about your company followed by information about you. The only reason seller(s) want information about you is to confirm that you are the right agent to sell their property. Briefly list your credentials. Keep your presentation under 30 minutes. Your presentation kit can be in a binder, as a PowerPoint presentation, or a web video of you presenting the information, or even web links. Most laptops can project images onto newer televisions. Brokers have meeting rooms where you can use an LCD television for your presentations. The tool you use for your presentation should be the one you feel has the best chance of interaction with sellers. For example, in PowerPoint, you can only go backward or forward, but using web links or a binder can take the sellers to any topic. While most brokerage firms have built custom presentation packages, not all firms have. Below are suggestions to include in your presentation package:

- Customize the title page with your seller(s)' name and information and include your unique selling proposition. Go early to take pictures from the outside to include them on the first page.
- A signed copy of a company letter on Code of Ethics similar to the National Association of Realtors®
- Information about brokerage services
- Names of satisfied homeowners and testimonial letters
- List of degrees and designations with a brief description of each
- Facts that will set you apart, such as your annual sales volume, percentage of your listings that were sold, listing-to-sales ratio compared to the average ratio, and percentage of the time your listings were on the market compared to the average listing
- Letter explaining all of the real estate steps and the process
- Information about their neighborhood
- Marketing, staging, and open house plans with a copy of some of your past ads
- List of sellers' most common objections and how you will overcome them
- Using as many pictures and graphics as possible, since people remember visuals before text
- Pictures of your office so that your sellers will identify with you, like a character in a movie
- Pictures of your receiving significant awards, especially if it will help your client
- Pictures of you in front of sold signs on sold listings.
- Pictures of what the subject area is known for; your prospects will feel comfortable if you are familiar with the area
- Listing agreement/Sellers' disclosures
- Colorful pictures of their property, used for suggesting improvements and showing how to stage it
- Comparative market analysis with photos of recently sold homes in the neighborhood
- Your personal agreements/Contact information

Preparing the Presentation Kit

Since the presentation will largely determine the flow of the meeting, it's important to be well prepared. Ask the homeowners for a time. An example is, *"Hello, Ms. Smith, I'm available on Friday at 5:30 p.m. and also on Saturday at noon."* Be sure to give the homeowners plenty of time to prepare or clean the property, maybe a day or two. If they need more time, this tells you four things:

- They are planning to work hard to impress you—they have plenty of cleaning to do.
- They have a busy schedule.

- They don't have a pressing need to sell.
- They may be talking with other agents.

If you try to set-up the appointment on the same day, you may get a negative reply. Don't be surprised what busy people's homes look like.

It is easier for homeowners to say yes if you set a time and date in advance. You will also need the extra time for your research. Check what other properties are selling for in the same area. Visit the neighborhood, see what other properties look like, and check for any For-Sale-by-Owners. Take pictures and ask other FSBOs their prices. This is an excellent way to meet FSBOs. They may be thinking about using an agent themselves. Check your MLS for listed, sold, and expired listings.

Tell the owners you would like to look at the outside first during your visit to give them time to clear last-minute things in case they have forgotten about you. Start taking notes and walk around the property. Look for ideas that will give the best curb appeal. Ask the homeowners about any improvements they have made since the purchase. Ask about the unique architectural features the house has and what they like about their home. Ask why they decided to buy the house, why are they selling, and if there is a selling price they have in mind. Gather the information for an accurate CMA, and ask for a return visit.

Pricing, Comparative Market Analysis (CMA)

Accurately pricing a property is important. The best way to accurately price the property is to use a **comparative market analysis, (CMA)**. Never use round prices; give the exact price. This shows accuracy. If the property is outside your area, try to arrive a day early, view what other similar properties have sold for, what listings have expired, and what listings are active. Fully understanding how to prepare a CMA is important. Your CMA should be as accurate as possible. Start a day early, ask homeowners' questions about their home, and use an actual listing sheet for questions. Take as many notes as possible; show the homeowners that you are gathering information in order to acquire the most accurate CMA possible. All homeowners want the highest price for their home, but some homeowners are unrealistic about the value of their home. For unrealistic homeowners, you need to explain that all lenders will order an appraisal before deciding to loan on the property and will never loan above appraised value. Below are reasons for not overpricing properties:

- First, even if the buyer were to offer the seller's price, the lender may not approve the loan.
- Secondly, the best chance to sell the property is in the beginning of the listing period. If the property is overpriced, it will drive away many genuine buyers.

- Thirdly, other agents will use the overpriced home to help sell other homes. For example, they will show the overpriced home first rather than show an equally compatible home for far less money.
- Fourth, the longer a home is on the market, the more neighbors will start wondering what is wrong with the home or the listing company.
- Fifth, it is a considerable amount of work for the sellers to maintain their home in showing condition. Sellers will soon tire and start thinking they have made a mistake by hiring the wrong agent.
- Sixth, often if the property is on the market for a considerable time, then it must be the agent who is not doing his/her job. The homeowners will start questioning the agent's duties. If the sellers are still unwilling to accurately price or to maintain the property, it is far better to thank the homeowners and walk away. As discussed in earlier chapters, listing overpriced properties can damage the real estate agent's career.
- Using a CMA is a real estate agent's way of accurately pricing the property without a charge. Most appraisers charge around $350 per property, and appraisals are good for only 45-60 days, depending on the lender. Since agents will use the same data appraisers use, most CMAs are accurate.
- To knowingly take an overpriced listing in hopes of later having the sellers reduce their asking price is unethical. The agent should be upfront; be honest about the listing price and the fact that the property may have to be reduced after a certain date. One of the agent's duties is honesty to his/her client.

If the sellers are still unrealistic after presenting the hard facts, suggest ordering an informal appraisal. Since the appraiser will work for the seller and not the lender, sellers are able to point out what they believe the value of their property is, and the appraiser's report will show the true value to the sellers and how the value was determined. Under new law, the lender or the agents can no longer pick the appraiser for a federal loan. The homeowner or the agent can pick the appraiser when a buyer is not trying to get a loan; however, the lender cannot use that appraisal.

When your CMA is ready for presentation, usually homeowners will want to know the price the moment you walk in the house. If you decide to give the suggested price, the battle is on; the remaining conversation will be defending the suggested price; therefore never argue with clients. Lay out your strategy for the appropriate time to give the suggested price. First, go over the CMA, showing the comparables. Make sure to personally visit each comparable. You should use only a handful (three-five comparables). The last thing in any presentation is price. The real estate rule is to show value before price.

Sellers Understanding **Real Estate (S.U.R.E)** means to an agent that you will surely get paid if you understand real estate rules. Buyers and sellers often slow down negotiations or withdraw because they do not understand how the real estate procedure works. Include the step-by-step process and how it works in your presentation package. Schedule enough time to explain the listing agreement, contracts, disclosures, marketing, and what they should expect from you, what you expect from them, and information on title closing. The special information booklet design from HUD details the real estate process for the sellers and buyers in English and Spanish. Be sure to leave copies with sellers. Explain safety measures, lockboxes, property tours, and open houses.

Marketing Plans

Homeowners will want to know how you plan to market and sell their property. If you have research, include it in your presentation kit. Include letters, post cards, ads, websites, broadcasting and examples of *MLS®* listings that you will use. If you plan to do door-to-door farming, explain how and when you will do this. If you plan to e-mail flyers to every agent, explain when and how many agents you will e-mail. Sellers do not want an agent to be vague on the plan to sell their home. They want the agent to have a clear vision on the steps he/she will take. The better you are able to explain the process, the more confidence they will have in you.

Ask your sellers how they would like to communicate. Would they prefer to communicate by Internet, phone calls, or by blog? If by phone, what part of the day would be best to call? During the listing period, keep an activity log book, and update your homeowners on a weekly basis.

Selecting the Right Real Estate Agent

Homeowners who have close contact with their agent have developed a sense of trust and will probably use the same agent. However, many agents will forget their clients, and these homeowners will be searching for a new agent. All homeowners have mixed feelings about their past agent(s). For example, if their past agent(s) failed to provide updates, having updates will be a major concern for homeowners. If they believe their former agent(s) failed to get the best price, their concern will be how you will get top dollar for their property. In the first meeting, ask seller(s) if they have sold a house in the past, what experiences they have had with real estate agents, and why they are selling. The goal is to find out what homeowners want and expect from their agent. If updates are important, bring it up during the presentation. If they are selling because they would like a larger home, then have information about larger homes

Prospecting for Sellers, Part II

in the area they prefer. The more initial information you gather, the better you will be able to overcome homeowners' objections.

Code of Ethics and Information about Brokerage Services

The National Association of Realtors and state associations have written codes of ethics. It is a good idea to download copies for your homeowners so that they will know about the strict code of ethics for Realtors®. Knowing that you are a professional and that you must abide by such a strict code of ethics may ease many of your homeowners' worries. You may even sign the code of ethics to show how serious you are.

Remaining Ethical and Focusing on Clients

Listing agents often start asking buyers financial questions in order to protect their client. The **Financial Modernization Bill of 1999**, also known as the Gramm-Leach-Bliley Act, protects individuals from having their financial information disclosed. The act states that you must have permission to inquire about an individual's financial status, and it restricts you from sharing a person's financial history. The Fair Credit Reporting Act (FCRA) and state agency laws also protect consumers. The FCR Act was designed to protect consumer credit privacy from both credit reporting agencies and from individuals who handle consumer reports. Anyone who provides credit information to another is considered to be a consumer reporting agency – including real estate agents, so most lenders are reluctant to allow others to view the consumer's report. Individuals should provide only direct knowledge to a third party.

Overcoming Sellers' Objections

Preparing for Overcoming Objections

Nearly all sellers will have some form of objection. In fact, most inexperienced real estate agents unknowingly create the opportunity for objections by asking the wrong type of questions and/or not being prepared to respond to common objections. Overcoming and handling objections are not the same. Overcoming objections is being prepared with the right scripts in order to respond to the majority of objections. The best way to eliminate an objection is to address it before sellers bring it up, then wait for sellers to bring it up, and have your script ready; this is overcoming an objection. Lack of preparedness to overcome the seller's objections will probably cause you to lose your opportunity. That is why the best you can do is to learn how to handle the objection. Below are the most common objections you will encounter, which you should be fully prepared to respond to:

- Honesty and loyalty
- Selecting the right real estate agent, (why should they pick you?)
- Cost of the sale, including your commission
- Overpricing of the home
- Condition of the home and the economy
- Understanding how real estate works, the unknown

Handling Sellers' Objections

Once your prospects voice their objection, it may be too late to overcome it; at this point you need to learn how to handle the objection. There is a simple rule whenever you encounter an unknown objection. This rule is called ACRES. To gain ground on your prospects, you must think in ACRES, which means the following:

- Acknowledge: you want to show your prospects that you understand their concerns.
- Concern: you want sellers to know that you care about their needs.
- Respect: show your prospect respect by not arguing and having an open mind.
- Evaluate: try to fully understand what your prospects are saying. Next try to draw a conclusion by examining real facts.
- Solution: try to provide a solution.

Commission Objections

Under the Sherman Anti-trust Act it is illegal to price fix. While most real estate companies charge between 4-7%, you are free to charge whatever commission you want. If you give sellers a range to pick from, they will select the lowest fee. When it comes to charging a commission, you should meet with either the manager or broker for a clear understanding of fees. You can relay this information as company policy. Once prospects realize they are getting exceptional service, paying your commission is usually not a problem. In fact, they are getting an extraordinarily good deal. Explain that if the property does not sell, there is usually not a fee to sellers. Most fees are negotiable. Prepare your cost analysis early, be honest, and give the homeowners a true picture of what can happen. For example, buyers sometimes require the sellers' financial assistances, as much as 6% of the sales price. The rough rule of thumb is sellers usually pay about 10% of the sales price to sell their home, but the price can vary, depending on several factors. Sellers want to know how much it will cost them to sell their home. When you prepare your presentation kit, be sure that the sellers' cost net sheet is in good faith. While the buyers will receive a Good Faith Estimate (GFE) from the lender, you should learn to prepare a closing estimate for your sellers.

Rules for Real Estate Success

Once you have the listing, you have to learn how to best service it. The number one reason that sellers switch agents is due to a lack of communication. It is very important that you have a system of communicating with your clients and customers. For example, e-mail your sellers every other Monday or on the 1st and 15th of the month. Leave updates; your clients will be expecting your status report to be on time. Just by keeping in contact, you will show that you are working hard to sell their property. If you don't contact them regularly, they will think you're not trying to sell their home. This is important because when it's time for changing the list price, extending the agreement, or presenting a low offer, they will likely be team players.

The method in which buyers search for real estate is changing. For help on selling listings, let's look at some 2009 statistics from the National Association of Realtors®. More buyers are searching the Internet before they decide to search for an agent because the MLS® is now public. In 2009, 92% of buyers used the Internet for finding real estate, and over 58% of buyers searched on their own to find the property before they searched for an agent. This indicates that the listings must be faultless. Buyers search property by price range; for example, for a property in their price range, they will input $200,000-$250,000. What this information implicates is that if you want to catch the buyers' attention, you need to change how you price properties. For example, the seller wants $250,000 and most agents would say, *"Why not put the property at $249,900 because the suggested price would be more attractive to buyers?"* What will happen is you will reduce your exposure to over 67%. Why? At $249,900, the property will be at the high end of a $200,000–$250,000 search range and usually an unaffordable price for most buyers. You may also lose buyers who input a range of $250,000 - $280,000, where you may have been the first on a very affordable list. By pricing the property at $250,000 an even number, you will capture both of the search variables, the search for under and over $250,000 range. Most buyers' search range will not start at $249,000, where most agents recommend. Another example is which numbers would be easier for you to read and remember, $214,755 or $210,000? Which number would you believe has room for negotiations? Be sure to use good pictures, especially the first picture, and include a video if possible. On your property description, word it directly to the buyers. Example, *"Hello, my name is Sam Seller. I will be happy to show you this ..."*

1. Plan how you will find For Sale by Owners.
   • Newspapers, Internet sites, driving in neighborhoods, asking friends, and ads

2. Ask your broker or manager about FSBO policy and rules.

3. Design an FSBO sign/flyer.

4. Research websites for finding FSBOs.

5. Research, write, and practice your scripts for approaching FSBOs.

6. Know the pros and cons of why homeowners decide to sell their own properties.

7. Know the five reasons why it's best not to list FSBOs.

8. Practice on presenting seller's net sheet.

9. Design an FSBO/seller presentation package.

10. Know the reasons why a FSBO/any seller would use you over other agents.

11. Understand when you should walk away from a seller. Here, we are all different, and only you know your limits.

12. Know and practice how to overcome the most common sellers' objections.

13. Know how to explain your commissions.

14. Practice your FSBO presentations.

Prospecting for Sellers, Part II

Rules for Real Estate Success

1. Property owners who have decided to sell their property without a real estate agent are called
   A. For sale by owners.
   B. Clients.
   C. Prospects.
   D. Buyers.

2. The biggest reason that property owners decide to sell their own property is
   A. Information on the Internet.
   B. Cost of commission.
   C. FSBOs can sell faster because they know their property better than real estate agents.
   D. Houses are easy to sell; anyone can sell real estate.

3. The only person who can legally sell FSBOs is a
   A. Real estate agent.
   B. Homeowner.
   C. A and B.
   D. Loan officer.

4. Where to find FSBOs is
   A. In newspapers.
   B. On Internet sites.
   C. Driving around the neighborhood.
   D. All the above.

5. A system where two sales agents would team up to try to encourage the FSBO to list his/her property is called
   A. The buddy system.
   B. The honor system.
   C. The fidelity system.
   D. Jail birds.

6. Smaller signs with your name and personal phone number that are placed on top or below the office sign are
   A. Public signage.
   B. Sign-riders.
   C. Cold calling.
   D. Door hangers.

7. SURE means
   A. Short sale farming.
   B. Door-to-door farming.
   C. Cold-call farming.
   D. You understand real estate.

8. ACRES means
    A. Accountability, Confidentiality Respectful, Ethical and be Safe.
    B. Acknowledge, Concern, Respect, Evaluate, and Solution.
    C. To be Obedient and Confidential.
    D. Equal to 45360 sq. ft.

9. An accurate way real estate agents have to price property is
    A. CMA.
    B. Short sale.
    C. REO.
    D. BPO.

10. Expired listings are
    A. Properties that available for sale.
    B. Short sale properties.
    C. Bank REO properties.
    D. Properties that did not sell.

11. Mnemonic means
    A. FSBO scripts.
    B. Starting a dialogue.
    C. The values you owe your clients.
    D. A type of learning to help make connections.

12. The Financial Modernization Bill is to protect
    A. Brokers.
    B. Buyers.
    C. Sellers.
    D. Any individual's credit from being disclosed.

CHAPTER 9
Property Staging

Objectives:

Understand how property staging

- Gives the property a competitive edge
- Affects buyers and sellers emotionally
- Affects negotiations
- Makes it easier to move
- Helps homeowners organize their personal items
- Protects sellers' valuables
- Gives the impression of a larger home and larger rooms
- Makes it easier to clean
- Communicates that a home is well-maintained
- Helps to overcome views on outdated properties
- Helps a home to sell faster
- Brings better offers

Terms:

- Buyers' remorse
- Cash incentives
- Curb appeal
- De-personalizing
- Moving kits
- Points
- Property staging
- Property tender
- The bad odor rule
- The rule of diminishing returns

Staging for a Competitive Edge

Why Staging

Staging is preparing a property for sale by maximizing its appeal while using the fewest dollars. Staged properties sell faster and gain better offers than those that are not staged. Staging is not the same as interior decorating or having a clean house. Interior decorating tends to be expensive. A property that has been decorated by a professional interior decorator is nice to look at, but it's not "home." While a home is not perfect, it feels right and offers the sense of 'belonging'. The purpose of staging is to give buyers the feeling of "home." "Home" is a feeling of being comfortable and able to mentally move into the house. The goal of staging is to focus on the buyers' senses, mentally drawing them into imagining themselves as the owners of the property.

Twelve Reasons for Staging

1. To give the property a competitive edge over other properties in the same area, encouraging better offers
2. To help the buyer(s) emotionally connect to the property
3. To enable the seller(s) to emotionally disconnect from the property
4. To encourage both parties to buy and sell, making negotiations much easier
5. To make moving and packing easier for the seller(s)
6. To help protect the sellers' valuables
7. To give the impression of a well-maintained property, indicating few if any repairs
8. To make it easier to clean and maintain because of less clutter and greater space
9. To help overcome views on outdated property
10. To give the property the appearance of a larger, more comfortable home
11. To shorten the time the property will be on the market for sale
12. To give buyers and sellers a sense of pride

Staging Enables Buyers to Connect Emotionally to the Property

Purpose of Staging

The purpose of staging a property is to enable buyers to envision themselves playing with their children in the family room, cooking in the kitchen, or having a cookout in the back yard with their friends. Buyers expect four things from a property:

1. To feel emotionally connected to the property

2. To get good value for their money
3. To have few, if any, repairs on the property
4. To have the property clean and in move-in condition

Sellers should be made aware that they will have to transfer their home from living to showing condition to get the most money in the shortest amount of time. For more information on staging, visit HGTV's website at www.frontdoor.com.

A staged property also helps alleviate the fear of making a purchase that the buyer will soon regret. Since a house is a very large purchase, most home buyers will experience some level of anxiety about the purchase, called **buyer's remorse**. You can help soothe their fears by creating an emotional connection to the property through staging.

Staging Enables Sellers to Disconnect Emotionally from the Property

Helps Sellers to Disconnect

Staging also helps sellers to disconnect emotionally from the property. They will feel it's no longer their home. As sellers slowly transfer their home from living to showing condition or from functional to presentation, they soon realize that their house no longer feels like their "home." Their pictures are no longer hanging on the walls, their personal items are not in sight, and their remaining furniture has been arranged to give the room the appearance of greater space, not of comfort to them.

After staging, sellers will feel that their house is no longer their home, and they will want to hurry up with a sale and move on with their lives. They may think that there is too much light coming into the rooms, the rooms are too clean, and there is too much space. They will miss the feeling of home.

Gaining the Cooperation of the Sellers

If the seller(s) seem/seems resistant to the idea of staging their house, you may have to put the seller(s) in the buyers' shoes. Have them view a few houses with you. After viewing the houses, ask them to state their likes and dislikes for both the interior and exterior of each house. Most sellers will list things that are unrelated to the property, such as clutter or small things like messy kitchens. Remind them that's how their buyer(s) will think when viewing their property. You might also want to give them a handout that lists all of the benefits of staging a property.

Meeting Sellers' Expectations

What Sellers Expect

Rules for Real Estate Success

What sellers expect from their real estate agent is knowledge about what to do and the ability to communicate that skill. For example, the homeowner may ask, *"Why should I stage? What is in it for me?"* They have an idea, but they want someone to clarify this point in an organized manner. As a professional, you should know how to clearly explain the purpose of staging in a 1-2-3 fashion. You might say the following:

Ten Ways Staging Will Benefit You

1. A well-staged property will bring you better offers.
2. Staged properties will sell faster.
3. Buyers will get the impression that since your property is well maintained, it will require few repairs. Properties that require fewer repairs will bring better offers.
4. You can take your time packing, which makes moving an easier task. By the time you're ready to move into your new home, you will already be packed and ready to move.
5. Since all boxes will be labeled, accounting for your items will be easier for you and the movers.
6. Packing will protect your valuables, such as jewelry items, during the sale.
7. Should you decide to clear unwanted items, staging will give the opportunity to organize or sell unwanted items.
8. Staging will give the property the appearance of a larger home.
9. The property will be much easier for you to maintain during the listing period.
10. The property will create a positive first impression.

Things to Remember when Staging a House

When a property is staged, a buyer's first impression of it dramatically improves. Ninety percent of a buyer's decision to purchase will occur within the first ten seconds of seeing the property. Buyers will first examine the property as a whole to measure the overall condition of the house, then they will solicit more specific information about the property. When buyers ask questions, the types of questions they ask will signal that they have either already eliminated the house and need confirmation, or they are mentally trying to move into the house.

Curb Appeal

When staging the property, don't get so caught-up with the inside that you forget all about curb appeal. After all, curb appeal is your first chance to make an impression. The idea is to grab the prospects' attention as soon as possible. There are thousands of homes for sale, so buyers will try to eliminate as many properties as they can before calling for an appointment. Internet searches followed by drive-by visits are the main way to eliminate homes. A property with little curb appeal may cause a perfectly good house to be eliminated. Have you ever heard of judging a book by its cover?

Depersonalize the Property

The objective of **de-personalizing** a property is to remove personal distractions from the property. For example, if the buyers walk into the living room and notice the seller's shoes are next to the couch, they will start wondering why the seller's shoes are in the living room. While noticing these little details, they are distracted from seeing the rest of the room. The seller(s) could have spent a great deal of time and money staging the rooms, or they may have even brought in a professional interior decorator, but all of this can be lost because of a small personal detail that distracted the buyer(s). If sellers want to sell the property for the greatest price and in the shortest time, they must start removing and packing all family pictures and anything personal that may cause a distraction. Remember that a buyer will never buy unless they first mentally move into the property. How can buyers mentally move into the property if the seller's pictures are still hanging on the walls? The same goes for arts and crafts, scrapbooks, or any hobbies. Seeing a seller's interests scattered about the house can be a major mental block for many buyers. Be sure that sellers are not at the property when buyers are looking at it. This is one of the reasons a FSBO should never show their own property, unless they are selling cheaply to an investor.

Making Moving and Packing an Easier Task for Sellers

Making Moving and Packing an Easier Task

One of the reasons homeowners hate to move is the difficult task of moving. Having to pack, and move their possessions to a new location and unpack is a considerable amount of work. They have to find a place for thousands of things.

One of the first things to do is to get the homeowners organized. All homeowners or renters have excessive items they will have to pack, move, and then unpack. Have homeowners sort through their personal items and start categorizing personal items into four groups:

- Group one — items that must stay in the house. These are essential items for everyday use.
- Group two — items that the homeowners can do without for a few months, but would like to keep, such as pictures, extra shoes, and winter clothing
- Group three — items to sell or give away to charities
- Group four — items to throw away

Provide Free Moving Kits

You can provide free moving kits to both buyers and sellers. You can provide them to sellers to help them as they remove their items in preparation for staging their house for sale. You can provide them to buyers to assist with moving into their new home. **Moving kits** should consist of empty boxes with your business label on them, large markers, a catalog book, and rolls of tape. Moving boxes come in all sizes, and most moving companies carry them. Try to find plain boxes without business logos on them.

Boxes usually cost about a dollar a box, and color labels usually cost another 30 cents. For about $50, just think about how often your customer will think of you throughout the year as the unpacked boxes (with your business label on them) sit around. It's not a good idea to recommend any one moving company because it can be a liability. It's better to provide a list from which your customers can choose.

Staging Helps to Protect the Sellers' Valuables

Protect Seller's Valuables

Before sellers pack their possessions, suggest that they take pictures of the personal property and their valuables for insurance purposes. It is also a good time to catalog their valuables. Boxes are often misplaced or forgotten. Moving is much easier if valuables are photographed and cataloged before they are placed into numbered boxes.

When your seller(s) move into their new residence, putting each box in its place is easier if they are labeled. For example, boxes labeled B-1 through B-8 go into the master bedroom, the box labeled B-2 goes into the master bathroom, and boxes K-1 through K-3 go into the kitchen, etc.

Some agents are concerned only with closing the transaction to the point of getting a check. After getting paid, they turn their attention to the next deal and forget all about the transaction they just closed. Most agents do not bother with providing service to their customers after closing on a house. If you continue to service your customer(s)/client(s), you automatically set yourself apart from the rest.

Staging Contributes to the Impression of a Well-Maintained Property

A Clean House

A clean house suggests that the property is a well-kept home that requires few repairs. Properties that require cleaning give the impression that the property may have hidden problems. Buyers may think if the seller lacks the pride to clean, what else may he/she be hiding?

- **Hire a Professional Cleaning Service** - you could hire a one-time service or a weekly maintenance service. A well-staged home will save the homeowner thousands of dollars in the end.

Staging Provides the Appearance of a Larger more Comfortable Home

Creating Visualization

Another staging rule is: *"An aid to visualization is space."* The greater the space buyers have, the easier the visualization is for them. When buyers walk into a room, they begin processing all the items in the room. The more items there are, the longer the processing will take. Even if buyers don't realize they are processing, it still takes effort. If sellers eliminate as many items as possible, processing the room is much easier for the buyer(s). This is not to say the room should be empty, but it should have only a few items that are appealing to the buyers' senses.

Creating Greater Space

In each room, try to give the perception of greater space. For example, if the bed and dresser are together, then divide them. Standing from the door way, move the bed to the furthest wall facing you and the dresser on the opposite wall, creating two defined spaces. This gives the perception of greater space. The same goes when trying to decide how to arrange, which furniture to remove, or which pieces are incompatible. Take note of any items blocking the pathway to other entries that are not allowing smooth traffic flow. If you decide to take staging seriously, look into ordering furniture templates from www.layitout.com. For example, templates for a full house at a cost of $99 are an excellent tool for buyers who want to know how their furniture will fit into any room. **Furniture templates** are flat colorful cardboard cutouts that are the square size to real furniture. You can include your photo or advertisement on your templates or leave instructions for buyers. Since templates are flat, this gives rooms the perception of greater space while still aiding buyers in using their imagination. To remove excessive furniture and items, suggest to sellers that they conduct an early garage or yard sale about a month before the house is on the market.

Keeping Rooms Simple

The fewer items there are in a room, the better. One large item is better than several smaller items. For example, having one large vase is simpler than several smaller vases because there are fewer items for the prospects to process.

Low-Cost Staging Tips

- **Use natural lighting** - get as much natural light into the rooms as possible, and use mirrors to reflect light. If you cannot get enough natural light into the room, use fashionable lamps to add more light. Natural sunlight tends to make rooms appear larger than they really are. Before showing a house, try to have the window blinds and doors open and the lights and ceiling fans turned on.
- **Use scented candles, air filters, block paint, and odor eaters** - The **rule about bad odors** is, *"If your buyers can smell it, you're not going to sell it."* A property that smells like smoke, old clothes or spoiled food is very difficult to sell. Every house has its own unique smell; usually cleaning will remove most bad odors. Try to find the source of any foul odors, whether they are from smoking, pets, old furniture, clothing, mold, or even ethnic cooking. Once the odors have been eliminated, try to use some refreshers. Be careful about adding strong scented candles, strong air refreshers, or too much bleach. Have the seller(s) purchase some type of aerosol odor removers, and then have them lightly spray bathrooms and family rooms before any showings. If the seller(s) have pets, suggest a pet boarding home at least until a contract is negotiated. If the property does have serious odor problems, such as mold or rotten wood, you should disclose this information to the buyer(s).
- **Apply fresh paint** – A fresh coat of paint can help a property that appears worn to look new. Be sure to use the right colors to make the room comfortable. Light colors, such as green, yellow, red, and brown gives the room a warm feeling. Dark colors reflect less space. Glossy pure whites on door and window trim gives the appearance

of cleanliness. Using darker paint for walls helps show the white trim wood-work. If you need help choosing colors, hire an interior designer or professional home stager.

- **Emphasize the uniqueness of older homes** - Older homes with old style cabinets, cupboards or old- fashioned bathrooms should show uniqueness rather than age. There are ample buyers who would be more comfortable with a distinctive home rather than a new home. Have the bathrooms painted. Small colorful floral arrangements and candles add to the uniqueness of an older home.

- **Clear-out old clothing from closets to create less clutter** - Stage garage sales and/or forward discarded items to a charitable organization of your choice. Sellers should be as organized as possible. Older houses were designed with smaller closets; however, today, larger closets are what buyers are seeking. Too much clutter gives the appearance that the closets are smaller than they are.

- **Remove cleaning supplies** - Visible cleaning supplies are like unclean houses; they are distractions for the buyers. Buyers don't want to be reminded about cleaning the house when they see a room. Have homeowners put away mops, brooms, laundry baskets, sponges, soap, or anything that may remind buyers of cleaning. A broom in the corner or a sponge in the sink may trigger dreadful thoughts of cleaning.

- **Storing Medicines** - All medicines should be labeled and stored in a safe place away from the public's view. Any old drugs should be disposed of and labels removed. Personal bathroom items such as toothbrushes and toothpaste should be stored in locked boxes away from the public's view. Medicines and personal care items are very personal, so why allow buyers to know the sellers' medical condition? Buyers don't want to know about sellers' medical problems. Some of these medical items build a mental picture of sellers moving about in a wheelchair or using an oxygen tank. Buyers now have developed a mental block, or worse. Exposing unnecessary medical equipment is the fastest way to kill a deal.

- **Remove pets** - Not everyone likes dogs, cats, birds, or other pets. Some people even have allergies to these animals. Large aggressive dogs are personal, and, if barking, can be very intimidating to buyers. They also pose a possible danger of biting someone. Suggest that sellers leave their pets in a kennel or doggie-day-care while showing the house.

- **Take a better look at the exterior** - Take a look at windows, interior drapes and its coverings, inside and outside the home. Are there hedges blocking your view? Does the tool shed need paint? Does the trash cans need to be moved? Stop and look through each widow. Check to see what buyers will see.

- **Property center point** - Fireplaces are usually the focal point of any family room. On cold days, light a fire to create a warm feeling for buyers to let them know that the fireplace works.

- **Lawn care** – Ask sellers to consider bringing in a professional landscaper, a few plants, and present a well-maintained yard and garage while the property is listed for sale.
- **Checking the Mechanical System** - Recommend to sellers that they have the air conditioner, heating system, or pool system inspected and repaired as soon as possible. Most homeowners have regular maintenance. As for the mechanical system, recommend using only professionally licensed companies. Using the neighborhood handyman or having sellers fix their own repairs may cause disclosure problems.

Early Planning

Start thinking about eliminating items that appear to clutter the garage, add a few plants, or maybe do some painting around the home. If you are using post cards or the letter system, this would be a great article: *"How to Prepare your Property."* Most people are thinking about selling months ahead and are waiting for summer when their children are out of school or when properties bring better pricing. Mail your newsletter early before the summer months, and give your prospects ideas on how to bring the greatest return for their home. Leave information, such as *"for more tips contact ..."* Do your research early during the off-season. For example, do research on how to fertilize grass, how to get it so green that it's almost blue. Do research on when to plant or which plants grow better in certain soils. Your letters should be so impressive that prospects think of you as the expert on how to prepare their home for sale. If you prepare your articles early, you will have time to edit before your mail-outs are distributed.

Staging Vacant Homes

Staging vacant houses involves preparing the property for showing in much the same way as new home builders do with model homes. Empty houses are difficult to sell. When the property is empty, buyers have a difficult time imagining how to use the space. Model homes are usually staged because the builder wants to make potential buyers feel warm, cozy, and comfortable – 'at home'. Interior decorators may use large colorful flower arrangements (natural or artificial), deep brown wooden picture frames, colorful candle arrangements, colorful towels and assorted green plants. Once the property has secured a contract, the items can be moved to a new location or stored and labeled. Garage sales, estate sales, dollar stores, and hobby centers are great places for decorating items.

Taking Videos/Pictures of Staged Property

Set a date to revisit the house after it has been de-cluttered, cleaned, and ready for showcasing. Now is a good time to take plenty of pictures or videos while the house is at its best. Try to take pictures/videos from each entry way. Take outdoor pictures two hours before sunset while you have plenty of light, and take several curb shots. Think like a buyers' agent. Those agents are trying to eliminate properties for their clients, from hundreds to a handful of properties. For the pictures that will be posted on the MLS or a personal website, ask yourself what may cause viewers to take a second look. Ask what would catch the attention of the viewer. Keep in mind the perception of depth, natural light, warm earth tone colors, de-cluttering, curb appeal, and space. Agents should complement the property with quality pictures or videos.

Property Tenders

A **property tender** is a person who is hired to live in the listed property that is vacant until it sells. A professional tender knows that it's his/her job to keep the property in showing condition. The tender will usually lease the property, pay very little rent, and pay all utilities. The tradeoff is the greatly reduced rent. Benefits for the homeowner include insurance savings, a well-maintained property, a professionally staged home, home security, help paying the mortgage, and a quicker sale. Tenders are usually more active during downturns in the economy. A property tender's job is to keep the home in showing condition 100% of the time. While some home tenders are licensed real estate agents, a license is not required, as long as the home tender does not discuss real estate with prospects.

Staging Encourages Better Offers

Staging = Better Offers

Express to your sellers that nearly 80% of callers come from the results of having good curb appeal. Do the mathematics. Will spending a few hundred dollars compensate and increase the number of appointments by 80% thus increasing amount of possible offers? Will painting the exterior at a cost of $500 provide a $2,000 greater return? Ask the sellers if there is a time frame in which they wish to sell. In real estate, the two best ways to sell a house is to sell it cheaply or stage it correctly. If the sellers are on a strict budget, suggest improving curb appeal as the most important, followed by the lighting, kitchen and bathrooms. Also, greater curb appeal increases the chances of better offers. Buyers often think houses with strong curb appeal are more likely to receive several offers, usually allowing buyers to present better offers. There is an old saying, "*You get what you pay for*," meaning if you want quality, you have to pay for it. "*If it's a cheap quality, then make a cheap offer.*" A well-staged home gives the appearance of better quality. Even, if all the sellers can get is the appraised value, the offers will be much better and more frequent.

How will selling staged homes help your long-term career? As mentioned earlier, sellers and buyers want facts. Since staged homes often bring better prices and faster sales, you can advertise your statistical facts. As you build your career, find what your listings-to-sales ratio is and the length of time your listings were for sale. Compare those statistics to the average listed home in your area. Here you can show your prospects statistical facts. Show your listings that sold for 10% more money and 20% faster than the average real estate agent in the same area.

Property Value

Pricing the property correctly is very important. Ask sellers if they would like to order a partial or an unofficial appraisal. A partial appraisal will cost much less than a full appraisal. The appraisal gives the sellers and buyers the actual price, an untrained real estate agent's CMA at best offers a price range.

CMAs are a good tool for real estate agents if they know how to do it correctly. For many agents, it gives a price range from which to sell the property, but oftentimes it causes more problems. If the agent suggest selling between $100,000 and $110,000, and of course the sellers would like the greater price. If the agent recommends a $100,000 price, they are giving the property away. All of this could have been avoided with a simple appraisal. After all, real estate agents are good at selling houses, and appraisers are professional at determining value.

Since the appraiser will be working for the sellers and not the lenders, show the property's interesting character. Ask what low-cost remodeling ideas would add the greatest value to the property. For example, old counter tops could be replaced with granite tops, rooms could be enclosed, a second bathroom added, or any remodeling that enhances the house. Appraisers are very good at suggesting improvements that would help sell the property with the greatest return per dollar. The last thing a seller(s) wants to do is invest $10,000 but get only $5,000 more for their home, which is called *"The rule of diminishing return."* If the seller(s) is planning major remodeling, suggest ordering a partial appraisal first.

Incentives to Help Sell the Property

In a slow market or to sell a difficult property, homeowners and builders will use some form of incentive. Staging properties is important, but not everyone has the means and funds to stage or do repairs. Here, homeowners can set aside money for those improvements.

Sometimes sellers are unable to complete repairs, therefore, offer cash incentives instead, **Cash incentives** are used as a bargaining tool and are paid to buyers at closing and funding. Determine what repairs sellers will complete, and for the rest of the repairs, determine the cost for each. Have the homeowners walk around the property looking for repairs or ask a contractor to do it for them.

Types of Incentives

The two basic types of incentives:

a) Incentives for the real estate agents
b) Incentives for the buyers (cash and non-cash)

The agent's incentives are often cash bonuses, whereas, incentives for the buyer can range from cash received for closing costs to non-cash items, such as home improvements and repairs.

Purchasing Non-Cash Incentives

First-time homebuyers rarely have items such as a stove, washer, dryer, lawn mower, or landscaping equipment prior to moving into their home. Buyers will appreciate new carpet, furniture, house repairs, a new roof, or even a home warranty plan. These non-cash items can be incentives, aside from cash financing assistance, to help them with closing costs. Sellers can even increase the sales price to give incentives to buyers, as long the sales price does not exceed the appraised value.

First Month's Payment

A seller's offer to pay for the buyer's first month's mortgage payment is an incentive. Paying the first month's mortgage is oftentimes less than a full month's payment, as the days remaining in the month are pro-rated. This type of incentive falls under the cash system. For example, if a full-month mortgage is $1,000 and the buyer closes on the 15th day of a 30-day calendar month, the first month's payment would be $500.

Buying Down the Interest Rate, (Points)

Sellers and builders are allowed to pre-purchase interest rates to a lower amount. When the interest rates are pre-purchased, this is called buying "points." **Points** are pre-paid interest rates. The idea is to lower the interest rate to make monthly payments affordable for buyers. The cost rule is one point is equal to one percent of the loan. To buy three points on a $100,000 loan, the cost would be $3,000. There are two options to buy down the interest rate. Option one is to buy the interest per year, which is called **Buy Down Points**. Option two is to permanently buy down the interest rate, which is called **Discount Points**. As long as the buyer(s) are able to afford payments in the first years, this allows them to qualify for the loan. Buying points for buyers falls under the cash system. For more information on Points (*Read: "Financing Real Estate*," Chapter 11).

Giving Sellers and Buyers a Sense of Pride

Showcasing the Property

The importance of staging is to allow homeowners to experience how other people feel when they perceive their showcased home. The seller(s) have done an enormous amount of hard work and spent a great deal money to make their home become the showpiece of the neighborhood. What a wonderful feeling it must be to have the best showpiece home in the neighborhood. Having the homeowners' neighbors and guests amazed at how inviting their home is gives them a sense of pride. Their home is being showcased, and they are thankful to the agent who made it possible. Showcasing a property is a good way to receive high recommendations from the seller(s) to their friends and family. Since the property is in show quality condition, now is a good time for open houses, updating pictures, or re-doing visual tours.

How to Reward Your Sellers

Schedule a time with homeowners when you will return after the home has been de-cluttered. Bring rewards, preferably plants, that will add to the property rather than adding more clutter. Better yet, bring plenty of encouragement. Show homeowners how impressed you are because, after all, you are asking a great deal from the owners.

Confirming the Professionalizing of the Real Estate Agent

Staging Designation for Real Estate Agents

Several schools offer specialty courses on staging if you are interested in learning more about it. You can even go as far as to earn a Professional Staging Designation. Think of it as an investment in your career. If you have a staging designation certificate, your farming community will notice that your listings display a better quality; they sell faster and cost less in repairs to your clients. Having your name associated with quality properties helps build your reputation in the real estate community.

1. Find where to buy empty moving boxes without logos. Design your first moving kit.

2. Go to several open houses for ideas on how to stage. In each open house, study how you can better stage the property.

3. Look for books and videos on staging.

4. Get information on staging designations.

5. Ask other agents if you can help with open houses, and study how they present.

6. Design a checklist for preparing properties for showing; for example, what to look for on the outside and inside of the house.

7. Design homeowner flyers for staging and showing.

8. Visit garage sales and stores for buying material for staging.

9. Visit model homes and staged homes that are listed for sale. Study how you would change items.

10. Go to YouTube.com for videos on staging.

11. Practice how to explain to sellers why they should stage their property.

12. Be able to go room-to-room to explain what items they will have to remove, what items to pack, and what items to move. Be able to give clear reasons for what you are asking.

13. Design your company labels for packing boxes.

14. Design a letter/flyer on staging/early planning that you can mail to homeowners.

Property Staging

Rules for Real Estate Success

1. What is preparing a property for sale by maximizing its appeal for the fewest dollars?
   A. Staging
   B. Farming
   C. Cold calling
   D. De-personalizing

2. Preparing the exterior of the home to grab the prospect's attention as soon as possible is called
   A. Staging.
   B. Curb appeal.
   C. The rule of diminishing return.
   D. The rule of the greatest gain.

3. To remove personal distractions from the property so prospects may visualize themselves as owners of the property is called
   A. Personal distractions
   B. The rule of diminishing distractions
   C. De-personalizing
   D. Buying points

4. The goal to staging for buyers is
   A. To meet the sellers' expectations.
   B. To help buyers to disconnect emotionally from the property.
   C. To help sellers to disconnect emotionally from the property.
   D. To help buyers visualize themselves in family rooms, cooking, playing with their children, and having family moments, or inviting guess for parties.

5. This happens when buyers think they have paid too much for the house, or for any reason, they regret trying to buy the property?
   A. Buyer's remorse
   B. Seller's remorse
   C. Buyer's mistake
   D. Buyers and sellers can legally break the agreement when buyers determine they are paying too much for the property.

6. Having empty boxes with your business label on them, large markers, a catalog book, and tape is/are
   A. A presentation kit
   B. A moving kit
   C. Goodwill boxes
   D. A marketing kit

7. A rule where sellers' improvements cost is greater than the return of money is called
   A. SURE, Sellers Understanding Real Estate
   B. ACRES, Acknowledge, Concern, Respect, Evaluate, and Solution
   C. The rule, if your buyers can smell it, you're not going to sell it
   D. The rule of diminishing return

8. The idea of lowering the interest rate to make monthly payments affordable for buyers
   A. Buy down points
   B. Points
   C. Discount points
   D. All of the above

9. To buy down the interest per year is called
   A. Buy down points
   B. APR
   C. Discount points
   D. All of the above

10. The purpose of staging is to
    A. Help buyers feel emotionally connected to the property
    B. Give buyers the sense of good value for their money
    C. Show few, if any, repairs on the property
    D. All of the above

CHAPTER 10
Prospecting for Buyers

Objectives:

Understand how to address the following:

- To find, prepare to work with, and establish rapport with buyers
- To be able to turn calls into appointments
- To categorize and qualify prospective buyers
- To narrow house searching for buyers
- To know how to preview and show properties to buyers
- To overcome buyers' objections
- To design the best scripts for the most common situations
- To design buyers' presentation kits
- To know what items lenders will need to approve a loan
- To establish rapport
- To close a sale and follow-up on the transaction
- To build a referral system and the importance of doing so

Terms:

- Buyer's presentation kit
- Categorizing buyers
- Determining category list
- Floor time
- HUD-1
- Leads
- Listings
- Opportunity time
- Referrals
- Sphere of influence

Benefits of Working with Buyers

The Psychology of Working with Buyers

Your job as a real estate agent is not attempting to control the buyer by getting him/her to sign a document or persuading him/her to select a house; rather, your job is to provide professional advice and an honest opinion (fidelity and integrity). You should play more of an advisory role and guide the buyer as you try to help him/her meet his/her real estate needs. Switching roles from that of a sneaky salesperson who applies pressure, trickery, and tactics to that of an advisor makes selling real estate less stressful and more enjoyable for everyone involved. Buyers don't want to be someone's next meal ticket; they do, however, expect honest service.

Establishing the Ten Steps to Working with Buyers

Successfully working with buyers is simply mastering the ten basic steps, which are as follows:

1. Finding buyers
2. Establishing rapport and working with buyers
3. Categorizing buyers/prospecting
4. Preparing your buyers
5. Qualifying prospects
6. Previewing and selecting the right housing for your prospects
7. Overcoming objections
8. Helping buyers get financing/mortgage lending
9. Closing the deal and to follow-up
10. Building a referral system

Finding Buyers

Buyers

Home buyers are everywhere, but how do you find them? Many of the previously discussed methods of marketing, sales, and prospecting for sellers are also useful when prospecting for buyers. Below are suggestions for generating leads for buyers. Examine each and choose the ones that best fit your personality. If you find that the method(s) that you choose are not working, you can always pick another and try it instead.

Sphere of influence, looking for family, friends, neighbors and co-workers for help to put the word out	Chapter 10
Building databases of sphere of influence, past clients and others.	Chapter 10
Buying leads	Chapter 10
Office floor time	Chapter 10
Working with old office files	Chapter 10
Selling HUD homes	Chapter 10
Building a database of buyers	Chapter 10
Build a working relationship with lenders	Chapter 12
Working with lenders/homeowners on pre-foreclosures	Chapter 12
Working with lenders/homeowners on foreclosures	Chapter 12
Working with lenders/homeowners on post-foreclosures	Chapter 12
For-Sale-by-Owners	Chapter 9
Expired listings	Chapter 7
Working with estate sales	Chapter 8
Garage sales	Chapter 8
Having listings	Chapter 7
Having open houses	Chapter 7
Farming	Chapter 7
Door-to-Door sales	Chapter 7
Conducting a weekly door-to-door campaign	Chapter 7
Yard signs	Chapter 7
Cold-calling/ telemarketing	Chapter 7
Working with builders	Chapter 7
Contacting renters	Chapter 7
Sending mail-outs to apartments	Chapter 7
Social networking	Chapter 7
Editorial writing	Chapter 7
Writing newsletters	Chapter 7
Sending post cards/e-cards	Chapter 7
Human resources	Chapter 7
Foreclosures	Chapter 7
Distributing business cards	Chapter 6
Using magnet car signs	Chapter 6
Names badges and apparel	Chapter 6

Distributing flyers in your area	Chapter 6
Hosting special events	Chapter 6/7
Having homebuyer seminars	Chapter 6
Working with attorneys	Chapter 6
Meeting private investors at seminars and foreclosure sales	Chapter 6
Supermarket posting and shopping carts	Chapter 6
Try contacting the chamber of commerce	Chapter 6
Joining church and social groups	Chapter 6
Trying classified ads and local magazines	Chapter 6
Considering radio ads	Chapter 6
Trying billboards	Chapter 6
Yellow pages	Chapter 6
Wearing apparel and name badges	Chapter 6
Sponsoring sport teams	Chapter 6
Visiting places like grocery stores or anywhere people meet and just start talking to people	Chapter 6
Providing post services	Chapter 6
Keeping in touch	Chapter 6
Surveys	Chapter 6
Developing a website	Chapter 4
Internet websites	Chapter 4
Talking Houses	Chapter 4
Blogging	Chapter 4

Sphere of Influence

You don't have to get the word out about your services all alone. It's easier and less expensive if you learn to use your **sphere of influence,** which is the group of people who know, trust, and like you and will recommend you. This army of people can be past clients, relatives, co-workers, merchants, business contacts, and friends. Why would anyone recommend you or avoid recommending you? If you are trustworthy, perform well, and people associate you with something they can be proud of, something that is unique, and/or something exceptional, they will recommend you. Once you demonstrate exceptional performance, people start associating themselves with you by calling you, "my realtor" with pride because you are the best in their eyes.

Most of your sphere of influence will refer you to their friends, family, and acquaintances out of a sense of pride. However, some of them may be unwilling to refer you; you may have to ask for their help. Many of your past clients may not understand the importance of referrals, so it's up to you to explain its importance. You should have a system in place for explaining the importance of referrals. A good time to ask for referrals is after closing and during your many visits and letters. You can ask for referrals via email, phone, snail mail, post cards, or in person. Asking for referrals should be part of your everyday to-do list.

Purchasing Leads

You can purchase leads from several sources; however, be careful about signing long-term contracts with lead providers. Read the fine print carefully, and do some research on each lead provider. Ask about the lead source, the success rate, and options for breaching the contract. Under RESPA, it is legal to purchase leads; however, it is illegal to pay for referrals from non-agents, which is a Section 8 violation. Marketing or paying for market leads is often confused with referrals. For example, is giving gifts to agents considered marketing or referrals? Again, paying for marketing is legal; paying non-agents for referrals is illegal. Rules for purchasing leads are as follows:

- Brokers are legally able to buy real estate leads from several Internet sites.
- Providers sell leads by zip code or per amount.

Lead providers also include companies that research county records for mortgages. These companies collect information on various types of loans and loan amounts and sell this information to brokers. Brokers who procure this information are able to use it to determine which loans need to be refinanced or which homeowners they may want to call.

Office Floor Time

One way of gaining buyer or seller leads is volunteering for office **floor time**. When working the floor, you are in charge of incoming phone calls and greeting walk-in prospects for a certain time period. A better word for floor time is **opportunity time**, an opportunity for sales. Each office has its rules for sharing leads. Be ethical; ask your broker for rules about sharing leads. Don't just show up and expect to sell a house over the phone. Again, this is another process. In opportunity time, your goal should be to get an appointment, not to make a sale. The appointment is used for Step 2, to make your sale or list a property. Be prepared by having your information ready, but most importantly, bring the right attitude. Rule: "You *get what you expect. If you expect to do well, you will.*" Items you should have ready when on floor duty are listed below:

- A welcome script
- Office inventory
- Internet ready for searching other listings
- Phone numbers of office agents
- Recent office ads
- Useful educational information for prospects
- Your schedule
- Knowing how the phone system works, and having a pen and pad ready
- Having a specially designed notebook for possible leads so that they are all in one location.

How to Turn Calls into Appointments

Turning a caller into an appointment is a five step process:

First, you must listen carefully to what the caller is seeking.

Second, you should compliment the property, or better yet, flatter the caller. For example, *"Yes, you just have to see this house. It has the most beautiful kitchen, would be great for family gatherings, and the schools are ranked the highest in our state,"* or, you can say, *"Nice choice, you have great taste. This home has..."* Rule: *"In sales, it's not about you; it's about them!"*

Third, you need to establish rapport. Try to start a dialogue on anything that might interest your caller. The rule here is, *"People like people who like them."* and, *"People will find you fascinating when you're fascinated by them."* Example, *"Wow, that's a big house. You must have a nice family."* Try to keep redirecting the caller to talk about what means the most to him/her. Afterward, you can say, *"I'm sorry, forgive me. Let me get back to your original question."*

Fourth, you need to be on a fact-finding mission. The questions you ask should be more open-ended versus close-ended. This builds for a better conversation. Examples of close-end words are: can, could, is, do, are, would, and have. It is easier for the caller to say "No" and not start a dialogue. Below are examples of close-ended questions:

- *Is there a price range?*
- *Is there a particular school?*
- *Do you have a requirement on bedrooms?*
- *Do you have any special requirements?*

Open-ended questions begin with, what, why, how, and when. Examples are below:

- *What kind of home are you looking for?*
- *How soon would you like to move in?*
- *When is a good time?*

Fifth, ask for an appointment. Following are examples of using close-ended questions, "*Would you like me to set an appointment? The house is vacant, and we can show it today.*" If your caller says, "*No, I was just calling,*" you should say, "*I understand. Would you like me to email you in a couple of weeks with new listings that are similar?*" At this point, it will be easier for the caller to say, "*Yes*" than to say "No" because two weeks or a few months is a long time away. If you can't get the appointment, get the next best thing: an email address. With email you can place buyers on an email drip campaign.

An example of an open-ended question is as follows: "*Mr. Jones, when would be a good time to show you this gorgeous Georgian-style home?*" As you have noticed several times, you should role play your scripts because your caller will ask the same questions in a different way every time you answer the phone.

Finding a Gold Mine

If you are starting off as a new agent, ask your broker for permission to go into old office files to contact past clients. Many of these clients have been forgotten by their agent or the agent may no longer be employed at the company. Start calling these past clients to introduce yourself, and ask if you can add them to your mailing list. Those old dusty filing cabinets of past clients can prove to be a gold mine of leads. Before you start your search, get the rules of contact from your broker/manager. Check for the rules concerning who keeps the files on past clients who belonged to former agents.

Listings

The most powerful way to find buyers is to have an inventory of properties, called listings. **Listings** are properties that are posted for sale by real estate agents, becoming a part of inventory homes. Buyers who call about a particular property have an idea of what they want and are usually serious buyers. Another excellent way of finding buyers is by having open houses. Once you have listings, you need to routinely have open houses. For more information on how to generate buyers by having open houses, read Chapter 7, *Prospecting for Sellers.*

Qualifying to sell HUD homes is easy. To start, you have to sign HUD's Selling Broker Certification forms. You will need to submit the following forms: SAMS 1111 Broker application and the SAMS 1111A Selling Broker Certification. Once this is completed, you can show, advertise, and submit offers on HUD homes. Upon closing a sale, HUD pays the broker a commission of up to five percent of the selling price if this was a condition of the offer the link for more information on how to register as a HUD brokers is hud.gov/offices/hsg/sfh/reo/hwtosell.cfm#register.

Establishing Rapport

Formally Establishing Responsibility

Establishing rapport in any type of sales is vital. Consumers must feel comfortable with the person with whom they are communicating; the relationship should be based on trust and respect. Legal duties and responsibility should be formally established. Ethics can be established by having a signed copy of the company's ethical protocol or the National Realtors® code of ethics signed before the consumers. To make your statement more official looking, think about using certificate paper.

Buyers appreciate some formal rules of conduct.

My Duties to my Client

Fidelity: I will always place your interests above my interests and all others.

Obedience: I will always be obedient to you within the law.

Loyalty: I will be completely loyal to you at all times.

Disclosure: I promise to never share any of your information unless I have your permission.

Confidentiality: I promise to inform you of all important issues concerning your property, and I will protect all confidential information.

Accountability: I promise I will earn your trust in handling your property, valuables, and care of your home.

Reasonable Care and Diligence: I pledge to do my best to stay informed of market conditions and all real estate matters and to communicate all important issues to you as soon as possible.

Signature _____ *Date* _____

Categorizing Buyers

Categorizing Your Sphere of Influence

You can break your sphere of influence into different categories. For example, find which sphere of influence has referred you in the past, or which is least likely to refer you. You may find fifty past clients who have not referred anyone to you. The next step is to ask why. What information can you mail or email to these fifty people? Did you miss something with these people, or are they too busy to repay you for your hard work? Do you need to make personal visits? The only way you can improve your referral business ratio is to ask questions and know how to categorize your sphere of influence list.

Categorizing Leads

Leads are people who may be considering using your services. There are strong leads, such as sellers who are looking for an agent to help them sell their property, or buyers, who are qualified to purchase a home. There are also weak leads, such as homeowners who are thinking of selling someday, but not now, or a buyer who does not qualify for a loan, but may qualify later. To save time and money, think of the group in which leads belong. You can categorize leads several different ways, such as when they will be able to buy or how loyal your prospects are. You need to know which leads to invest your time in and which leads will produce next month, next year, or even bring you more leads. To improve your selling ratio, do not concentrate on working with any one type of lead, but know how to carefully select your leads. The only way to determine the type of lead is to ask several questions and have it pre-qualified by a reputable lender. Since you can work with only a limited number of buyers at a time, it's important to know which ones to invest in and which ones to save for later or leave for your competition.

Categorizing Buyers

If you're an exclusive buyers' agent, it's wise to predetermine the kind of buyers you will work with and decide how best to use your time and money by **categorizing buyers**. Since you can show houses to only a few buyers, working with the wrong buyers or borrowers can be costly. Sometimes after you have used your gas and time, the buyer may choose to write the contract or to purchase the property using another agent or for any other reason, decide to not buy; they may even refuse to accept your calls or email. Consequently, the first thing you should do is determine how motivated your buyers are, their financial qualifications, how soon they are planning on moving, and then sign them up exclusively. To categorize buyers, do the following:

- Eliminate window-shoppers and have them pre-qualified by a reputable lender. Usually, if they are willing to spend the time to qualify for a loan, they are serious. The loan officer can tell you how cooperative they were. If arrangements were made early, and they had all of their required documents for the lender to review, they are motivated.
- Find out how soon they are thinking about buying a house. Interview your prospects, and try to place them into one of three or four categories.
- Find out if your prospects are willing to work with you.
- Are your buyers realistic about finding the right house? Buyers often want a fantastic deal, a perfect home on a low budget, or they have to see every house in the MLS. If you have shown houses in their price range, but they are persistent, there are larger homes for their price range. Buyers will come to you with ideas of what they want. It's up to you to set realistic boundaries as soon as possible. Maybe one of their friends bragged about the home he/she purchased. If you decide to work as a buyers' agent, your success will largely depend on your ability to place buyers into the different categories. See the example below.

Type of Groups	Purpose of Groups	Time Allowed per Group
Group one	**Need** housing now and have realistic boundaries	80%
Group two	**Want** a house soon but are still a little unrealistic	10%
Group three	**Desire** housing someday but are not committed to an agent	7%
Group four	**Dreaming** of housing as a long-term goal, not loyal to anyone, unrealistic or unable to buy	3%

Determining Category

You need to **determine the category** in which to place your prospect by asking questions to discover how soon buyers will need housing, how committed they are to buying a house, and if they can buy today. For example, ask buyers the following questions:

- If you find the right home today, are you willing to make an offer today?
- How long have you been thinking of buying?

- Have you used another real estate agent?
- What is your present living situation? Is there is a lease agreement? If so, when does it expire? Is there another house you need to sell?
- What is your price range?
- Have you been pre-qualified by a lender?
- Do you have the funds for a down payment (5%), closing costs (1-2%), and prepays (1-2%)?
- Are you willing to spend the time to look for a home?
- Do you have a time frame?
- Are there any special property needs?
- What is your perfect home (price, location, schools, bedrooms, etc.)?
- Do you have a wish list?
- What are your absolute deal breakers?
- Are there any problems or objections to buying today?
- Why are you moving?
- Are you ready to sign an exclusive agreement?

Be direct. By asking hard questions, you will narrow your search and quickly know in which group your new prospects belong. Look at their housing and financial situation. Do they need housing now or later, and do they have the financial resources to purchase? How ready are they to apply for credit and how strong is their loan application? Below are definitions of groups:

- Group one is usually easier to work with and will probably purchase a house soon. They are ready because they need a house and usually they know exactly what they want.
- Group two is harder to work with because they do not need a house now; they are willing to wait for the right one.
- Group three will buy someday, but not anytime soon. They have a desire to buy a house or investment, not because of a need but more of a want.
- Group four is most likely to waste your time and money. We call these people dreamers or window shoppers.

Many new real estate agents make the mistake of working hard with the first buyers they meet. You need to learn how to categorize your buyers quickly because you may end-up wasting too much time and money with a group four buyer if you don't. Group four buyers are the hardest to work with. They are the most discriminating, most demanding, and uncooperative buyers. Even worse, they will be too demanding on the contract after they finally find the right house. Learning to categorize your buyers will help you avoid getting discouraged because you have worked with so many of the wrong types of buyers. How to overcome objections and how to work with buyers who experience buyer's remorse is discussed later in this chapter.

Even if your prospects fall into group one, if they do not respect your profession, demand more than you are willing to offer, and are unwilling to follow your professional advice, it may be better to walk away. If you can determine what category your buyer(s) fit into, you will save valuable time by choosing to not work with them. Instead, you will work with buyers who respect you and your profession and who are reasonable. You are not going to be the perfect match for all prospects in group one. If you don't think a relationship with a buyer is a good match, cut your losses early and move-on to the next prospect. Some people have too many personal issues, so don't take it personally if it doesn't work out with some buyers.

Keep in touch with groups three and four and move them up to a higher position as time permits. Remember, you cannot win over all buyers. In the long-run, working with percentages is what will make you successful. Pawning groups three and four off to another agent isn't the answer either. Doing so may just make the situation worse. If, however, both you and the prospective buyer(s) understand your roles in the process, things will work out in favor of both parties. The best thing to do is to plan to use approximately 10% of your time staying in touch with buyers from groups 3 and 4 by emails, letters, phone calls, and personal visits. Don't forget these are the same people who will refer other buyers and sellers to you. Just because buyers are in group 4 doesn't mean they don't know of people who would be in group one. Once you have filtered-out prospects from group one, be professional and set your boundaries—make it clear what services they should expect from you. If you work with only one type of buyer, let them know. If you do not answer calls after 10:00 p.m., let them know that as well.

The Importance of Building a Database of Buyers

Another reason for categorizing buyers is to build an Excel database. The moment you start your career, you will start receiving calls from prospects. These prospects may have called about a listing from a newspaper ad or from a referral. Start saving your prospects' information. The idea is to build large Excel databases of buyers, sellers, friends, family members, investors and other professionals. The more organized the database, the better.

How impressive would it be if sellers called you about listing their property and you brought your presentation kit, which included a list of 1,200 prospective buyers 1,400 real estate agents, and 400 other professionals, such as title companies and loan officers? Your best buyers may be in group one, but referrals are in groups two and three. While some buyers may be in group three for credit repair, they still would like to know that you are thinking of them. Investors would also appreciate information on good deals you found from MLS or bank short sales.

Preparing your Buyers

Exclusive Agreement

When working with buyers, make sure to ask for an exclusive agreement. Inexperienced agents often fail to ask for an agreement for fear of rejection. This is business; ask for an exclusive agreement. For information on how to ask buyers for an exclusive agreement, read Chapter 5, *"How to Overcome Exclusive Agreement Objections."*

Buyers' Presentation Kit

You should have a presentation kit for buyers, just like you should have one for sellers. If your buyers are already convinced they will use your services, however, there is no need to present them with the kit. Your presentation kit for buyers should include all of the items that are required for you to sell a property. The items in your kit largely depend on your established relationship. Your **buyer presentation kit** should contain some of the items below:

- Information about your professional services
- Career facts: your listings to sales ratio, number of homes sold, the average time your listings were on the market, and your percentage of happy clients. Compare all of these facts to the market average. Show the difference between your services and the average market services.
- A formal agreement of what your client should expect from you
- A list of how you will overcome your buyers' major concerns
- A list of what lenders will need to qualify the applicant
- Contact information: cell phone, work phone, address, and email
- A way of obtaining information on what the buyers' housing interests are, such as number of rooms, location, floor plans, and schools
- A step-by-step guide to buying a house and an explanation of the procedure
- Lender's qualification letter
- Blank contracts
- Maps of buyers' interest points
- MLS printouts
- Pricing information on homes that were sold fitting the buyers' needs
- Notepad for taking notes on each home visited

Similar to working with sellers, you should work to gain the buyers' trust in two parts: information and presentation. Ask buyers questions to build their presentation kit, and include that information in your folder. If schools are important to your buyer, gather information about each school. Information about community centers may be what the buyers are looking for. This information will build the buyer's desire to want to live in the subject area. Keep careful notes of what buyers are saying about areas and houses. Ask open-ended questions on each property. For example, if kitchens are important, ask, *"How did you like the kitchen in house number one compared to house number two?* or, *"How was the floor plan compared to the other house?"* After about five houses, buyers will be confused about which house had what items. Your job is to keep the buyers organized on the different properties.

Qualifying Prospects

Meeting the Applicants

The three reasons for qualifying buyers are as follows:

- To find their personal needs, such as type of housing, schools, bedrooms, layout of rooms, location, etc.
- To determine if they are financially able to qualify for a loan, the amount, and when they can expect to purchase.
- To close the transaction quickly

The best way to know if you have strong buyers is have your buyers pre-qualified by a reputable lender first. If they have a large down payment, what is the maximum sales price, loan amount, and when can they start looking? Schedule to meet applicants at the lender's location or your office, but, always pick a convenient location away from distractions. If three hours are required to complete the loan application, let your applicants know in advance. Be sure they have a list of what items to bring to the loan officer. The meeting should be well-planned and organized, preferably using a step-by-step loan application process. It is very important that you understand lender's requirements; doing so will help you know if you have a good prospect and be able to close in record time. Below is a sample checklist of what items the applicant needs to provide to the lender. Ask your lender for their stalking/order sheet so that you can explain to your clients what items are required to close and move into their home in weeks not months. Yes, explaining mortgage loan requirements is the lenders' duty, but it is your money. While loan officers are working with hundreds of customers and making a few hundred, you are working with a few clients and making thousands. By giving the loan officer everything they need, in the order they need it will close your deal in record time. For more information on how to quality applicants see, Chapter 11.

Y/N Checklist for Taking a Loan Application	
	Identification, Driver's License, and Social Security Card/IRS-TIN
	Last two years of tax returns with all schedules, W-2s, and 1099s
	Two of their most recent paycheck stubs
	Two-three months of the most current bank statements, personal and joint (all pages)
	Mortgage payment booklet, property deed, or lease agreement
	Name and address of landlord for the past two years
	Copy of the executed Earnest Money Contract
	Copy of divorce decree, if applicable
	Copy of DD-214 & Certificate of Eligibility, if applying for a Veteran loan
	An authorization letter to check the applicant's credit
	List of all creditors who will not be on the credit report
	If self-employed, will need financial statements (CPA Letter)
	A list of all assets, value amount, and time owned (hard and liquid assets)

Previewing Properties and Selection of Housing

Viewing Properties

When selecting which homes to visit, preview as many as possible in your office. Use your needs, wants, and likes list, and keep notes as your buyers preview the properties. Your main goal is to reduce the final list to fewer than ten properties and later to show six or fewer. This list should comprise the very best properties that are available for your buyers' needs. Your buyer should know that this list is the best one to suit his/her needs. When buyers have the best, why should they look elsewhere? If the initial list didn't work, start over, reassessing their needs; again, the showing list should remain less than six properties.

Finding the Perfect Home

First-year real estate agents often make the mistake of trying to find the perfect home for buyers who insist on relentlessly searching for the "holy grail" of homes. Your job is to educate the buyer that the perfect home doesn't exist. Finding the holy grail of homes for a buyer may require a tremendous amount of work and is usually impossible to find. Instead, think of your client's housing needs as a temporary solution. Explain to buyers that in the old days, people purchased their home as if it were their final purchase. Today, we're a mobile society, and moving in five – seven years is normal. Therefore, focus on searching for housing that will accommodate the buyers for the next few years, and, of-course, you must take an individual's situation into account. In a few years, the family's housing situation or employment circumstances may change. Your buyers may even desire living in a different neighborhood by that time, so why frustrate everyone by searching for the perfect dream home? Suggest that your client(s) consider residing in a home where they will be happy for the next few years, and in the future, when they are ready and have the means, search for a larger home in a different neighborhood, or even in another city. For example, if you are working with a young couple who is planning a family, but is working near downtown, why even bother to show them homes that are too far away? Their present needs are urban living, but in a few years, it may be rural living. If you happen to find their dream home, that would be great, but don't overwork yourself or your buyers. Save yourself time and money and your buyers' frustration by narrowing your search just as you do with clothing, cars, and items that are easily replaceable. If you make your buyers' housing experience an enjoyable one, it's likely they will look forward to searching for a more permanent home in the next few years. This is called the Buyers' Cycle.

House Searching Should be Exciting, not Frustrating

Buyers become frustrated when they are shown too many houses; this is called getting the buyers "*house drunk*." When this happens, there is a good chance that they will switch brokerage firms. To avoid frustrating your buyers, do your homework; make an orderly checklist of your buyers' needs, wants, and likes before searching active listings. Prepare a list of your buyers' requirements. Your first step is to eliminate properties from your computer or even preview the properties by e-mailing digital pictures to your buyers from the property locations to give them a mental picture. Email pictures using your cell phone. Most cell phones today have email and photo capability. Previewing properties saves time and frustration for both you and your buyers. The rule is the more properties buyers view, the more frustrated they will become. After a while, all of the properties become blurred. Viewing properties is fun at first, but it can quickly become exhausting. Using a digital camera is handy when viewing several houses. These digital pictures, combined with a priority list, will help prevent buyers from getting house drunk.

Don't be afraid to ask a well-seasoned agent for help. Watch how the seasoned agent masterfully shows homes in terms of value before focusing on the price, how they carefully watch the buyers for clues, and how they slow showing down or quickly move on to the next room. Watch how they will guide buyers from room to room, presenting the "show," allowing buyers to emotionally connect to the property. Observe how they can reduce hundreds of properties to only a handful from which buyers can select. Notice how they show properties in terms of the buyers' needs.

Showing Properties

Buyers hire real estate agents to find housing, but what they really want is an exciting experience in the least amount of time with minimal frustration. Suggestions for showing properties are as follows:

- Preview properties using your computer to eliminate as many properties as possible before driving to them.
- Take notes of the buyers' needs, wants, and must-haves to help them narrow down what is truly important to them. Make adjustments to your list as you continue to show them properties.
- If your buyers still want to look at houses, suggest that they do drive-by viewing to see the properties' curb appeal.
- Call the listing company for an appointment as soon as possible to give sellers time to do last minute touch-ups.
- Don't show more than six properties in a day in order to keep the buyers from becoming house drunk or frustrated.
- Ask your buyer(s) if they would like some water before you start.
- It's best to preview each property personally, but if that is not possible, at least do a drive-by to become familiar with the routes.
- Plan your showing, and know the best route you will take.
- Try to take the scenic route and park across the street for curb appeal to give buyers a wider view of the property. Never park in the driveway, in case the sellers are trying to make a quick exit.
- Be sure that your vehicle has plenty of gas.
- It is best not to take children to showings; they can create problems and are a distraction. If there is no choice, ask to split the kids into two cars. Teenagers are more concerned about losing their friends than having a new home. Try to have teenagers ride with you so you can explain the schools, shopping, and social events in the area. They are not losing friends, but have a unique opportunity to find new ones.
- While buyers are examining the outside, you have time to unlock the house and turn on the lights.
- Check the different types of lock-boxes, and be familiar with each one.
- If buyers ask about the price, first tell them what the monthly payments are. The monthly amount is far less than the sales price, so break the price into smaller amounts.

- Try keeping your personal opinions to yourself unless your buyer(s) ask for advice.
- Ask open-ended questions about how the buyer(s) feel about the property.
- If you were able to preview the properties from your sheet of needs, wants, and likes, you can point out the benefit of each property.
- Don't rush your buyer(s); be sure to give them plenty of time to view each property. Let them touch as much as possible; this is a part of emotionally connecting for the buyer(s).
- Take pictures and notes of what buyers like about each home; they will soon start forgetting which property has what features.
- Before you show any property, act like a tour guide and entertain your buyer(s). When you start your sales pitch, first try to sell the community. You should know what is new in your farming community. Know how schools perform, what new businesses are moving in, and have information about board members of the neighborhood association, if there is one.
- Don't try to cover 100% of what the property has to offer while you are showing it. Let your buyer(s) use their imagination. For example, for unusual rooms, instead of making suggestions, first ask your buyer(s) for their ideas; let them participate in the showings. If your buyer(s) don't have any ideas, make suggestions. An example of an open-ended question is, "Would the room make a good study for you?"
- The kitchen area is important; if your buyers are a man and a woman, the woman usually makes the initial decision to buy over 80% of the time. Look for detail; try to ask open-end questions, allowing them to emotionally connect.

Buyers usually buy emotionally. Once they like a certain property, they will start looking for reasons to justify their purchase.

How Many Vehicles to Use?

Whether to use one vehicle or two when showing properties will depend on the buyers. Here are some simple rules when it's acceptable to use one vehicle:

- The buyer(s) is/are unfamiliar with the area or are from out-of-town
- The properties you are showing are in different areas
- You need to take a scenic route to sell the area

When it's acceptable to use two vehicles:

- The buyer(s) is/are familiar with the area
- The buyer(s) has/have children or family members with them

- The properties are in the same area
- It is company policy
- If you decide to use more than one vehicle, be sure that the people in the other vehicles have a cell phone, map, or GPS

Tips for Showing Properties:

- Help your buyer(s) complete a buyers' requirement sheet.
- Carefully reduce the number of showings showing fewer than 20 houses, especially if the buyer(s) are from out-of- town.
- Once you have the list down to the top 20 houses, use your computer or have buyers do drive-bys to reduce the number of houses to fewer than six. If the buyer(s) is/ are out-of-town, you might do the drive-bys or preview each house yourself.
- Make appointments without the buyer(s) present, and ask if there are any recent offers. Don't be surprised if the listing agent says, "Oh, we have several offers."
- Prepare your material, have a digital camera, map, GPS, notepad, and car ready.
- Meet with the buyer(s) and discuss price, schools, parks, shopping, and plan your route.
- If the buyer(s) don't know the area, drive slowly, so they can see what the community offers.
- Don't be a chatterbox and talk about your personal life—act as a tour guide.
- Take control; slowly walk your buyer(s) from room to room.
- Ask for small commitments; take notes on the buyers' opinions.
- Ask the buyer(s) what they think, and go over your buyer's requirement sheet. The requirement sheet will also help you remain objective. Take more notes.
- Try giving the buyer(s) the time they need to absorb their environment. Top producers introduce the feature and give buyers time before asking for small commitments.
- Take pictures of what the buyer(s) like about the house.
- Repeat the same with other houses.
- Try having the buyer(s) enter each room without you. Stand a foot outside of each room to give your buyer(s) a better view of the rooms. You can explain that they can get a better feel for the rooms without you in them. While you may believe you're important, sometimes you are a distraction. When buyers are examining different rooms, they need their space, so don't choke them with your presence.
- Keep the same pace and emotions as your buyer(s) do.
- Try refraining from getting overly excited; stay calm during showings.
- Never try to control the showing; let your buyer(s) get involved.

Below is an example of how to help distinguish your buyers' true needs from a feature they would just like to have. During the showing, buyers may become confused about their real needs. If you are working with several buyers, you may also forget or be unsure of your buyers' needs or must-haves. That's why you have a list. The requirement list below isn't set-in-stone; use it as a guide. Ask questions to separate your buyers' wish list from their real needs. Buyers may not always know what they do want, but they will know what they don't want.

Buyer Requirement Sheet

Name
Address
Phone number Work number

Description of requirements

Price range	
Down payment	
Down payment assistance	
Type of loan	
Interest rate	

Item	Need	Want	Wish	Dreaming
Type of living room:_____				
Number of bedrooms: _____				
Number of bathrooms:_____				
Need of breakfast room: _____				
Need of central A/C: _____				
Two stories: _____				
Square ft. range:_____				
Type of yard: _____				
Lake front: _____				
School district /school: _____				
Area/zip code: _____				
New home				
Year built				
Used home				
Subdivision				
Attached/detached garage				
Garage				
Fireplace				
Pool				
Community center/ pool				
Size of kitchen				
Closets				
Corner lot				
Washer and dryer				

Overcoming Buyers' Objections

Knowing how to overcome objections means the difference between having a career or short-term job in real estate. New agents and some seasoned agents have a tendency to lower their commissions in order to get the sale because of their fear of rejection. The problem with this is that it lowers your income, but doesn't earn your client's respect. Giving-up commissions is a temporary solution, but it doesn't really solve your problem. Below are rules on how to overcome the buyers' objections and not lose commissions or respect:

- When working with buyers, sellers, or investors, never give your price amount until you have firmly established the value of your services. How can clients agree to your price if they have yet to understand the value of your services? Consumers normally shop for a product first, and then find out about pricing. Your presentation package should show the value your buyers will receive.
- Ask small non-commitment questions. For example, "Mr. Johnson, are there any community regulations preventing us from placing our real estate sign in your front yard?" "Would putting your property on the MLS before summer be a realistic goal for you?" "How soon will you be ready to start looking for a home?" These are small non-commitment questions that will later add to the total commitment sale. Here you are not asking the final question, but small questions. After several of these questions, you will know if your buyers are ready. Buyers have fears as well; these types of questions don't commit the buyers, but they do reveal how the buyers are thinking. You are testing the waters before you ask the final direct question.
- If the buyer(s) start asking several questions, chances are they are thinking about buying that house. Before you ask if they would like to make an offer, first test the water. Ask non-commitment questions. For example, ask "What do you think about this property"? If the reply is encouraging, ask another question, "Do you think your family will be happy here?" Now that you have two favorable answers, ask the big one, "Are you ready to make this your home?"
- If your buyer(s) ask for a part of your fees, don't be afraid to say no. Of-course, be polite and thank your buyer(s). Most of the time, they are only testing you. Gaining their respect is much better than getting the sale. Try giving your buyer(s) time to digest your reply. Pause for at least five seconds. One way to maintain control is by not responding immediately. This gives you time to gather your thoughts, and the buyer(s) are often just thinking things out loud. They will often agree to your commissions. A long pause in a conversation is a very powerful communication tool.

- Listen carefully and acknowledge your buyers' objections. Make it clear that you understand their objections. You may say, "Yes, those are very important issues!" While another real estate rule is never to defend the property, sometimes it's a minor issue that can easily be corrected. You might say, "Yes, you are right, the rooms are out-of-date. Do you think that a nice warm color as the backdrop to your furniture would make a difference?"
- Never attack or argue about objections. Be professional and remain calm.
- Address the objection with an open-ended question to provoke thought.
- If possible, address each objection with facts or even elaborate on how to overcome objections. For example, if your buyer(s) disapprove of the dining room color, you can say, "Would you like an estimate? Would you like some contractors' phone numbers?" Try turning a negative into a positive. You might also say, "That's good. Now you can select whatever colors you like. Behr paint has some beautiful colors; you should see this year's pallet of colors!"
- If the buyer(s) insist on having new carpet, you may say, "Other than the carpet, how do you like the house?" Here, you are trying to pinpoint the buyers' real objectives. You can also say, "If the house had new carpet, would you make an offer?"
- The reason professional agents ask many questions early in the relationship is to overcome objections. Buyers' objections are real concerns for them; the sooner these objections are known, the easier it will be to overcome them.
- Before you reply, ask for clarification. Give your buyer(s) time to fully clarify their thoughts.
- Ask about deal breakers. What are the non-negotiable must-have features? Also what are the absolute not-haves? Pets, houses close to apartments, or older homes are examples of not-haves.
- Agents often move too fast. Some people need more time to think about the big decision. Give the buyer(s) time as they think about/discuss each room.
- Many buyers get nervous because they do not fully understand the financial involvement. Carefully pick a loan officer who will accurately answer any questions the buyer(s) may have and a lender who gives all federal disclosures on a timely schedule. Once this is done, you don't have to spend your time answering questions about monthly payments, mortgage insurance, etc. Your focus is on qualifying your buyer(s) on their personal needs, not financial matters.
- If the objection is that they are not sure how the real estate procedure works, distributing HUD's Information Booklet for Consumers is a good idea. One of the best ways to overcome objections is to educate buyers.

Financing (See Chapter 11)

Qualifying your prospect(s) means the likelihood of their getting approved for a loan. The how to qualify process is discussed in more detail in Chapter 11, *Financing Real Estate.*

Closing and Follow Up

Closing

The final step in the real estate transaction is the closing. The buyer(s) has/have qualified for the loan, the property has met the lender's guidelines, and the sellers have qualified to sell their property. Now what can happen? Buyers and sellers can have remorse. It's rare for sellers to have remorse because they usually have selected another home and are excited about the move. Buyers are typically the ones who express remorse. There can be several reasons for this: the most common ones are job security, misunderstanding, discomfort about the property, and self-doubt. They start thinking subjectively about all of the negative things that can happen. After all, a 30-year loan is a big commitment. Be prepared, always know what scripts you will use, respond with objective answers, such as the investment of a good education or the value of the home.

Buyers may think they have good reasons to stop a contract, but self-doubt is usually what holds them back. Your job is to find out why the buyers are having second thoughts. If there was loan fraud involved, this shouldn't be overlooked; the penalty for loan fraud is $10,000, and the punishment could be applied to you if you knew about it. If the buyer has received a layoff notice from his or her employer, discuss this with the lender, even if the buyer is in a full contract.

Attending Closings

Meet with real estate agents and borrowers at closings. Real estate closings are a rich source of leads. Title companies close most of the residential real estate transactions. Closings are often filled with real estate agents, brokers, attorneys, buyers, and sellers.

Loan officers rarely attend closings (fewer than 10%). Remember this rule of thumb: "*Whoever doesn't attend the closing will usually be blamed for any mistakes that are made.*"

By federal law, upon request, a HUD-1 or HUD-1A statement shall be ready one day before closing. The **HUD-1** is the final breakdown of all expenses for all parties in the transaction. Have the title company fax or email your copy as soon as possible. Do your mathematics and check for mistakes. If anything is not clear, you have time to discuss whatever is not clear with your broker, lender, or the title company. If you are a new agent, meet with the title agent, and discuss each item line-by-line. Make sure that no surprises await your client(s) at closing. Arrive at least 30 minutes early. Lenders and title companies are able to make corrections even during closing. Ask for a new HUD-1 statement for new changes. Make it a point to personally meet title closers in your area, and exchange business cards. Title companies do have referrals and walk-ins, and those leads can be yours!

Building a Referral System

Keeping in Contact

Remember, *"If you forget your borrowers, they'll forget you."* If you fail to keep in contact with past clients or customers, they will forget about you. By keeping in constant contact with customers/clients, they will keep referring future business to you. **Referrals** are the business leads from past clients or friends that are sent to you. Suggestions for building referrals are as follows:

- In addition to using all of the strategies and marketing tools at your disposal, always remember that in this line of business, the greatest tool you can use to your advantage is your personality (inclusive of your character, attitude and the manner in which you relate to people). Plan your visits, even send postcards or make calls weeks in advance.
- As you build your referral base, remember that friends will tell their friends about your business ethics. They will say the most wonderful things about you: how smart you are, how good you are at your job, or how much they trust you. Some callers may even have an image of you as a superman or superwoman and therefore may expect nothing less than super service from you. Consequently, if you have a busy workload, it is in your customers' best interest to be honest about the services they can expect from you. Set the rules and parameters of the business relationship early, so as not to disappoint your callers and avoid losing future referrals.
- Instead of your telling the world how great you are, building a referral base is like having an army of happy homeowners saying wonderful things about you. Quality service leads to an increasingly satisfied clientele. What is wrong with saying, "Can you do me a really big favor and tell your friends to call me if they need a good Realtor®?" or you can say, "Do you know of any friends or family members who are looking for a home?"

- Try drafting a letter and asking your happy homeowner to email it to all of their friends. This letter can contain news or pictures of your new happy homeowners, business cards, new listings, or educational material. Ideas for letters are almost endless.
- Before the computer age, typed letters were considered more professional than hand written ones. Today, this rule has changed; a handwritten letter now gives a personal touch. If you need to write a few letters, try handwriting them, a lost art due to computer technology. What would our business school teachers think after insisting for years to never handwrite but to always type? Typed letters still have a formal place, but letters to past clients aren't always formal.

The Importance of Referrals

How important are referrals? The National Realtors Association estimates that nearly 50% of buyers will come from referrals. If the average agent gets 50% of referrals, what percentage can you get if you have a referral marketing system in place? If you were to find housing for an average of 100 buyers per year and worked for 10 years, and 80% of those loyally referred one prospect per year, which would be 800 new buyers per year. If you mail four letters per year to 100 previous clients at a cost of 50 cents each, the total mail-out cost would be $200. Even if you received one referral for the sale of a $200,000 home, the profit could be an estimated at $6,000. Now estimate the profits if you were to mail out four letters to 1,000 former happy clients for ten years. Why ten years? Because, building a referral base is a long-term committed business relationship as in a retirement system. Activities you can do to promote referrals are the following:

- During the off season, plan annual trips to visit all of your past clients. For example, you may decide to take yearly pictures of your past clients' house, or their children, if possible, yearly calendars. These calendars will, of course, have all of your marketing information. It doesn't have to be calendars. It can be for any reason, even a simple hello visit. The point is to personally visit clients at least once a year to let them know that you are still in business, especially if you're transferring to another company. Simply by mailing letters or cards four times a year will not substitute for your personal visit. Your clients have to actually see you, talk to you, and relate to you if you want to continually get their referrals.
- Your cards and letters should always have something that is important for your clients; for example, information on how to protest property taxes or hurricane information. Always look for important information that you can share. Why is educational information important? This business is a give-and-take type of

business. Give your clients valuable information now, and you can ask for their help later. Think about the old rule of benefit. What is likely not to work is your writing about how great you are and asking for their support. Where is the benefit to your clients?

- Should you decide to use the referral marketing system, remember like all other types of marketing, in order for your referral marketing system to work, it has to be continuous and consistent, like putting funds away for retirement. Keep a database of all referrals; that way, you will know your referral percentage, who to send Thank-You letters to, and whom to visit.

A Form of Retirement

Think of referrals as adding to your retirement. As you decide to retire, bring in apprentices or co-workers to work your rich referral base. If you have buyer leads, let your trusted apprentices do the work. If you have seller leads, let the word of mouth do the rest. Once you have built years of quality service, the nightmare begins when you finally decide to retire. Retiring won't be easy, you will need help.

All of those referrals will keep calling long after you retire. Now you have to decide what to do with all of the calls that come-in on an almost daily basis. If you give-up your license, you cannot get paid for selling your referrals. So, you will have to decide whether or not you trust an apprentice to take care of a business that took you a lifetime to build?

1. When looking for buyers, select which types of sources you would like to use. Number your sources from one to twenty, from the most favorable to the least favorable.

2. Ask about working floor time.

3. Ask your broker or other agents' advice on which purchasing lead company has better results.

4. Examine the buyer's representation agreement. Be knowledgeable and comfortable using such forms.

5. Practice presenting a buyer's exclusive agreement.

6. Develop a script that tells buyers why they should have representation.

7. Design a script that tells buyers why they should use your services.

8. Develop a buyers' presentation kit. You can later change the content, but for now, you need some direction.

9. Research which software you will use for developing a database of buyers.

10. In your management contact software, add categories of buyers.

11. Design a company Buyer's Requirement Sheet.

12. By using your management contact software plans, you can often contact prospects and clients.

13. Find the top producers in your office, they just may be looking for a dependable buyer's agent.

14. Make sure to have phone numbers of every agent in your office.

15. Make sure other agents in the office know that you are available for open houses.

16. Ask your office manager about old files.

17. Research your requirements for selling HUD homes.

18. Have a checklist of loan officers.

19. Start going to broker open houses. Ask the agents for a tour. You will need to know who the agents are and the inventory of homes.

20. Ask other agents how you can master the craft of reducing the numbers of homes that you will show.

Rules for Real Estate Success

1. The people who know, trust, and like you, who will spread the word about you are called
   A. Sphere of influence
   B. Leads
   C. Floor time
   D. Listings

2. A term real estate agents use which refers to people who may be thinking of using your service is
   A. Listings
   B. Prospect leads
   C. Floor time
   D. Office duty

3. The time period used taking incoming phone calls and greeting walk-in prospects in the office is called
   A. Executive's agreements
   B. Door greeter
   C. Floor time
   D. Office duty

4. Properties that have been posted for sale by real estate agents are called
   A. Executive's agreement
   B. Office duty
   C. Floor time
   D. Listings

5. A real estate broker or salesperson acting as an agent for another agent is a fiduciary. Special obligations that are imposed when such fiduciary relationships are created are called
   A. Fidelity
   B. Office duty
   C. Floor time
   D. Listings

6. When the agent faithfully performs his/her duties and follows the instructions of his/her client, unless the request is either unreasonable or unlawful, is called
   A. Fidelity
   B. Obedience
   C. Disclosure
   D. Office duties

Prospecting for Buyers

7. When the agent obtains and gives any information that is relevant to the client, it is called.
   A. Commingling
   B. Categorizing
   C. To disclose/disclosure
   D. Reward system

8. The reasons for determining the category of your prospects is to
   A. Work smart
   B. Not to waste your time with prospects who will not buy
   C. Determine` great, good, and bad buyers
   D. All of the above

9. A term used for separating buyers into groups that are most likely to buy soon compared to groups
   that are less likely to buy is called
   A. Categorizing
   B. Commingling
   C. Fiduciary
   D. Grouping

10. Business leads from past clients or friends that are sent to you are
    A. Easy money
    B. Referrals
    C. Gold mining
    D. Silver digging

CHAPTER 11
Financing Real Estate

Objectives:

Be able to identify and understand the following:

- The importance of qualifying prospects
- The risk factors that lenders consider before approving a loan
- The types of income that you can use to qualify the borrower
- The importance of credit reports to lenders
- Mortgage Terms
- The different types of loan products
- Conforming loan requirements
- Identifying the main difference between FHA and VA
- The methods that VA uses to analyze income

Terms:

- Available income/effective income
- Conforming/prime lenders
- Debt-to-income ratio (DTI)
- GSE
- Housing ratio
- Loan application
- Non-conforming loans
- Pre-approved/pre-qualified
- Risk-based pricing
- Total living ratio
- VA loans

- Certificate of Eligibility
- Credit scores
- FHA loans
- Hard assets
- Liquid assets
- Loan to value (LTV)
- Payment shock
- Residual income
- Sub-prime lenders
- VA entitlement
- Yield spread premiums

The Importance of Qualifying
Prospects in Marketing and Sales

Rules for Real Estate Success

Not all prospects will qualify for a mortgage loan. Knowing lenders' guidelines will help convert a greater percentage of prospects into buyers, thereby, resulting in more sales. While some prospects may be just short of qualifying, it may take others months or years to qualify for a mortgage loan. While lenders will order credit reports and financially qualify borrowers, you should understand the guidelines lenders use in order to better help and categorize your prospects. By knowing what lenders expect (stacking order) and how they approve loans, the time it takes to qualify and close your clients buying transaction is shortened. You will be able to help your clients understand what lender requirements are and be able to present those items in the exact organized order required. Doing so can shorten the loan process from months to a few weeks. While qualifying applicants is the loan officer's responsibility, it's your income and your clients that will be looking to you for a smooth transaction.

An example of a credit issue, if the buyer's credit score is 620 and all other requirements are satisfactory, a ten-point improvement is fairly easy to obtain in 30 days, which gives the prospect a credit score of 630, which is a qualifying score for most lenders. While loan officers know how to qualify borrowers according to their company's guidelines, they may not be creative enough or willing to overcome qualifying issues. After all, they will make hundreds while you make thousands. They have several applicants (customers) while you have a few buyers (clients).

Financially Qualifying the Applicant

It is best to have your prospect(s) **pre-qualified** for a price range before spending your time showing houses so that you know the exact price range of houses to show. To **pre-qualify** is to measure how much home an applicant can purchase. To **pre-approve** is to verify the applicant's income, employment, and credit history. You can also use this opportunity to be sure that the buyer is willing to sign a contract. The reasons that you should pre-qualifiy/pre-approve are covered in Chapter 10.

Mortgage Lending

Most lenders sell their loans as mortgage-backed securities to secondary investors but keep the servicing rights to the properties. Some of these investors are:

- Insurance Companies/private investors
- Federal National Mortgage Association (FNMA) Fannie Mae
- Federal Home Loan Mortgage Corporation (FHLMC) Freddie Mac

- Federal Agricultural Mortgage Corporation (FAMC) Farmer Mac
- Government National Mortgage Association (GNMA) Ginnie Mae

The largest investors are government sponsored enterprises, better known as Fannie Mae and Freddie Mac. These types of loans are packaged into bond-type securities representing an undivided interest in a pool of mortgages. Since secondary investors will purchase the loan, they set the guidelines for primary lenders to follow. Lenders' guidelines are to approve loans based on two factors: the qualification of the property and the borrower. The settlement agent or title insurance company gathers the information for the qualification of the property. Property qualifying steps are listed below:

1. Obtain an appraisal report; it must meet the lender's requirements.
2. Obtain a survey; it must meet the requirements of both the title insurance company and the lender.
3. Obtain the title policy; it must meet the lender's requirements.
4. Gather all legal documents: the deed, promissory note, and mortgagee clauses.
5. Be sure that the homeowner's insurance meets the lender's requirements.
6. Get a flood certificate, which is a federal statute and lender requirement.

Lender's Requirements for Borrows

1. Identification
2. Credit scores and recent credit history
3. Down payment, loan-to-value (LTV, loan amount compared to value of property); the greater the down payment, the safer the investment.
4. The borrower's income and debts (DTI, comparing debt-to-income)
5. The type of property, whether the property is for residential, investment, or commercial purposes
6. The collateral, whether the property is a good safe investment
7. Mortgage terms (number of years); longer terms mean a greater risk
8. Type of loan product/program
9. The loan follows state and federal requirements

Credit Scores and Recent Credit History for Qualifying Borrowers

Credit Scores

The lender's greatest risk factor is credit scores and credit history. **Credit score** is a statistical model, which predicts future performance or the probability of default and delinquency based on prior experience.

Most lenders prefer the tri-score method, which is using the middle score, <u>not</u> the average score from the three bureaus. If a request from only two credit bureaus is ordered, the lowest score is used. If there are two people applying for a loan, lenders will normally use the lowest middle score of the two. There are only three credit bureaus, which are the following:

Experian/FICO score www.experian.com, (888) 397-3742
Trans-Union/Empirical score www.transunion.com, (800) 916-8800
Equifax / Beacon score www.equifax.com, (800) 685-1111

Credit bureaus sell information to credit agencies, which, in turn, assemble and organize the information for retail mortgage lenders. In mortgage lending, a credit score of 620 is considered the minimum score for grade "A" loans, which are acceptable by standard Fannie Mae/Freddie Mac underwriting. Interesting credit score information is below:

- Most of the information in a credit report is deleted after seven years, except for a bankruptcy, which is deleted after ten years.
- Credit information is continuously being updated to reflect the latest information on a person's debt and payment history.
- Making late payments of 30 days or more will have the greatest negative impact on credit scores, especially if it is a mortgage payment.
- Inquiries are also recorded. To the lender, inquiries are an indication that the borrower is seeking new credit or extension of available credit. Historically, a high number of inquiries reflect a higher degree of risk, especially if they are recent 30-day inquiries.
- Automobile and mortgage inquiries within a 45-day window are counted as one inquiry for scoring.
- If an applicant's credit report contains mistakes, they can be corrected. The applicant must contact each of the credit bureaus or the credit agency for corrections.
- For corrections, under the **Fair Credit Reporting Act (FCRA)**, the credit bureau or credit agency must complete an investigation within a 30-day period of the original credit bureau notification. Subsequently, the company <u>must</u> provide a written notice of the results within five days after completion of the investigation, including a copy of the credit report if it changed based on the dispute.

Credit Score and Credit History

In today's market, lenders are intensely credit-score driven. Credit score and credit history will usually determine the type of underwriting and/ or approval. One of the first things a lender does is order a credit report that shows debts, payment history, inquiries, a list of all creditors, and a credit score.

Credit scores can range from 300-850. As a general guideline, prime lenders target applicants with credit scores that range from 620-850. **Prime/conforming lenders** are lenders who accept low-risk loans and sell loans to **government sponsored enterprises (GSEs)**, such as Fannie Mae and Freddie Mac. The sub-prime market will accept scores as low as 400, depending on the lender's guidelines.

Sub-prime lenders or **nonconforming lenders** are lenders that accept high risk **non-conforming loans** that do not meet GSE guidelines. Since the dividing line between the prime market and sub-prime market seems to be a 620 credit score, scores over 620 usually have better pricing. Credit scores from 620-670 are acceptable but are still considered risky. Conforming lenders usually require full documentation and verification of all documents. This is referred to as "full doc loans." Conforming loans are those that meet GSE guidelines.

Credit scores over 670 are considered grade "A+" loans, not a substantial risk. Therefore, most lenders require less documentation. These loans can be streamlined and are called low/no doc loans. Scores of 620 and below are usually unacceptable for Fannie Mae/Freddie Mac's guidelines; therefore, they are considered nonconforming or sub-prime loans. However, Fannie Mae/Freddie Mac have been known to purchase low credit score loans if the borrowers were able to provide other compensating factors. See each lender for compensating factors.

Non-prime lenders are willing to accept a higher risk, such as charge-offs, collections, or even bankruptcy, as long as the total amount is under $5,000. Additionally, few lenders will approve loan applications with a history of late student loan payments, child support, or IRS tax liens. See mortgage risk tip sheet below:

Underwriting	FHA	VA	CONFORMING	SUB-PRIME
Credit Scoring	None but subject to lender req. (FHA-620+)	None but subject to lender requirements	620+ FICO less than 620 subject to mortgage ins. availability	400-800
Down-payment	5%	0	5% Standard GSE	Each lender has its own guidelines.
Debt Ratios	31/43 %	41/41 %	28/36 %	55/55 %
Gifts allowed	Yes	Yes	Borrowers must have at least 5 % of own funds	Each lender has its own guidelines.

Underwriting	FHA	VA	CONFORMING	SUB-PRIME
Seller Contributions	6 % X Sales Price	4 % X Sales Price	Over 90% LTV = 3 % less than 90% LTV = 6 % less than 75% LTV = 9%	Most lenders 6%
Reserves	2 months	2 months	2 months	Usually none
Mortgage Ins.%	UPMIP 1.5 % monthly. 05%	0-4.99% dn. 2.0% 5-9.99% dn. 1.50% 10% + dn. 1.25%	See mortgage ins. chart	Usually none required
Cash on hand	3 % of acquisition	Closing cost Reserves	Enough cash for Down-payment Closing cost Reserves	Enough cash for Down payment Closing cost Reserves
Co-borrower allowable	Yes	Yes	Yes	Yes

Calculating Credit Scores

Scores are a mathematical formula designed by the three credit bureaus. The software that is used doesn't have feelings, understand variables, or even remember the past. Knowing how scores are calculated can help applicants improve their scores. Real estate agents can make better decisions about how soon to work with applicants with low scores. Scoring should never be taken personally; it is simply a mathematical system of adding or subtracting points based on existing variables. Below is the mathematical formula for credit scores.

- 35% of the score rate is determined from payment history (late and on-time payments):
  a. Recent late payments will weigh more heavily than old late payments. The older the late payment, the less it will affect the scores.
  b. Current to 12 month payments = 40 %
     13-24 month payments = 30%
     25-36 month payments = 20%
     accounts greater than 37 months = 10%

- 30% of the score is based on loan balance ratio, (total loan limit compared to loan balance):
  a. 50% or less of loan balance starts the deducting of points
  b. 70% or less of loan balance results in a larger deduction of points
  c. A low loan balance on any one account also reduces the scores. The loan balance needs to be spread over all accounts.

- 15% of the score is based on the length of credit history:
  a. The older the credit history, the more credit cards the consumer may have before points are taken from the score.

b. A good amount of credit cards are three-five for revolving accounts on old history (25-30 years) and less than three revolving accounts for new credit history.
c. High revolving accounts over $30,000 are considered installment accounts.

- 10% of the score is based on the type of credit (installment or revolving):
a. Installment accounts usually increase the score.
b. Revolving accounts decrease the score.

- 10% is based on the current accumulation of debt such as
a. The number of recent inquiries in less than 12 months, which can reduce the score by 10%. All mortgage inquiries within a 45-day period are considered as one inquiry. More than five-seven inquiries per quarter can drop the credit score by 15 points, depending on whether the consumer has new or old credit. For those persons with new credit, the score can drop as much as 30 points.
b. Opening new lines of credit drops the score for 30-days, but increases the score over a long-term period.

Tips on How to Build a Good Credit Score

- Pay bills on time. Your bill-paying history serves as an indicator of how you will be pay them in the future.
- Credit scores emphasize the most recent payment record. The older the late payment, the less it will affect credit scores. Lenders are more concerned about recent lines of credit.
- Pay at least the minimum monthly amount required. You can pay more, but never pay less.
- Transfer revolving debts to installment or consolidating debts. It usually takes 30-60 days for credit scores to change after corrections are made. Try to have more installment accounts than revolving accounts.
- Keep credit card balances low. Don't "max out" your credit cards. Accounts should have more than 50% of available credit. One factor that can drive-up credit scores is the total percent of credit available from all lines of credit.
- Be careful regarding paying off and closing accounts. Closing loans that have a large credit line available can negatively affect credit scores. Pay down accounts to under 50%, but never close accounts.
- Opening new accounts will increase the available credit ratio. If you are going to open new accounts, do so months before applying for a loan. Requesting new lines of credit during the loan period may cause the lender to perceive that you are creating a higher debt ratio.

- Never open or apply for new credit, such as a car or boat loan, during the loan application period. Most lenders will request a final credit report before funding and closing.
- Collection accounts over 3 ½ years old are still a part of history, but have little effect on scores. Most conforming lenders will not accept loan applicants who have outstanding collection accounts.

Down Payment

Down Payment

The minimum down payment is 5% for conventional loans, 3% for **FHA loans**, and 0% for **VA loans**. A larger down payment, however, brings less risk to the lender; therefore, there is less need for documentation, a faster approval, and a better interest rate. For example, a 95% Loan-to-Value loan (LTV) will have a better interest rate than a 100% LTV loan. Fannie Mae considers the down payment a primary risk factor. **Loan to value (LTV)** is the amount of money the lender will loan or risk to the lender. The **down payment** is the money the borrower is using to secure the loan or risk to the borrower. LTV + Down payment = Value (sales price).

Prime Lenders prefer that borrowers apply a down payment of 20% or purchase mortgage insurance in case of default. Most sub-prime lenders do not demand mortgage insurance. It is not permissible for applicants to borrow the down payment money because of the additional risk to the lender. Lenders will verify all down payments and demand that all funds are seasoned for at least 60 days for GSE loans and usually 30-60 days for sub-prime loans.

Borrowers' Income and Debts; (DTI, comparing debt-to-income)

Borrowers' Income and Debts

The third most influential risk factor is income. Lenders use three income factors below to determine applicants' repayment ability for residential loans:

1. Amount of income calculated as the average gross monthly income compared to the purposed debt
2. Type of income
3. The stability and durability of income

The housing price is determined by the applicant's income. The lender will determine the true debt-to-income ratio. Inform the lender of the price-range in which your applicant is seeking to purchase. Knowing the price of the house helps the lender determine a safe price range. Lenders measure the amount of stable gross monthly income the applicant will have available to determine repayment risk. The rationale is that if the applicant's housing expenses exceed a certain percentage of his/her income, then the likelihood of default on repayment of the loan increases.

To determine how much house the applicant can afford, lenders will measure the amount a borrower owes (debt) as opposed to how much the borrower is able to earn (income). This combination is referred to as the debt-to-income ratio. **Debt-to-income** is the amount of monthly debt compared to gross monthly income.

The debt-to-income ratio is calculated by dividing the total monthly housing debt by the gross monthly income. Lenders use gross monthly income, not net income.

For example:

$1000 total proposed monthly mortgage debt
÷ $ 4000 total gross monthly income
= .25 DTI (25% debt-to-income)

In the above example, 25% of the borrower's income goes toward paying the housing debt. This leaves 75% of gross income available to pay for other expenses.

Conforming/GSE, FHA, and VA lenders use two types of debt ratios which are

- **Housing ratio** (front-ratio), which measures the proposed housing expense.
- **Total living obligations ratio** (back-ratio), which measures the combination of proposed housing and living expenses.

Debt-to-income ratios are	
Conforming/GSE	28/36 %
FHA	31/43 %
VA	41/41 %

Financing Real Estate

While all lenders use DTI ratios to measure risk, loans sold to GSEs use ratios as a guide. For example, Fannie Mae and Freddie Mac have 28/36 DTI ratios, but will accept loans up to a 65% DTI if the borrower can compensate with other factors, such as a large down payment.

As the debt ratio is lowered, the applicant's position with the lender is more favorable. As the debt ratio increases, so does the risk factor. This leaves the borrower with less money to pay for other expenses. Lenders are concerned with how much money the homeowner will have after all monthly debts are paid. This is referred to as the **available income ratio** by conventional lenders and **effective income** by FHA. The various types of stabilized gross income are weighed differently, as follows:

- **Self-employment**: The lender weighs the likelihood that the borrower will be able to continue making monthly house payments. In order to determine stabilized income, the lender will most likely require a few years of income documentation. Self-employed borrowers may be required to have larger down payments, depending on the overall risk.
- **Bonuses**: If the borrower is using bonuses to qualify for a loan, he/she must show the lender that the bonuses were stable and will be continuous.
- **Wages and salary**: Normal wages and salary are the safest acceptable income for the lender; however, lenders usually become concerned when the borrower switches occupations often (unstable employment), since this may pose a greater risk.
- **Overtime pay**: Like bonuses, the lender expects overtime to continue in the future.
- **Part-time pay**: Like bonuses and overtime pay, lenders prefer stable part-time income to continue in the future. Prime and sub-prime lenders have different rules for part-time employment, such as uninterrupted employment for two years and a strong likelihood of continuation.
- **Temporary agency employment**: Most lenders will not accept temporary agency employment. Once the applicant finds full-time employment outside of the agency, the income is permissible after two years.
- **Employment gaps have time limits**: Each lender establishes the period of time an applicant can have gaps in his/her employment. For example, for a prime full-doc-loan, the period cannot exceed six months. If it exceeds six months, an exception is required. All prime loans with over one month of unemployment require a reasonable explanation stated in a signed letter of exception.
- **Employment/self-employment conversion**: If the borrower changes from a W-2 wage earner to a 1099 employment, the new status will require two years of 1099 forms, even if the borrower is in the same job for the same company. In this case, an option is to pay for a no-doc product loan.

- **Retirement funds and rental income**
- **Public assistance income**
- **Co-signer's Income**: this refers to a co-borrower who will be obligated on the note but will not necessarily occupy the property. The primary borrower and the co-signer are each fully liable for the entire loan balance.
- **Child support**: most lenders require an official divorce decree with two to three years remaining.

For calculating wages or salary, lenders use gross monthly income, require two years of similar type of employment, verified by two years of tax returns, and up-to-date check stubs.

In order for the lender to measure debt-to-income ratios, employment income must be reduced to gross monthly income for calculations. Using the right calculation is essential. For example, if a borrower earns $800 gross income per week, what amount will be used for monthly income? The correct answer is $3467. There are 52 weeks in a year.

Income conversion calculations:

- Annual: gross yearly income /12 = monthly income
- Weekly: gross weekly income X 52 /12 = monthly income
- Bi-weekly: gross bi-weekly income X 26 /12 monthly income
- Semi-monthly: gross semi-monthly income X 24 /12 = monthly income
- Hourly: pay per hour X number of hours per week X 52 / 12 = monthly income

Types of unacceptable sources of income:

- Foreign income, unless by an American company
- Unverified income
- Income by other family members
- Temporary agency income
- Unemployment compensation
- Part-time employment less than two years
- Job gaps over six months
- VA school benefits

Assets/Net Worth

An applicant's net worth, or assets, is important because it reveals their financial strength. The greater the borrower's financial strength, the lower the investment risk and the better the interest rates.

Assets are divided into two parts: hard and liquid assets.

Hard assets are assets such as real estate, automobiles, and other personal property. The borrower's cash reserves (funds left after closing) also help strengthen the overall financial status.

Liquid assets, such as money in banks, stocks and bonds, earnest money, 401K plans, gifts of funds and reserves to be held by the lender are even more important. Lenders require verification for any type of liquid asset. Lenders prefer at least two months of house payments as cash reserves. Types of liquid assets that can be used for down payment, closing costs, and monthly reserves are as follows:

- Checking and savings accounts
- Earnest money held by the escrow agent
- Bonuses and commissions
- Rent money
- Mutual funds
- Life insurance proceeds
- IRA, 401(K), or Keogh funds
- Charitable organization gift programs and housing grants
- Sale of real estate (requires a HUD-1 settlement statement)
- Public assistance income
- Seller's contributions on the real estate contract
- Gift funds (require a gift letter)

Seller Contributions as Assets

In real estate transactions, sellers are able to contribute to the buyer's expenses on owner occupied properties; however, contributions are limited to the following guidelines:

- GSE loans – 3% x sales price < 90% LTV
- GSE loans – 6% x sales price > 90% LTV
- GSE loans – 9% x sales price > 75% LTV
- FHA loans – 6% x sales price
- VA loans – 4% x sales price
- Most sub-prime – 6% x sales price

Gift Funds as Assets

The applicant can use 100% of a gift for a down payment for all FHA and VA loans. For conforming conventional loans, the guidelines are:

- 95% LTV loans - gifts are not permitted, borrowers must make a 5% down payment

- 90% LTV loans - gifts are limited to 5%
- 80% LTV loans - gifts are unlimited, 100% of down payment can be a gift

For all gifts, the donor must provide the following:

- Evidence of the relationship between donor and recipient
- The dollar value of the gift
- Testimony that the gift is not to be repaid.
- His/her signature
- The address for which the gift is intended
- Evidence of the donor's source of gift
- Checks or wire transfer evidence to the recipient

Gift donors can only be from the list below:

- Direct relatives
- Employer
- Municipality
- Nonprofit organization

Collateral

Types of Properties

There are several types of properties, with each having different lending guidelines, as follows:

- Residential loans usually have longer terms and better rates, as they are considered a safer investment than commercial or investment loans, which bear more risk.
- Residential investment loans (two-four units) because they are a higher risk for the lender, demand higher rates and larger down payments as opposed to one-unit residential property loans.
- Commercial/investment borrowers have shorter repayment terms; the secondary market for commercial loans is made-up of private investors. Most loans are kept in a portfolio, which are held by the original lender. Of the three types of borrowers mentioned, commercial borrowers are considered the highest risk. Greater risk will demand higher interest rates.

The seven (7) items lenders demand to determine the quality of the subject property are:

1. Appraisal report
2. Survey
3. Homeowner's Insurance
4. Flood Certificate
5. Legal Instruments: Deed of Trust/Mortgage
6. Warranty Deed with Vendor's Lien
7. Promissory note, Name of Affidavit, Assignment of Mortgage and Title Comment/Title Policy

Lenders and mortgage insurance companies are concerned that if the loan is foreclosed, the property will not maintain its value. Most lenders require an appraisal that is less than 90 days old. The appraiser determines the present value and notes any conditions that the lender needs to know about.

While the survey, title policy, homeowner's insurance, and flood certification are important, they are not considered pricing issues.

Mortgage Terms (number of years); Longer Terms are a Greater Risk

Mortgage Terms

As a general rule, the shorter the terms, the better the interest rate; fewer years means less risk for the lender. For example, a 30-year term loan will demand a 6% rate, whereas a 15-year term may qualify for a 5.5% rate. **Term** is the number of years or the length of the contract.

Types of Loan Products and Programs

Loan Products

Other risk factors that can influence the interest rate are the type of products and/or program the borrower selects. These products/ programs include the following:

- Fixed rate mortgage
- Adjustable rate mortgage/convertible
- Bi-weekly mortgage
- Balloon/two-step reset mortgage/convertible mortgage

Rules for Real Estate Success

- Blanket mortgage/Package mortgage
- Graduated payment mortgage/ buy-downs
- Reverse annuity mortgage
- Home equity loan
- Construction loan/permanent loan
- Bridge (gap) loan
- Combo (piggy-back) loans
- Interest only loans
- Affordable housing loans
- Fannie Mae loan programs (affordable housing program)
- FHA Programs
- Manufactured home loans
- Points, discount points, and basis points
- Full-doc-loans
- FIFA, Full income/Full Asset
- SIFA, Stated Income/Full Asset
- SISA, Stated Income /Stated Asset
- NINA, No Income/No Asset, No Ratio, NO Doc
- Wavier of escrow accounts and no impounds

Usually, each of the products listed above carry a different interest rate. For example, if the applicant prefers a fixed rate mortgage as opposed to an ARM, the risk to the lender would increase the rate. Again, mortgage lending is a risk-based business, so the cost of the risk is transferred to the borrower.

Before deciding whether to approve an applicant, mortgage lenders look at other information besides credit, down payment, income, and assets. Lenders are concerned with payment shock. This is the difference between what the borrower currently pays and the proposed payments. If the new house payment is more than twice the old house payment, it usually results in **payment shock**.

Types of Underwriting

Knowing the risk factors also helps determine the choice of underwriting. When applying for funds, each type of loan has its own requirements. The types of underwriting include:

- Conventional conforming (Traditional & Fannie Mae's My Community - Freddie Mac's Home Possible)
- Conventional non-conforming (Alt A, sub-prime and hard money)
- FHA/VA
- Affordable housing

Fannie Mae and Freddie Mac's Underwriting (GSE)

Conventional conforming provides better interest rates for borrowers who have good credit scores, low debt ratios, and are able to fund at least 5% for their down payment. Conventional means private lending or loans not insured by FHA or guaranteed by VA.

Government Sponsored Enterprises (GSE)

GSEs are federal-related corporations that are privately owned, such as Fannie Mae and Freddie Mac. GSE loans are limited to 80% LTV; if the lender's LTV is more than 80% of the loan, the borrower will be required to purchase mortgage insurance for the difference.

Federal Housing Administration (FHA) Insured Loans

Who is the Federal Housing Administration (FHA)? A large part of our community believes that FHA is some type of government lending program. In fact, **Federal Housing Administration (FHA)** does not lend funds; its role is that of a government mortgage insurance agency (Mutual Mortgage Insurance Plan). Like private mortgage insurance, FHA charges the homeowners **mortgage insurance premiums (MIP)** for accepting the loan default risk. **MIPs** are mortgage insurance premiums paid to the Federal Housing Administration.

In the 1990s until 2007, the FHA insured a small percent of mortgage loans and was considered a relic during this time. During 2007-2008, these sub-prime lenders, however, had turbulent times, with a large percentage of their loans going into default. These loans usually didn't have mortgage insurance coverage, which caused a large percentage of lenders to go out of business and left the rest with stringent guidelines. During this period, the FHA was able to regain its share of mortgage loans.

FHA Guidelines

FHA guidelines are the following:

*   Applicant's verification of income is necessary for at least two years.
*   FHA allows homeowners to carry a greater housing debt over conforming loans. Housing debts generally cannot exceed 31% of monthly income, which is called the front ratio.
*   Back ratio is the housing expenses plus any recurring charges called fixed payments, which cannot exceed 43% of effective monthly income.
*   FHA will accept a 5% down payment.

Rules for Real Estate Success

Veterans Administration Loans (VA) are loans that are guaranteed partially or fully by the Department of Veterans Affairs. Like the FHA, the VA does not loan funds but charges fees to **guarantee** the veteran's loan amount, which are called **VA loans.**

A VA loan guarantee (**entitlement**) is available to only qualified veterans for their personal residence.

Income for VA loans is analyzed using two income methods:

- **Debt-to-income ratio** not to exceed 41%
- **Residual** income (left over money after housing, taxes and recurring obligations)

The debt-to-income-ratio should not exceed 41% of gross income, and the down payment can be zero dollars. Like FHA, there is a consumer cost to guarantee the loan amount, which can vary from 0-2% of the loan amount.

Financing Real Estate

VA funding fees are based on the down payment amount.				
Veterans dn payment	Veteran %	Vet Multiple user %	Nat'l Guard %	Refinance %
0 -< 5%	2.00%	3.00%	2.75%	2.75%
5%-<10%	1.50%	1.50%	2.25%	2.75%
10% or more	1.25%	1.25%	2.00%	2.75%
All refinance fees are .05%				

Entitlement means the maximum VA guarantee that is available to the veteran for the purchase of a home. The current maximum limit is set at $60,000. If the veteran bought a home early for $20,000, the remaining entitlement would be $40,000. Veteran's **Certificate of Eligibility** (notice that the veteran is eligible for a loan) can be ordered by using VA form 26-1880 or if the lender has access to ACE (Automated Certificate of Eligibility system), the veteran will also need to show discharge papers or Form **DD-214**. After March 1, 1988, Veterans Affairs formal approval is required to assume VA loans.

State and Federal Requirements

Consumer Protection

There are several federal and state laws that were designed to protect consumers. Part of being successful in real estate sales is being able to protect your clients and play fairly with customers. Two examples of federal and state laws are as follows:

- The Good Faith Estimate (GFE), which the borrower(s) receives from the lender before the third business day, should match the final HUD-1 Statement at closing. If the lender/loan officer adds fees without a reason to the final HUD-1, this may be fee packaging. The only way to protect your customer is to ask your buyer for a copy of his/her GFE. Another area of concern is Yield Spread Premiums, or Broker fees.
- Lenders are concerned with junk fees and predatory fees, and if the consumer's higher payments are caused by the mortgage broker's premiums. The total mortgage brokers' fees cannot exceed 5% of the loan amount, or lenders and GFEs will not accept the loan. Brokers' profits are made in two areas: one is through charging the applicant a direct fee or a percent of the loan amount, and the other is through increasing the interest rates from wholesale to retail. The difference from increasing the interest rate is known as **Yield Spread Premiums.** Some junk fees may be legal but unnecessarily adds to the cost of the loan. When mortgage brokers/bankers increase their profit margin is by adding Yield Spread Premium, this will result in a higher interest rate for the borrower. For example, if the broker increases the wholesale rate by two points as a profit for himself/herself, this would increase the interest rate by 1/4 of a percent for the full term of the loan.
- Note: from 1999-2007, nearly every applicant could qualify for some type of mortgage loan. There were many so called Sub-Prime lenders that make it possible to purchase a home with no down-payment, few requirements, and with terrible credit scores, but at very high interest rates. The hidden profits these lenders made were enormous.

Rules for Real Estate Success

1. Ask your office manager or broker if he/she has a preferred-list of loan officers.

2. Most season agents have already selected the very best loan officers, and they may share their list.

3. Start your own list of loan officers and the programs they offer.

4. Ask about any special financing programs.

5. Ask if there is a lender's list of what buyers/borrowers should bring for approval.

6. Ask about credit agencies that are professional with credit solutions.

7. Check for credit seminars and mortgage lending workshops.

8. Ask your loan officers about tips to identify and separate good from bad buyers; be careful not to violate any Fair Housing Laws.

9. Understand what fees a loan officer can charge.

10. Understand how to read and explain an HUD-1 statement.

Financing Real Estate

1. Loans that can be sold to Fannie Mae/ Freddie Mac are called
   A. Jumbo loans
   B. Conforming loans
   C. Non-conforming loans
   D. Sub-prime loans

2. Conventional conforming lender's debt ratios are:
   A. 31/43 %
   B. 28/36 %
   C. 41/41 %
   D. 55/55%

3. VA's standard qualifying housing ratios are
   A. 29/41%
   B. 41/41%
   C. 28/36%
   D. 36%

4. Loan amounts that exceed Freddie Mac and Fannie Mae's guidelines are called
   A. Conforming
   B. Non-conforming
   C. Prime loans
   D. FHA loans

5. The mark-up of interest rates from the wholesale price to retail is called
   A. Broker Fees
   B. Yield Spread Premiums
   C. An administration Fee
   D. A and B

6. VA entitlement means:
   A. Funds available for a Veteran
   B. Guaranteed money by VA
   C. That the veteran is eligible for a loan
   D. A or B

7. Credit scores:
   A. A statistical model which predicts future performance
   B. Are the types of collateral guaranteed by lenders
   C. Insurance premiums known as MIPs
   D. A and B

8. GSEs are:
   A. The funds available for a Veteran loan
   B. Federal related corporations that are privately owned
   C. A part of the Federal Housing Administration
   D. B and C

9. In real estate, to pre-qualify an applicant means:
   A. For the lender to estimate a housing price range from which the applicant can afford
   B. For the lender to know exactly what the applicant can afford by verification
   C. To determine the eligible of a property
   D. None of the above

10. To pre-approve an applicant means:
    A. For the lender to estimate a housing price range from which the applicant can afford
    B. For the lender to know exactly what the applicant can afford by verification
    C. To determine the eligible of a property
    D. None of the above

11. Which is not a collateral/property requirement?
    A. Funds
    B. Survey
    C. Appraisal
    D. Legal instruments

12. The minimum credit score acceptable by Fannie Mae and Freddie Mac is:
    A. 720
    B. 650
    C. 620
    D. 400

CHAPTER 12
Closing and Post Services

Objectives:

To be able to understand and do the following

- Know what post-closing services that are available
- Be aware of how to market Real Estate Owned (REOs) properties
- Write an effective REO resume
- Know where to find REOs
- Know how a short sale works
- Know the requirements of a hardship letter
- Work with loss mitigation departments.
- Loan modifications

Terms:

- Broker Price Opinions (BPO)
- Days on Market (DOM)
- Deed-in-Lieu of Foreclosure
- Forbearance
- Government Sponsored Enterprises (GSEs)
- Hardship Letter
- Loan Modification Agreements
- Loss Mitigation Departments
- Post-Closing Services
- Real Estate Owned (REOs)
- Short Sale
- Special Mortgage Forbearance Agreements

Post-Closing Services

There is a huge need for real estate agents and loan officers to provide post-closing services. **Post-closing services** are services provided by lenders, real estate agents, and attorneys after the property is purchased. Post-closing services can be very lucrative for real estate agents and loan officers who are willing to learn and train in such services. The post-closing services are divided into three main areas.

Three Types of Post-Closing Services

1. In **Pre-foreclosure,** lenders have programs which help homeowners keep their home. Since homeowners are not transferring title but changing the status of the loan, most states require a mortgage license to work in forbearance, repayment plans, and loan modifications. Below are three pre-foreclosure programs:

   - Forbearance
   - Repayment Plan
   - Loan Modification

2. In **Foreclosures** status, lenders have programs for homeowners to leave their home, but still avoid foreclosure. In this case, the title will transfer, so a real estate agent or attorney is required. Below are four foreclosure programs:

   - Trustee sale
   - Deed in lieu of foreclosure
   - Mortgage Assumption
   - Short sale

3. In **Post foreclosure,** the property was foreclosed and the lender, investors, or mortgage insurance company purchased the property at auction. The property now belongs to the lender, investors, or mortgage insurance company, which is known as **real estate owned (REO).**

   - Bank, real estate owned (REOs)

Pre Foreclosure Services

Pre Foreclosure

Forbearance or to forbear-lenders/investors have special departments called Loss Mitigation to help consumers with plans to repay any late payments and to avoid future late payments. Most often consumers are often unaware of these special departments that are set up to help homeowners to avoid foreclosure. All lenders have Loss Mitigation departments: the goal for these special departments is to avoid losing money, which is usually caused by foreclosing.

A **special mortgage forbearance** agreement is an agreement between a lender and a mortgagor (homeowner) that contains a plan to reinstate the mortgagor and not to foreclose.

Fannie Mae's goal is to let borrowers know that foreclosures and short sales are preventable. Fannie Mae estimates that in over half of all foreclosures, borrowers fail to communicate with the lender/servicer, thus failing to use their options. Fannie Mae has contacted its servicing agents with a wide range of workout solutions and incentive fees for servicing agents to assist borrowers. What real estate agents can do for past clients is to be available in a time of hardship and be able to offer guidance on housing financial matters. On Forbearance or Workout Agreements, since lenders are reluctant to pay real estate agents any type of commission and usually homeowners don't have it, some real estate agents are hesitant to help and would rather wait for the sale to assist. Agents should give all clients the same respect, whether past or present. A truly professional agent simply treats their past buyers as present clients. Past transactions should be treated as clients. In this case, the reward is good will and further referrals. Think of it this way: if your real estate agent was available for you and did all he/she was capable of to find solutions to help you save your home, would you recommend that person to all your friends?

Workout Plans to Help the Homeowner Keep their Home

A **Temporary Forbearance** is a special mortgage forbearance agreement that will normally allow the mortgagor to delay monthly mortgage payments. The minimum time is usually four months, and the maximum can be up to eighteen months. Under a temporary forbearance, the homeowner is expected to continue with his/her monthly payment even after the forbearance agreement is over and at the same time, catch up with all past due amounts. Therefore, the payments can actually double because the catch-up payments are added to the normal payments. A temporary forbearance is not a good option for most homeowners, but again, it depends on the hardship. Under a temporary forbearance, government-sponsored enterprises (GSEs) are usually notified, but approval is not required. **Government-sponsored enterprises** are federal corporations that are privately owned, such as Fannie Mae and Freddie Mac. Each lender has the right to decide which type of agreement is best for the overall situation.

Repayment Plan

The homeowner makes monthly payments under forbearance or the repayment plan, which includes past due amounts, or the homeowner can elect to pay the past amount in a lump sum.

Loan Modification

The best type of agreement for a long-term hardship is a loan modification. **Loan Modification Agreements** can change the entire term and conditions of the loan, such as reducing the interest rate or changing the type of loan from an ARM to a fixed rate loan, from 30 years to a 40- year mortgage. Whether the modification is for one year or 30 years depends on the hardship and investors. Borrowers can add any late payments, interest, and attorney fees to the principal balance on this type of plan. Whether real estate fees can be added to the principal depends on the investors, though usually, they cannot be. Some non-prime lenders and all prime lenders require that homeowners are at least three months late before the servicing company can start any modification to the original loan agreement.

Since this type of agreement is not transferring title, the forbearance or loan modification agreement is without settlement or closing at a title company. The lender prepares the new loan documents, and the mortgagor agrees to no additional closing costs to the consumer.

Before there is any kind of forbearance agreement or loan modification, however, the mortgagor must prove hardship status. The lender or investors who have the loan will require the following items:

- A hardship letter
- Appraisal
- Check stubs
- Bank statements
- Tax returns
- List of assets
- A detail list of monthly expenses
- A credit report

Hardship Letter

The **hardship letter** must explain the nature of hardship, whether the situation is temporary or long term and the desire to keep the home. The final agreement must be approved by its investors and all interested parties. For example, if the loan belongs to Freddie Mac, then the agreement must meet lender, mortgage insurance, and Freddie Mac's guidelines.

Rules for Real Estate Success

If the property has mortgage insurance, then the investor/lenders are encouraged to assist the homeowner or lose the possibility of insurance coverage. Mortgage insurance policy expects lenders to try at least three workout programs before they agree to pay.

Loss Mitigation Departments

The Loss mitigation department/Asset Management is to minimize losses for its investors. If the loan is without mortgage insurance coverage, then the investors decide the best agreement for the company. For example, if the loan balance is $210,000 and the present sales value indicates $176,000 plus 9-10% in closing costs, $2,000 in attorney's fees and monthly upkeep and insurance for another 1%, the investors loose upward of $60,000 on the file. In this case, the investors are more likely to work on an agreement for the mortgagor to keep his/her home.

Foreclosure Services

Workouts Plans for Homeowner to Leave their Home but Still Avoid Foreclosure

When a forbearance repayment plan or loan modification agreement does not work, or the homeowner decides he no longer wants the property, there are still options to avoid a costly foreclosure and to leave the property owners with minimal credit damage. Fannie Mae has a program that will pay homeowners up to $5,000 if the homeowner cooperates and does not damage the property.

Mortgage Assumption

Another option is to check with the lender/investor to see if he/she is willing to waive the due-on-sale clause. During years 2008-20011, because of the slow economy, property values were dropping at a historical rate. Many lenders consider waiving the due-on-sale clause to qualified borrowers. Real estate agents can earn a commission because this is an actual transfer of property ownership.

Deed-in-Lieu of Foreclosure

Deed-in-Lieu of Foreclosure is the last option before an actual foreclosure. **Deed-in-Lieu of Foreclosure** occurs when the homeowner voluntarily conveys the property to either the lender or the mortgage insurance company. The lender contacts a real estate firm to market the property for sale as a REO (real estate owned). In this way, the lender hopes to receive the property sooner and in better condition. Lenders usually require the property to be in the market for sale for 2-4 months without a reasonable offer before they accept the property. Lenders prefer that homeowners try every option before they agree to a Deed-in-Lieu of Foreclosure.

Short Sale

Short sale agreements are another way real estate agents can help their clients avoid bankruptcy or foreclosure. A **Short sale** happens when the lender agrees to sell the property for less than the amount owed. The proceeds from the sale of real estate are insufficient to satisfy the liens on the property. The lien holder forgives the homeowner of the remaining debt. In this type of arrangement, the homeowner provides evidence of financial hardship. The forgiveness of debt can be considered income. The homeowner will receive a 1099A (Forgiveness of Housing Sales Debt) or 1099C (Cancellation of Debt). See Mortgage Forgiveness Debt Relief Act of 2007 below to check if your client will be affected by the 2007 Forgiveness Act.

Mortgage Forgiveness Debt Relief Act- from IRS website: www.irs.gov

What is the Mortgage Forgiveness Debt Relief Act of 2007?

The Mortgage Forgiveness Debt Relief Act of 2007 was enacted of December 20, 2007. Generally, the Act allows exclusion of income realized as a result of modification of the terms of the mortgage or foreclosure on your principal residence.

What does that mean?

Usually, debt that is forgiven or cancelled by a lender must be included as income on your tax return and is taxable. The Mortgage Forgiveness Debt Relief Act of 2007 allows you to exclude certain cancelled debt on your principal residence from income.

Does the Mortgage Forgiveness Debt Relief Act of 2007 apply to all forgiven or cancelled debts?

No, the Act applies only to forgiven or cancelled debt used to buy, build or substantially improve your principal residence or to refinance debt incurred for those purposes.

What about refinanced homes?

Debt used to refinance your home qualifies for this exclusion, but only up to the extent that the principal balance of the old mortgage, immediately before the refinancing, would have qualified.

Does this provision apply for the 2007 tax year only?

It applies to qualified debt forgiven in 2007, 2008 or 2009.

If the forgiven debt is excluded from income, do I have to report it on my tax return?

Yes. The amount of debt forgiven must be reported on Form 982, and the Form 982 must be attached to your tax return.

Do I have to complete the entire Form 982?

Form 982, Reduction of Tax Attributes Due to Discharge of Indebtedness (and Section 1082 Adjustment), is used for other purposes in addition to reporting the exclusion of forgiveness of qualified principal residence indebtedness. If you are using the form only to report the exclusion of forgiveness of qualified principal residence indebtedness as the result of foreclosure on your principal residence, you only need to complete lines 1e and 1f you kept ownership of your home and modification of the terms of your mortgage resulted in the forgiveness of qualified principal residence indebtedness, complete lines 1e, 2, and1 0b. Attach the Form 982 to your tax return.

Where can I get this form?

You can download the form at IRS.gov, or call 1-800-829-3676. If you call to order, \ please allow 7-10 days for delivery.

How do I know or find out how much was forgiven?

Your lender should send a Form 1099-C, Cancellation of Debt, by January 31, 2008. The amount of debt forgiven or cancelled will be shown in box 2. If this debt is all qualified principal residence indebtedness, the amount shown in box 2 will generally be the amount that you enter on lines 2 and 10b, if applicable, on Form 982.

Can I exclude debt forgiven on my second home, credit card, or car loans?

Not under this provision. Only cancelled debt used to buy, build or improve your principal residence, or refinance debt incurred for those purposes qualifies for this exclusion.

If part of the forgiven debt doesn't qualify for exclusion from income under this provision, is it possible that it may qualify for exclusion under a different provision?

Yes, the forgiven debt may qualify under the "insolvency" exclusion. Normally, a taxpayer is not required to include forgiven debts in income to the extent that the taxpayer is insolvent. A taxpayer is insolvent when his or her total liabilities exceed his or her total assets. The forgiven debt may also qualify for exclusion if the debt was discharged in a Title 11 bankruptcy proceeding or if the debt is qualified farm indebtedness or qualified real property business indebtedness. If you believe you qualify for any of these exceptions, see the instructions for Form 982.

Is there a limit on the amount of forgiven qualified principal residence indebtedness that can be excluded from income?

There is no dollar limit if the principal balance of the loan was less than $2 million ($1 million if Married filing separately for the tax year) at the time the loan was forgiven. If the balance was greater, see the instructions to Form 982, Page 4.

Is there anything else I need to know before filing?

Yes, because the Mortgage Forgiveness Debt Relief Act of 2007 was passed so late in the year, The software systems used by tax preparers and at the Internal Revenue Service need to be updated to accept the revised Form 982. The IRS expects to be able to process the new Form 982 electronically on March 3, 2008.

Investors, lenders, and mortgage insurance companies must all agree to a short sale. The homeowner writes a hardship letter to the lender. If the lender agrees to the request, either the lender or the homeowner requests that a real estate agent sell the property at a loss to the lender. The property is sold, and the debt to the lender is forgiven. Before the lender grants the request, lenders look at the following circumstances as indicators whether to grant a hardship case:

- Unemployment
- Type of employment
- Divorce
- Bankruptcy
- Medical illness
- Death
- Property value/balance

If the homeowner has any type of large assets, the lender is unlikely to grant a short sale. Large assets are an indicator to the lender that the homeowner has the ability to pay-off the difference. Sometimes, the lender will enter into an agreement to pay the difference and to be repaid by the homeowner over a short term. The final short sale agreement will depend on the homeowner's circumstances and investor's guidelines. Examples of assets are as follows:

- Bank funds
- 401K /retirement
- Stocks and bonds
- IRAs
- Real estate
- Two or more automobiles
- Business assets

In a short sale where real estate agents are involved, the fiduciary relationship is still between the sellers and the real estate broker, not with the lender.

Finding Short Sale Properties

Finding short sales are much the same as finding listings. You must advertise for them. Lenders will often select the real estate agent. In this case, you must send your resume to lenders and mortgage insurance company's Loss Mitigation departments or asset management.

Post Foreclosure Services

Real Estate Owned

Real Estate Owned (REOs) are properties lenders have purchased from the homeowner, that are being listed for sale by real estate agents. The lender may require the property to be maintained and repaired while refunds for agent's repairs may take up to 60 days. The best way to gain short sale listings is from lenders, investors, mortgage insurance companies, credit unions, real estate investment trust, or asset management companies (middleman for the inventors/lenders). These departments and companies want results. Below are the three items all investors expect from real estate agents:

1. That you completely understand how REOs work.
2. That you are able to sell the property.
3. That you get the highest and best price in the shortest amount of time with the lesser amount of liability.

REO Resume

Most lenders require your name to appear on their approved vendor list before they send you business. To be on the lender/asset management list of approved agencies you will need an effective resume. Some lenders will require an electronic posting of your resume and others will prefer a hard copy. Below are tips for preparing an effective REO package:

- Your name and contact information
- W-9
- Proof of your E&O insurance policy
- Copy of General Liability Declarations
- A copy of your real estate license
- A resume having a REO type of headline.

Other items to include are:

- Describe what REO training, experience, or designations you have.
- Include your **sales volume** and the **amount of time** to sell each home, **days on market (DOM).**
- Include what maintenance and repair services you offer.
- Address what area you best service (zip code, and city).
- Include what special trades you have, such as a finance background, FHA broker, or license and bonded contractor.

Packaging Yourself as an REO Expert

Packaging yourself is very important. There are several ways, such as having the following:

- A marketing brochure with your Unique Selling Proposition, "Your REO expert."
- An Internet address or email that reads for example, REOyourname. com
- A Letterhead that reads "Sold 10 million in sales"
- A background in computer technology, since most lenders will communicate by website.

Broker Price Opinions (BPO)

Asset management companies will need to know the property value in order to determine what price to sell the property and the cost of the sale. They will either call an appraiser or ask a real estate agent to determine the value. When they solicit a real estate agent's opinion of value, it is called a **Broker Price Opinions (BPO).** BPO reports pay from $50 to $200 dollars. One of the best ways to gain REOs is by offering to do BPOs. Accepting BPO assignments is a good way to know the asset management people (one foot in the door).

How to Find REOs

Every lender has a Loss Mitigation department or will use an asset management company; however, many are out-of-state. Try calling local banks, credit unions, and mortgage insurance companies for information on their Loss Mitigation departments. If you have the money, you can join any of the many REO training centers to acquire a complete list of all Loss Mitigation departments in the United States or search for REO conventions. First, find the contact person. You can do this by calling or sending letters to departments asking for the right contact person. Next, send your resume to all of the Loss Mitigation departments/asset management. Be sure to ask for their stacking order sheet. While most stacking order sheets are similar, it's best to have it exactly the way they want it. You can search MLS properties that are REOs and try a tax search for the investors.

Keeping REOs

Like regular clients, you must constantly contact your REOs. For example, for every closing, send flowers, and Thank You cards. Like buyers and sellers, REOs are people who will forget you as soon as you forget them. Be careful and complete your paperwork and keep your contact person updated on REO properties.

Conclusion

From reading the text, you will find that a career in real estate can be exciting and rewarding, but offers many challenges.

Many decisions will be made throughout the course of your career. One of the first decisions that you will make is whether to work full-time or part-time, whether to work as an agent only or to become a broker, whether to generalize or specialize (working with buyers and sellers or working with buyers only or sellers only). You will have to decide whether or not to take all the training courses necessary to keep-up with this exciting and rewarding field of real estate.

This ever-changing, ever-growing field allows the freedom for independent employment, which means, bottom-line, an unrestricted, unlimited income. This freedom also allows for a more independent time schedule. However, that does not mean that you will not put-in your time. Success in real estate requires much hard and intelligent planning and work. You will work long hours, weekends, sometimes at night, sometimes on holidays. Building a successful business demands your dedication.

Building your business is a process; you cannot simply start listing and selling instantly. Your business is built on the foundation you lay. This foundation requires many stages of preparation. First, you must create a workable, but affordable marketing plan. Get business cards and learn how to use the latest computer technology. Next, you will have to make contacts. Do not allow fear or shyness to interfere with your meeting people; they are, after all, your business. Tell everyone you come into contact with about your business and do not hesitate to ask for referrals. Once you have made contacts, create a dependable database; keep adding to it and keep it updated. Always be prepared: handout business cards, talk with people, be ready to answer any question, be ready to overcome objections – know your scripts. Set realistic goals; without them, you will not have a clear and focused plan for building your business and achieving your success. You will need to learn real estate procedures, such as: staging a house and holding an open house. Also, you will have to understand such procedures as real estate finance and post-closing services. These are some of the steps/stages you must take in order to build your business' foundation and to attain success.

Your success will come not only from working hard, being dedicated, using the latest technology, being prepared, and/or possessing knowledge of real estate procedures. Always remember that your success, and more importantly, your reputation will come from your use of strict ethical practices. Make no mistake, your clients and colleagues will judge your character as well as your business by the ethics you incorporate into your life and business dealings. Constantly use the consistent set of real estate rules, as set forth by your State Real Estate Commission.

Enjoy what you do; your clients will know whether you do or don't. Find and use the absolute and best tools that will help you reach your goals and achieve the success you so 'richly' deserve. Use the information –tools- you have learned from the contents of this book; make it a part of your permanent Real Estate Reference Book Collection. Having reference material will prove useful because during your career, you will find yourself wanting to try something different or refresh an old idea.

Sincere wishes for the best of success and good fortune.

1. Ask your local bank if they have a loss mitigation department contact person, a phone number, or email address to start you in the right direction. Let your local bank officer know what you are trying to do, he/she may have suggestions. Pay close attention to the terms bankers use.

2. Most major banks have seminars on preventing foreclosures as well as on how to work with short sales; ask to be on their training list. For this you will have to contact each bank's central office.

3. Research for loss mitigation/foreclosure/short sale seminars in your area.

4. Find where public real estate auctions are held.

5. Talk to your broker about what information the office may have.

6. Search out REO/foreclosure agents in the *MLS*®

7. Research for loss mitigation/foreclosure terms and information on the Internet.

Closing and Post Services

1. What are the services provided by lenders, real estate agents, and attorneys after the property was purchased by the homeowner called?
   A. Post-closing services
   B. Forbearance
   C. Loss mitigation
   D. Short sale

2. To delay or to stop any action; in mortgage lending it is to refraining from taking legal action to recover the real property is called
   A. Post-closing services
   B. Forbearance
   C. Short sale
   D. Broker Price Opinions

3. A department designed to avoid losing money caused by foreclosing on properties is called
   A. Broker Price Opinions
   B. Forbearance
   C. Loss mitigation department
   D. Post-closing services

4. An agreement between a lender and a mortgagor that contains a plan to reinstate the mortgagor and to not foreclose is called
   A. Stop Now Program
   B. Broker Price Opinions
   C. Short sale agreement
   D. Special mortgage forbearance agreement

5. A formal agreement to change the terms and conditions of the loan, such as to reduce the interest rate or change the type of loan is called
   A. Loan modification agreement
   B. Hope Now
   C. Save my Home program
   D. Fannie Mae Gold Star

6. When the lender agrees to sell the property for less than the amount owed is called
   A. Long sale agreement
   B. Short sale agreement
   C. Loan modification agreement
   D. Repayment agreement

7. When the homeowner voluntarily conveys the property to either the lender or the mortgage insurance company in exchange for forgiveness of the loan amount is called
   A. Grantee Deed
   B. Contract for Deed
   C. Deed-in-Lieu of Foreclosure
   D. Section 32 mortgage

8. What explains the nature of hardship that determines whether the request is a temporary or long-term agreement?
   A. Section 32 mortgage
   B. Forgiveness of debt
   C. Homeowner's affidavit
   D. Hardship letter

9. What are GSEs?
   A. Government-sponsored enterprises
   B. Government real estate properties
   C. Guaranteed stock entitlement (VA)
   D. Guaranteed sellers eligibility (FHA)

10. In real estate what is a BPO?
    A. Banker price opinion
    B. Broker price opinion
    C. Broker pending offer
    D. Broker property owned

11. In real estate what is a REO?
    A. Government-sponsored enterprises
    B. Real estate opinion
    C. Real estate offer
    D. Real estate owned

Chapter Test Answer Sheet

Chapter 2	Chapter 3	Chapter 4	Chapter 5
1. A	1. C	1. D	1. A
2. D	2. A	2. B	2. E
3. C	3. D	3. A	3. D
4. B	4. E	4. C	4. B
5. D	5. A	5. A	5. D
6. D	6. A	6. D	6. D
7. A	7. C	7. D	7. B
8. D	8. D	8. A	8. B
9. B	9. C	9. D	9. B
10. A	10. B	10. C	10. B
11. A	11. B		11. D
12. D			12. A
13. A			13. D
14. B			14. B

Chapter 6	Chapter 7	Chapter 8	Chapter 9
1. D	1. A	1. A	1. A
2. E	2. B	2. B	2. B
3. C	3. C	3. C	3. C
4. D	4. D	4. D	4. D
5. D	5. A	5. A	5. A
6. B	6. B	6. B	6. B
7. C	7. C	7. D	7. D
8. C	8. D	8. B	8. D
9. A	9. A	9. A	9. A
10. D	10. B	10. D	10. D
11. A	11. C	11. D	
12. D	12. D	12. D	
	13. A		
	14. B		

Chapter 10	Chapter 11	Chapter 12
1. A	1. B	1. A
2. B	2. B	2. B
3. C	3. B	3. C
4. D	4. B	4. D
5. A	5. B	5. A
6. B	6. D	6. B
7. C	7. A	7. C
8. D	8. B	8. D
9. A	9. A	9. A
10. B	10. B	10. B
	11. A	11. D
	12. C	

Glossary

A

ABCs of real estate sales (Always Be in Control): a real estate rule, meaning that if an agent is going to close the transaction, they must maintain control.

Absentees: property owners who do not live on the property.

ACRES: Acknowledge, Concern, Respect, Evaluate, and Solution.

Advertisement: a commercial message in any medium promoting, directly or indirectly, a credit transaction. Generally, advertising is when the consumer is left with the means to contact the promoters.

Affiliated Marketing: when a company has agreed to pay the host a commission to help sell its product. Internet ad payments will depend on three basic payment systems. One is the pay per click, pay per lead, or pay per sale.

Agency: in real estate, the term agency refers to the relationship between two individuals, one having the legal power to act on behalf of the other while representing the individual's best interest.

Annual Percentage Rate (APR): the interest and certain closing costs the buyers will pay at settlement.

Antitrust Laws: prohibit monopolies and sustain competition in order to protect companies from one another and protect consumers from unfair business practices.

Available income: how much money the homeowner will have after all monthly debts are paid.

B

Being a One-Man Show : in real estate is to be self-employed having the same business duties as a CEO.

Benefit words: words like "free" in a sentence that attract the listeners' attention.

Blogs: chronological journals over the Internet or online diaries with the latest entries on top by date. It serves as an online media, such as a discussion forum. Blogs can be personal or for business.

Body language: nonverbal communications; includes eye movement, voice tone, gestures, posture, and greeting.

Broker fees: fees that the brokerage companies charge. An example is mortgage brokers; before 2011 brokers could legally charge consumers a fee know as Yield Spread Premiums, which is increasing the interest rate to earn a profit.

Broker open house: a pre-open house to show other agents the property that is for sale.

Broker Price Opinion: a real estate agent's opinion of value.

Buddy system: in real estate, two or more agents would team up to solicit business in a certain area.

Business etiquette: a set of manners or social conduct in a business situation, a set of rules that govern the way people socially interact with one another in business.

Buyer's presentation kit: a presentation kit that includes the items that are required to list a property for sale.

Buyer's remorse: when buyers experience some level of anxiety about purchasing the property.

C

Calculating credit scores: the mathematical system of adding or subtracting points based on lending variables.

CAP: advertisment should include the following three items: **C**ompany, **A**gent, and **P**roperty information.

Cash incentives: are used as a bargaining tool which is paid to buyers at closing and funding.

Categorizing buyers: to group buyers in an order most likey to buy.

Certificate of Eligibility: Veteran's notice VA form 26-1880 that the veteran is eligible for a loan.

Cold calling: making unsolicited phone calls.

Comfort zone: the area in which you feel comfortable talking to homeowners. It may be where you live or work, maybe an area where you enjoy visiting.

Company marketing: the dollar amount paid by the brokerage to promoting the office.

Comparative market analysis(CMA): a tool used by real estate agents to accurately price a property.

Comparing debt–to–income (DTI): the amount of monthly debt compared to gross monthly income.

The debt-to-income ratio is calculated by dividing the total monthly housing debt by the gross monthly income.

Competency: your obligation to be knowledgeable about real estate

Conforming lenders: lenders who accept low-risk loans and sell loans to **government sponsored enterprises (GSEs),** such as Fannie Mae and Freddie Mac.

CPS Selling Rule: all properties will sell for the highest dollar if the following three items are met:

Cooperation, Price, and Service.

Creating a Sense of Importance: to convey to the caller the sense that the property is valuable and in demand.

Credit score: a statistical model, which predicts future performance or the probability of default and delinquency based on prior experience. Credit scores range from the 300's to 850.

CSIR: Customer Service Index Reports or clients' evaluates of your services.

Curb appeal: to showcase the exterior of the home to grab the prospect's attention as soon as possible.

D

Days on Market: how long the property has been on the market for sale.

Debt-to-income ratio: the amount of monthly debt compared to gross monthly income. The debt-to-income ratio is calculated by dividing the total monthly housing debt by the gross monthly income.

Deceptive Trade Practice Act: a federal law to protect consumers from unfair and deceptive acts.

Deed-in-Lieu of Foreclosure: occurs when the homeowner voluntarily conveys the property to either the lender or the mortgage insurance company.

De-personalizing: a property is to remove personal distractions from the property.

Direct approach: to directly ask prospective customers for their business.

Discount points: to permanently buy down the interest rate.

Discount real estate broker: a brokerage firm that offers services at a discount price or accepts a lower or no fee.

Domain name: the offical name of a website.

Door-to-door sales: selling or making door to door calls.

Drip campaign: to put your contacts on a regular mail-out plan.

E

Effective income: FHA's ratio on how much money the homeowner will have after all monthly debts are paid. This is also referred to as the **available income ratio** by conventional lenders.

Ethics: what we perceive is right or fair, and how our ethical belief influences our decisions and behavior in society.

Exclusive listing agreement: a legal contact that stipulates the conditions of the listing between a seller and a broker. The broker becomes the exclusive agent of the seller.

Expired listings: property listings that were for sale on the *MLS®* system, but the contract period expired, and the property did not sell.

F

Fair Housing Act, FHA: The1968 federal law that makes it illegal to discriminate on the basis of race, color, religion, sex, national origin, physical handicap, or familial status in connection with the sale or rental of housing. These individual classes are known today as the "protected classes."

Farming for prospects: focusing on a particular group of people or a geographic area. You can farm for buyers or sellers, apartments or houses.

Fee packing: when the lender's fees are much higher at closing or in the HUD-1 closing statement than on the GFE by adding illegal junk fees.

FHA guidelines: standards FHA uses for loan applicants.

*FHA loans (*Federal Housing Administration): FHA charges the homeowners mortgage insurance premiums (MIP) for accepting the loan default risk. MIPs are mortgage premiums paid to Federal Housing Administration.

Fidelity: in real estate is the relationship between a broker or salesperson and their client. Acting as an agent for another is a fiduciary. Special obligations are imposed when such fiduciary relationships are created. As a real estate agent, the primary duty is to represent the interest of the client. The agent's position must always be clear to all parties involved. The agent must remain faithful and not place the agent's personal interest above the client's interest

Fiduciary: the relationship of trust betwwen the broker and hi/her client.

*Financial Modernization Bill,*125: known as the Gramm-Leach-Bliley Act, protects individuals from having their financial information disclosed. The act states that you must have permission to inquire about an individual's financial status, and it forbids you from sharing a person's financial history.

First 30 Day Action Plan: Developing a 30 day action plan to prepare for a real estate career after receiving a license.

First awareness: to be the first person prospects will think of when they decide they need a real estate professional or be the first person someone would recommend to their friends and family.

Flip video™: a small hand-held video camera to take digital pictures or video. What makes the Flip Video™ different from other digital cameras is its simplicity in uploading files to social networks and in editing videos for websites.

Floor time: being in charge of incoming phone calls and greeting walk-in prospects for a certain time period. A better word for floor time is opportunity time, an opportunity for sales.

For Sale by Owner: a property that is being sold by the homeowner without the assistance of a real estate agent; a person who is selling their property without help from a real estate agent.

Forbearance: also known as a Workout Agreement; an agreement between a lender and a mortgagor (homeowner) that contains a plan to reinstate the mortgagor and not to foreclose.

Foreclosure: the legal act of taking back the property from the mortgagor/homeowner.

FSBO process: a process that real estate agent will use to list the For Sale by Owner property.

Furniture templates: flat colorful cardboard cutouts that are the square size to real furniture. You can include your photo or advertisement on your templates or leave instructions for buyers. Since templates are flat, this will give rooms the perception of greater space while still aiding buyers in using their imagination.

G

GEM: the three things buyers expect from a property which are: **g**ood value for one's money, **e**motional connection to the property, and the property be in **m**ove-in condition, clean, with few, if any repairs.

Generalize: a real estate agent who preforms many functions, a "jack-of-all-trades" selling real estate, insurance, mortgages, and property location, or helping both buyers, and sellers.

Geographic farming: when agents farm in a particular physical location; they farm for sellers to acquire listings. In this type of farm method, agents are better able to concentrate on being known as an expert in their particular area.

Global Positioning System (GPS): transmits precise microwave signals, enabling GPS receivers to determine their location by speed, direction, and time. GPS was developed by the Department of Defense. In 1983, President Ronald Reagan issued an order making GPS available to American civilians for free. Today, GPS has become widely used as a worldwide aid to navigation. GPS comes in several applications: in cell phones, handsets for walking or hiking, for boating, and even for the real estate agent's automobile.

Goals: stating what you want to achieve.

Government Sponsored Enterprises (GSEs): federal-related corporations that are privately owned, such as Fannie Mae and Freddie Mac. GSE were set up by the federal government to buy mortgage and issue mortgage-back securities to be sold as common stock.

H

Hard assets: assets such as real estate automobiles, and other personal property, unlike liquid assets, hard assests takes more time to convert to money.

Hardship Letter: explains the nature of hardship, whether the financial situation is temporary or long term and the homeowner's desire to keep the home.

Housing ratio: two types of debt ratios which are

Housing ratio: a mathematical ratio by lenders that measures the proposed housing expense. The purpose is to measure whether the loan applicants can afford the house payments.

HUD-1: the final settlement statement of charges for both sellers and buyers.

I

Individual marketing: the advertising dollar amount paid by the agent (promoting the individual agent).

Institutional marketing: the marketing amount paid by the franchise (advertising dollars promoting the franchise).

Integrity: the special obligation by the agent to exercise integrity when discharging responsibilities. The agent must be prudent and cautious in order to avoid misrepresenting anything, either by commission or omission.

K

Kaizen: the Japanese word for continuous improvement.

Kickback: the act of giving or receiving unearned gifts or funds; an illegal act by a real estate agent, a loan officer, or by any individual receiving funds from the sale of a house without performing a required act.

L

Liquid assets: items that are easily converted to cash such as money in banks, stocks and bonds, earnest money, 401K plans, gifts of funds or reserves to be held by the lender.

Listing campaig: the process of building an inventory of properties for sale.

Listing pipeline: maintaining a certain amount of listings per month. The goal is set a system to have an ample amount of properties for sale and always be replacing the sold listings with new listings.

Listings: the properties that are for sale.

Loan application: the formal application to purchase real estate.

Loan Modification Agreements: a legal agreement to change the terms and conditions of the loan, such as reducing the interest rate or changing the type of loan from an ARM to a fixed rate loan, from 30 years to a 40- year mortgage. Whether the modification will be for one year or 30 years will depend on the hardship and investors.

Loan to value (LTV): the amount of money the lender will loan or the risk to the lender.

Loss Mitigation Departments are departments that are designed to minimize losses for its investors.

M

Magnetic car signs: magnetic advertisments that are placed on the agent's vehicle.

Marketing: refers to how a salesperson attracts prospects to their business, such as putting an ad in the newspaper that would generate leads

Marketing niche: a unique marketing plan, one that is uniquely performed by a salesperson.

Marketing plan: designing a plan to generate leads that will turn into commissions.

Mnemonic: any learning technique that an aid to a person's memory. An example would be a short poem or keys words used to help a person to remember something, particularly lists, however, a mnemonic may be visual, kinesthetic or auditory that relies on associations.

Mnemonic strategies: employed to facilitate learning by creating connections where the connection is not immediately obvious to the learner.

Morals: the feelings of what is right and wrong as a community or group.

Mortgage insurance premiums (MIP): mortgage insurance premiums that Federal Housing Administration (FHA) charges the homeowners for accepting the loan default risk.

Movie Marker: a Microsoft™ video software package designed to make videoing easy.

Moving Kits: a marketing tool consists of empty boxes with business labels, large markers, catalog book, and rolls of tape. Moving boxes come in all sizes, which most moving companies have.

N

National Do-Not-Call: a federal laws that details the telemarketing sales rules (TSR) which applies to any plan, program, or campaign to sell goods or services through interstate phone systems. This includes telemarketers who solicit consumers, often on behalf of third party sellers. It also includes sellers who provide, offer to provide, or arrange to provide, goods or services to consumers in exchange for payment.

O

One-stop center decision: a one-stop real estate office that offers several services such as residential real estate, commercial real estate, leasing, mortgage lending, insurance, investments, and title work services. Attorneys, surveyors, appraisers, interior designers, engineers, investors, hard moneylenders, and real estate schools may be housed in the same office. This concept was developed to make home purchasing easier, less expensive, and more attractive to consumers. Real estate buyers and sellers would shop or go to one office instead of having to go to different people and locations.

OPECC Rule: a training recommendation which means to observe, practice/role play, evaluate, commit, and confidence.

Open house: having the property available, or open, for the public to view.

P

Payment shock: the difference between what the borrower currently pays and the proposed payments. If the new house payment is more than twice the old house payment, it usually results in financial shock.

Perpetual sales: a marketing approach created by the number of listings gaining momentum and continuing to grow.

Photo Story Software: a Microsoft™ digital storytelling easy-to-use software package that uses pictures, graphics, and audio, to create a digital story for web publishing.

Photographic book or **coffee table book:** a collection of photographs made into a professional quality book. The images are printed on heavy stock paper with 30–100 pages per book. There are several companies such as Shutterfly™, Apple™, Kodak gallery, Picaboo, Mypubisher, Lulu.com, and many others who can create these books at a reasonable price.

Points: when the interest rates are pre-purchased to a lesser amount, this is called buying "points." Points are pre-paid interest rates. The idea is to lower the interest rate to make monthly payments affordable for buyers. The cost rule is one point is equal to one percent of the loan. To buy three points on a $100,000 loan, the cost would be $3,000. There are two options to buying down the interest rate. Option one is to buy the interest per year, which is called **Buy Down Points.** Option two is to permanently buy down the interest rate, which is called **Discount Points.**

Portable data transfer devices: function as a data storage device that fits into your computer's USB port. This allows you to easily carry your files with you or transfer them from one computer to another. These devices come in all shapes and sizes and are small enough to carry in your pocket.

Post-closing services: services provided by lenders, real estate agents, and attorneys after the property is purchased.

Post-Sale Service: services provided after closing that will help build long-term relationships with clients.

Power scripts: grouping words to give the best anwers to address nearly any question a prospect/client may have.

Pre-approval: verifying the applicant's income, employment, and credit history, usually made by a lender.

Pre-foreclosure: the homeowner is having difficulty with mortgage payments and working with the lender to make correction and update the account

Pre-qualified: to give prospects a price range and the likelihood of being able to purchase a property. To pre-qualify is to measure how much home an applicant can purchase without extensive verification.

Professional image: a projection of personal characteristics, such as manners, qualities, and values, it will be the first image that comes to client's mind when needing a service.

Property tender: a person who is hired to live in the listed property that is vacant until it sells.

Prospecting: the act of searching for potentially new customers, clients, or purchasers for the possibility of a desirable real estate transaction outcome.

Q

QR code: a matrix, or a two dimensional bar code. QR codes can be used to read text, open a URL, or display pictures with the use of a digital camera phone. The QR codes are modules arranged in a certain square pattern.

Real Estate Own Properties (REO): properties that lenders have purchased at auction and are being listed for sale by real estate agents.

Real Estate Settlement Procedures Act: a federal act that requires lenders to be more effective in providing advance disclosures of settlement costs to home buyers and sellers. Under RESPA, lenders must give several disclosures in advance and give the timeline for each disclosure.

Really Simple Syndication (RSS): a way to subscribe to websites and help save viewing time on the Web, the frequently updated works such as news headlines, blog entries, and video are organized in a standardized format.

Referrals: the business leads from past clients or friends.

REG. Z, **Truth-in-Lending Act, TILA, (1968):** a federal act to promote the informed use of consumer credit by requiring disclosures about its terms and cost. The regulation also gives consumers the right to cancel certain credit transactions involving a lien on a consumer's principal dwelling.

Rule of benefit: a theory that decisions made will depend on the benefits or rewards the decision maker will receive.

S

S.U.R.E; Sellers Understanding Real Estate: means that the agent will surely get paid if both the agent and consumers understand real estate procedure. Buyers and sellers often slow down negotiations or withdraw because they do not understand how the real estate procedure works.

Sales skills: refers to the manner in which the agent will personally interact with the consumer in order to sell a product.

Scrapbook: a collection of ads, cards, and letters that the agent can use in marketing.

Short sales: happens when the lender agrees to sell the property for less than the amount owed. The proceeds from the sale of real estate are insufficient to satisfy the liens on the property. To help the homeowner avoid foreclosure, lien holders or lenders and insurance companies will agree to accept less than they are contractually owed. The lien holder forgives the homeowner of the remaining debt.

Sign-ride: the smaller signs with the agent's name, personal phone number, and web site address that are placed on top of or below the office sign.

Social Media: a term used to describe internet sites that allow users to participate in sharing of content. Today social networking sites have become a venue for people to share thoughts, ideas, information, and they allow for interactive dialogue among people who share similar interests. It allows Internet users to keep in contact with friends, friends' friends and beyond. Social media is establishing connections with friends and family.

Social networks: online communities where information is shared instantly such as Facebook™, Twitter™, My Space™, and Linkedin™ to communicate as a social group.

Special mortgage forbearance: an agreement between a lender and a mortgagor (homeowner) that contains a plan to reinstate the mortgagor and not to foreclose.

Specializing: working and fully focusing in one segment of real estate sales; the idea is to provide the best service possible in a concentrated area.

Sphere of influence: people who know what services you offer and who are willing to recommend those services to their friends and family. The groups can be teachers, co-workers, doctors, and family members.

Staging: preparing a property for sale by maximizing its appeal using the fewest dollars.

Supra Keys System: consists of special computerized lock boxes used by real estate professionals across the United States. They are made to easily attach to any doorknob or railing. Each box has a storage compartment to hold keys. This allows real estate agents to go directly to the house for showings and records who has access to the property.

Survey: the measurement of house boundaries and the exact location of the house.

T

Target your audience, means to zero-in to whom you plan to market.

Tasks: building blocks of a major goal; actions are broken-down into a simpler form to attain a desired goal.

Telemarketing sales rules (TSR): see National Do-Not-Call.

Testimonial letters: the letters that clients write wonderful things about the agent.

The Card Trick: a marketing tool designed to have clients, friends and family distribute the agent's business cards.

The rule of diminishing return: when the homeowner invests more into their property than the investment will return.

Time management: to perform the greatest amount of work in the least amount of time

Total living obligations ratio: conforming/GSE, FHA, and VA lenders use two types of debt ratios to determine whether the applicant is able to make mortgage payments. The two ratios are housing ratio (front-ratio), which measures the proposed housing expense and total living obligations ratio (back-ratio), which measures the combination of proposed housing and living expenses.

Trigger terms under Reg Z: certain advertising word groups used by lenders that require full disclosure. They are: the amount or percent of any down payment, the amount of any payment, the number of payments, the repayment terms, and the amount of any finance charge. If the

U

Unique Selling Proposition: a marketing concept introduced by Rosser Reeves of Ted Bates and Company during the 1940s. USP is based on advertising a product so unique consumers will want to switch products. The idea is called a proposition tagline. An example of a proposition tagline is, "Coke®: *'The Real Thing'*."

V

Veterans Administration (*VA loans):* guarantee the veteran's loan amount for a fee. Veterans Administration does not mortgage or fund mortgages but will guarantee loans for veterans.

Virtual Tours, are video presentations designed to give prospects the sense of being at the location.

W

Webinars: web-based seminars in which the presentation is conducted over the web. The presentation is in real time and interactive. The viewers and presenters are able to interact with one another in real time.

Webcasts: prerecorded files, which lack the interactivity webinars have. To view a webinar or a webcast file, the viewer needs only three things: an internet connection, a phone, and a computer or a smart phone.

Y

Yield spread premiums: Before 2011, were used by lenders to mark-up the interest rates from the wholesale rate to retail. The mark-up of interest rate was profit to the lender and the consumer would pay back the cost over the term of the loan. However, they are now illegal.

Index